Merely Players?

Merely Players? Actors' accounts of performing Shakespeare marks a significant departure in Shakespeare studies by placing the Shakespearean performer in the role of critic. It draws on three centuries' worth of actors' written reflections on playing Shakespeare and recognises these individuals as valuable commentators in the field of Shakespeare studies. The book features the testimonials of various performers throughout history, including:

- Ellen Terry
- Henry Irving
- John Barrymore
- Flora Robson
- Michael Redgrave
- Juliet Stevenson.

In bringing together the dual worlds of academia and performance, *Merely Players?* offers a unique resource for the Shakespeare scholar and theatre-lover alike.

Jonathan Holmes is Lecturer in Drama at Royal Holloway, University of London. He has previously published work in *Shakespeare Survey*, *New Theatre Quarterly* and *Studies in Renaissance Drama*, and also works as a theatre director.

Merely Players?

Actors' accounts of performing Shakespeare

Jonathan Holmes

Routledge
Taylor & Francis Group

LONDON AND NEW YORK

First published 2004
by Routledge
II New Fetter Lane, London EC4P 4EE

Simultaneously published in the USA and Canada
by Routledge
29 West 35th Street, New York, NY 10001

Routledge is an imprint of the Taylor & Francis Group

© 2004 Jonathan Holmes

Typeset in Baskerville by Keyword Typesetting Services Ltd
Printed and bound in Great Britain by TJ International Ltd, Padstow, Cornwall

British Library Cataloguing in Publication Data
A catalogue record for this book is available from the British Library

Library of Congress Cataloging in Publication Data
Holmes, Jonathan, 1975–
    Merely players?: actors' accounts of performing Shakespeare/
Jonathan Holmes.
        p. cm.
Includes bibliographical references (p. 184) and index.
    I. Shakespeare, William 1564–1616 – Stage history.
    2. Acting. I. Title.
    PR3112.H58.2004
    792.9'5 –dc22   2003016866

ISBN 0–415–31957–9 (hbk)
ISBN 0–415–31958–7 (pbk)

To the reader, health; to the writer, wealth;
and to both, both.

Robert Armin

Contents

Acknowledgements

Gratitude is first of all due to the AHRB, who for three years awarded me a full scholarship and without whom it would not have been possible for me to undertake this project. Thanks also to colleagues in The Department of English at The University of Birmingham, The Shakespeare Institute and The Shakespeare Centre, and to the librarians at the latter institutions, for providing the resources and support necessary for me to complete this book. I am grateful to John Drakakis for allowing me access to unpublished work in relation to his forthcoming Arden edition of *The Merchant of Venice*, to Tony Davies for providing the wherewithal for me to air parts of my work at conferences in Stirling, Dublin and Cambridge, and to Russell Jackson for his help and advice. Talia Rodgers and Diane Parker at Routledge provided good-humoured and kind support throughout the latter stages.

I would also like to acknowledge the following for permission to quote from previously published material: to Steven Berkoff for permission to quote from *I Am Hamlet*, © Steven Berkoff, 1989; to Cambridge University Press for permission to quote from essays by Patrick Stewart on Shylock, Sinead Cusack on Portia, Donald Sinden on Malvolio, Michael Pennington on Hamlet and David Suchet on Caliban in *Players of Shakespeare 1*, edited by Philip Brockbank, 1985, © Cambridge University Press, reprinted with permission, essays by Ian McDiarmid on Shylock, Juliet Stevenson and Fiona Shaw on Rosalind and Celia, Frances Barber on Ophelia, Antony Sher on the Fool and David Suchet on Iago in *Players of Shakespeare 2*, edited by Russell Jackson and Robert Smallwood, 1988, © Cambridge University Press, reprinted with permission, essays by Gregory Doran on Solanio, Ralph Fiennes on Richard II, Penny Downie on Queen Margaret, Anton Lesser on Richard III, Simon Russell Beale on Thersites and Philip Franks on Hamlet in *Players of Shakespeare 3*, edited by Russell Jackson and Robert Smallwood, 1993, © Cambridge University Press, reprinted with permission, essays by Christopher Luscombe on Moth and Gobbo, David Tennant on

Touchstone, Richard McCabe on Autolycus, David Troughton on Richard III, Julian Glover on Friar Lawrence and Derek Jacobi on Macbeth in *Players of Shakespeare 4*, edited by Robert Smallwood, 1998, © Cambridge University Press, reprinted with permission; to Harvard University Press for permission to reprint from *Mimesis as Make-believe: on the foundations of the representational arts* by Kendall L. Walton, Cambridge, Mass.: Harvard University Press, © 1990 by the President and Fellows of Harvard College; to Routledge for permission to reprint from *From Acting to Performance*, London, 1997, by Philip Auslander; and to The Women's Press for permission to quote from *Clamorous Voices: Shakespeare's Women Today* by Carol Rutter.

Many friends have provided stimulating conversation and provocative argument at points throughout the composition of this book. Thanks therefore to Marion Thain, Rebecca Lingafelter and, as always, to Pete, Nick, Tom and Deirdre. Special thanks must go to Peter Hinds for his rigorous and perceptive criticism over coffee and wine at The Cross, and thorough proofreading undertaken without the benefit of such incentives.

Finally, by far my greatest debt is to Peter Holland for precise and wise counsel, unstinting encouragement and continuing and generous friendship. Many of the better ideas in what follows are his, and it would be a considerably lesser endeavour were it not for his input.

Sometime a paradox

Shakespeare has embodied his characters so very distinctly, that he stands in no need of the actor's assistance to make them more distinct, and the representation of the character on the stage almost uniformly interferes with our conception of the character itself.

W. Hazlitt[1]

To analyse performance from the point of view of the actor is like describing a meal from the point of view of the entrée.

S. Booth[2]

I

The subject of this book is actors' accounts of their experiences of playing Shakespeare. Actors have set down in print their analyses of and reflections on the performance of Shakespeare for over 250 years.[3] In the latter half of the twentieth century this steady stream of publications became a flood, with the year 1984 alone seeing sixteen British actors publish accounts of acting in theatrical productions of Shakespeare plays. Such accounts, though varied in form, are distinct from anecdote, autobiography or memoir in their focus, which is not the actor's biographical self but rather one principal focus of his or her job – performing Shakespeare.

Shakespeare is unique among playwrights in that actors can construct whole careers from performing almost exclusively in his plays, and be labelled great within their profession for doing so. On the so-called legitimate English stage, at least until the middle of the twentieth century and to a very large extent since, all actors who are called great are players of Shakespeare, and all who specialise in Shakespearean performance have a potential claim to greatness.

For an actor engaging with Shakespeare, then, there is more at stake than simply a challenging job. And since the beginning of the twentieth century, not only have actors had to negotiate the position of this writer within their own profession; they have had to deal with his dominance within another, arguably more monolithic, structure: the Academy. The clash of these two competitors over what Terence Hawkes has called 'meaning by Shakespeare'[4] has not been lessened by the ever-expanding Shakespeare industry at large, which has resulted in the performance of Shakespeare within prominent institutions such as the Royal Shakespeare Company becoming to a considerable extent one more stop on the cultural tourist trail.[5] In substantial ways, success by an actor in a major Shakespearean role is an economic achievement; it has the effect of a promotion within the profession, recognition outside it, and the attraction of a position within the mythology of the dominant cultural icon of Western, and possibly global, art.

Despite the extraordinary number of works published each year on Shakespeare and discussing all aspects of this phenomenon, a fraction of these are concerned with the work of actors. Even within the subset of Performance Studies much labour is devoted to an examination of the product, the semiotics of the performance, but little to an investigation of the processes of creating that performance, and almost none to listening to the voices or reading the words of those immediately responsible for that act of creation. Considering the sheer quantity of material written by actors about performing Shakespeare, the length of time such material has been emerging, and the increasing regularity with which it is being published, it seems at the least paradoxical and at the most frankly bizarre that there has been no attempt critically to analyse at least a fraction of this corpus. This book begins to redress that balance.

My intention is to examine the ways in which actors discuss in print their negotiation with the perceived authority of the Shakespearean name. The subject is not so much the performance itself, but its rhetorical embodiment in subsequent or contemporaneous accounts of that performance; not simply the process by which a performance is constructed, but the strategies of invocation through which the process is sanctioned. In doing this the aim is to initiate progress in a hitherto neglected area of Performance Studies: the discussion of Shakespearean performance by the performer.

It is my contention that not only are the views of actors sophisticated and perceptive enough to be placed alongside more conventional criticism as commentaries on the production of Shakespearean meaning, but also that these accounts encourage new insights into the particularities of such production. To this end, my methodology in preparing this book has been predicated on three kinds of reading: readings of actors' accounts, readings of comparable and connected criticism, and readings of the plays themselves. The intention behind this is to situate these accounts both critically and performatively as part of a wider discursive field, while at the same time flagging up their distinctive identities within that field.

In addition to the obvious signifier of Shakespearean performance, I have developed a theoretical foundation for this argument through an exploration of the concept of mimesis. I define this concept in Aristotelian terms as 'imitation' or 'representation',[6] and follow theorists of drama and poetry since Sidney in attributing to it centrality in the composition of an artefact.[7] So much writing by actors focuses on the problematic nature of representation – whether through verbal or physical characterisation, or more abstractly in the form of dealing with the strangeness of a 400-year-old text – and so much of Shakespearean drama obsesses about the representational and imitative relationship between art and the world that this seemed like a natural, indeed overdue, conceptual premise from which to start.

My discussion, then, looks at the work of actors through the prism of criticism and theory in order both to rehabilitate these individuals as valuable commentators in the field and also to contextualise their own ideological preoccupations. These, no more than any other, are not transparent or naïve texts: they are as loaded with preconceptions and politics as any other, and therein lies much of their interest.

II

A similar project, in many ways the starting point for my own, was undertaken in 1997 by W.B. Worthen. In his excellent book *Shakespeare and the Authority of Performance*, Worthen devotes a fifty-six-page chapter to 'acting and the designs of authority'.[8] It is as eloquently written and reasoned as the rest of his work, reaching conclusions as to the relationship between an actor's appropriation of the authority of a Shakespearean text and an interpretation of the text itself:

> Actor training produces a performance that attempts to elide body, text and author. History, indeed difference of any kind disappears into the absent nature of the body itself: the natural body speaks the author's voice.[9]

Useful arguments such as this accumulate to produce an image of the actor's training existing naïvely at odds with the demands of the historicised, pluralist, Shakespearean text. Worthen substantiates this thesis, and indeed all his conclusions pertaining directly to the ideologies of performance as understood by performers, by direct reference to two works – the *Players of Shakespeare* series and Simon Callow's *Being an Actor*. The latter is cited only twice, extremely briefly, at the end of Chapter 3. Worthen's argument, then, rests almost entirely on evidence gleaned from a single source – the *Players of Shakespeare* series.

Though the series contains many accounts by different actors, Worthen cites them sparingly, and the reader would be forgiven for assuming that the scope of actors writing about Shakespeare is restricted to half a dozen names from one source. Such an approach is not only of limited value for analysis; it also displays a methodological naïvety absent in the sections of the book that deal with the more traditionally intellectual concerns of scholars, theorists and directors. Actors' discourse is presupposed to be transparent in a way that the work of scholars clearly is not, and Worthen makes selected, highly context-specific quotations stand as generalisations about actors' understanding and use of Shakespearean authority. He appears so eager to appropriate the authority of the actor's words that he falls victim to that lack of discipline and insight he attributes to those same actors. As the first chapter of the present study will demonstrate, even the source he does use is far from compliant with his arguments about training and technique.

My first chapter therefore focuses on the engagement with both theatrical technique and Shakespearean text as discussed in the *Players of Shakespeare* series, the most extensive and comprehensive archive of actors discussing their approaches to this playwright in existence. In *Players of Shakespeare 3* Ralph Fiennes discusses the processes of writing about performing Shakespeare:

> Actors are often wary about putting into print their emotional response to a part; it is something private that manifests itself in rehearsal and performance and is not easily articulated. With Shakespeare especially the actor is party to something essentially profound, which, whatever the production does to the play, almost always comes through in some form to the audience.[10]

Acting Shakespeare here is to engage in a form of mysterious alchemy that may be dispelled if explained, and which literally incorporates the figure of the absent writer as a channel for communication with the audience. Moreover, for actors used to the presence of the writer in the rehearsal room, dealing with the weight of interpretation of a Shakespearean 'classic' without such reassurance can be daunting. When directing his first non-modern play in several years in the form of Farquhar's *The Recruiting Officer*, Max Stafford-Clark writes:

> It was only when we began rehearsal for *The Recruiting Officer* in June that I needed George [Farquhar] every day. I realised that it was the first time in over fifteen years I had been in rehearsal without a writer. I don't always get on well with playwrights. Their obsessions are the banner we directors fight under and this doesn't always make for an easy relationship. But I missed George terribly ... I dropped into the

habit of writing to him every night when I got home ... I came to
depend on a nightly exchange of views with George.[11]

The value of a present author is to sanction interpretation and to endow
closure, limiting the spiral of signification, and to provide authority.
Fiennes is understandably uneasy about rationalising a process that for
him is difficult enough to begin with, involving as it does the daunting task
of negotiating the great genius of western culture, and doing so in the guise
not of an actor but a commentator. Henry Irving a century earlier con-
fronts similar anxieties:

> Not that it would be an altogether desirable practice for actors to take
> the public into their confidence with regard to everything they did or
> wanted to be done. That might excite the wrath of some of our friends,
> who, to the rest of our misdemeanours, would add that of trespassing
> on their preserves.[12]

Within this wry comment on the attitudes of critics it is perhaps possible to discern a possessive attitude towards Shakespeare, whom Irving,
more than any performer before or since, was concerned to identify as
an actor who wrote plays.[13] Irving is also here appropriating the 'pre-
serves' of other fields, scholarship and aesthetic criticism, to sanction his
own work, laying claim to both a primary discourse and its metalan-
guage, desiring to control both production and reception. In this fashion, the theatre was to be located as the true home of the bard, rather
than the study, and the actor his principal interpreter, rather than the
scholar.

The position of Irving and others in regard to theatrical traditions of
imitation and appropriation, what Harold Bloom has called 'the anxiety of
influence',[14] is the subject of Chapter 2. This section of my argument
examines how actors locate themselves in a tradition of performance;
approaches to a role can be determined as much by the previous players
of that role as by any supposedly fresh response to the text. As Harriet
Walter writes in a discussion of her performance of Lady Macbeth:

> In the months leading up to rehearsals I ... pored over other actors'
> accounts of playing the part. It was comforting and exhilarating to
> commune with these ghosts, to feel part of a tiny band of people who
> had shared this rare and particular task down the years; but in the end
> I felt nearer to them than to Lady Macbeth.[15]

The construction of a part is a combination not only of technique and
textual interpretation, but of a strong response to histories of playing,
and of traditions existing within the profession itself. Such histories are

inevitably both political and imitative, involving as they do the endowment of genealogies to a famously itinerant craft.

Harriet Walter's Macbeth, Antony Sher, an actor who has written
prolifically on the subject of performing Shakespearean drama, is particularly candid about the initial intimidation experienced when first making
contact with such a powerful cultural icon. In Sher's experience, 'reading
Shakespeare is sometimes like looking through a window into a dark room.
You don't see in. You see nothing but a reflection of yourself unable to see
in. An unflattering image of yourself blind.'[16] Looking through this glass
darkly, what is evident is Sher's own personality staring back.
Shakespearean characterisation becomes a process of identifying yourself
in the dense tangle of the text, which comes to reflect your own personality
– not so much holding a mirror up to nature as to an image of your own
nature. These operations of identification and confrontation with a role
and with the author are explored in particular in Chapter 3, which deals
with the most canonical role of all: Hamlet. This section distils the argument formulated in the previous chapter concerning traditions of inheritance and imitation, and narrows the focus to reflections on playing the
most celebrated part in drama. In important ways this experience can be
seen to highlight the concerns of all actors playing Shakespeare, crystal-
lising as it does relationships with the profession, the academy, other
players of the role, the actor's performance self, and the socio-cultural
position of the playwright. Playing Hamlet can be seen as the defining
experience of playing Shakespeare.

Though Irving was determined to locate himself in a theatrical genealogy stretching back to Shakespeare himself, it was one that operated
according to strictly patriarchal conditions, including a kind of primogeniture – epitomised literally in William Davenant's claims to be
Shakespeare's son.[17] Juliet Stevenson in *Clamorous Voices* speaks passionately
of clearing away the detritus of such a moribund tradition, asserting:

> There's always been a tradition of actresses in this country who ques-
> tioned the received ideas about Shakespeare's women and who brought
> their own sense of female integrity to the role. But those were individuals
> making personal choices. What has happened in the past ten to fifteen
> years is that the women's movement has come along, providing a frame-
> work for those instincts – a framework that has structured those possi-
> bilities of re-examination, not just for actresses but for audiences too.[18]

Clamorous Voices is very much about the construction of an alternative
tradition to the heavily masculine and linear one epitomised by the
Hamlet experience – one of 'Shakespeare's Women Today', as the book's
subtitle informs us. Such issues of gender in Shakespeare, in particular in
the context of this book, are the focus of Chapter 4. In this I examine not

only accounts of playing female characters, but also the scrutiny devoted by these particular actors to broader political concerns of the positioning of women within the Shakespearean canon, and of Shakespeare within western society.

III

Clamorous Voices is interesting not least because of the close links forged by an academic and a group of practitioners, to a large extent removing established boundaries. This and other texts show that working on a Shakespearean role is not all about an aversion to or a fear of what Michael Bogdanov has called 'the gelatinous blancmange of academia'.[19] The relationship of scholars with performance, which has been and continues to be mutually rewarding, is a thread running throughout my analysis. Irving, as has been mentioned, made great efforts to appropriate the discourses of academia as well as the stage, not least by means of the edition of the complete works that bore his name, *The Henry Irving Shakespeare*.[20]

Another point of intersection between the two disciplines can often be located in the actor's research activities. David Suchet approaches a role via the routes of scholarly investigation,[21] and Simon Russell Beale also employs essentially academic practices in preparation for rehearsals.[22] Occasionally, results of these methods anticipate scholarship. Gordon McMullan's excellent recent edition of Fletcher and Shakespeare's *Henry VIII* places deserved emphasis on the connections between this play and the approximately contemporaneous *The Winter's Tale*, and is among few examinations of the play to begin fully to tease out these resonances: 'Generically and iconographically, *The Winter's Tale* and *Henry VIII* have a great deal in common, and certainly more than "late play" critics have generally cared to acknowledge.'[23] Connections had been made at length over three decades previously, however, in the introduction to a 1954 Folio Society reprint written by the actor Flora Robson. After playing Paulina in Peter Brook's 1951 *The Winter's Tale*, Robson wrote the commentary on the play in which she remarks:

> It fell out quite naturally ... that I should see more and more affinities between the people in the play – Leontes, Hermione, Perdita – and those of the childhood of Elizabeth I: her towering, jealous, heir-hungry father; Anne Boleyn and Elizabeth herself.[24]

Robson goes on to point to the closeness of composition of both plays, commenting:

> When Shakespeare was working on *The Winter's Tale* he had his head full of the events of the reign of Henry VIII ... all these ideas

overflowed to colour and transform a simple fairy tale with the totally real passions of a remembered king, queen and princess.[25]

Or, as McMullan remarks: '*Henry VIII* begins, in a sense, where the earlier play leaves off, dramatising the political and social ramifications of the unease signalled even within its reconciliations.'[26]

Robson goes on to identify textual parallels between the plays, some of which are also cited in McMullan's edition, and she also finds connections between Hermione's speeches in court and the records of Anne Boleyn's statements at her own trial.[27] It is interesting to note that, while both Robson and McMullan use much of the same evidence, the one piece of information McMullan does not include is Robson's account, highly relevant though it is. An added irony of this in the case of both *The Winter's Tale* and *Henry VIII* is that without the editorial activities of the actors Heminges and Condell, no text of either play would have survived.

Actors, as Edward Burns makes clear in his otherwise highly actor-friendly *Character, Actor and Being on the Early Modern Stage*, are in no way to be considered the new critics, as he writes: 'I am not suggesting that we instate any actor as a "critic" of Shakespeare.'[28] Regrettably such academic disparagement remains the trend, despite the increased benevolence of the academy, and Renaissance Studies in particular, towards theatre practitioners. As Charles Frey commented in a review of *Players 2*: 'It is good to be reminded, perhaps, that many actors do have strong and often persuasive interpretations of their own.'[29] The condescending 'perhaps' locates the remark firmly in the tradition of the Johnsonian dancing dog. Frey is marvelling not that it is done well, but that it is done at all. His agenda is revealed in all its wounded conceit when he comments huffily, 'much less often do they seem to profit from the interpretations of Shakespearean critics'.[30] Shakespearean performance is portrayed as having been impoverished from its lack of contact with criticism, which operates as a kind of benevolent patriarch, guiding the children of the stage in the right direction. Actors' accounts are too often at best considered footnotes to discussion. The present study is manifestly an attempt to rectify this discrepancy, allowing the actor's voice to be heard where often it is ignored or censored.

Talking of Stanislavsky's *An Actor Prepares*, Michael Redgrave has written:

> Stanislavski's book is like some great mirror, wherein a man can see, standing close to the glass, the first mirrors of his soul, his own eyes, and in them, the tiny shape of the surrounding countryside; standing further back, he sees his setting reduced into a frame, and somewhere in that frame, looking curiously impermanent, the figure of himself.[31]

As with Sher looking into Shakespeare, Redgrave here figures the actor's task as one of visual imitation, holding up the mirror to nature, in Hamlet's over-cited phrase, in which his own self is reflected back. For Sher, this is a sign of failure, as the self must be assimilated into the text. For Redgrave pursuing Stanislavsky, it is a virtue, as the self becomes the fiction, 'reduced into a frame', and any dramatic text is resolutely sidelined. Sher operates in a system of mimesis that is indirect and dependent on the authority of the dramatist. Redgrave in contrast appropriates the authority of the teacher above that of the author, being concerned to sanction the production of an independent performance self which then uses the author's words as a vehicle for expression. Both men employ a distinct understanding of mimesis in order to compose their onstage selves, both as actors and characters. In both cases their identity is pluralised, whether through fragmentation or multiplication, while remaining unfixed and 'impermanent'. Plenitude is a result of absence.

Such an equal aptitude for so many things was characterised by Plato, famously, as dangerous and to be excluded in case it provoked dissent or, worse, madness. Diderot, in the *Paradox of the Actor*, is also aware of this possibility: 'In the great comedy, the comedy of the world, the one to which I always return, all the hot-blooded people are on the stage; all the men of genius are in the pit. The first are called madmen, the second are called wise men.'[32] The mimetic act is insane, precisely because it forecloses one identity in order to open up a proliferation of other selves. The paradox of being everything and nothing is sufficiently disruptive as to constitute a condition of insanity. Such a condition also begins to blur the distinctions between 'stage' and 'pit', as the boundaries between sane and mad are transgressed.[33]

In support of his hypothesis that actors do not undergo the emotions they portray, Diderot points to the example of Garrick, who, he claims, was notorious for the artificiality of a method that produced startlingly realistic results. As Joseph Roach in particular has demonstrated, the debt of Diderot to the 'English Roscius' was enormous. Familiar to the *philosophes* from his Paris performances of 1764, comprised principally of monologues from Shakespeare, Garrick 'became the central exhibit in their taxonomy of genius, a natural phenomenon to be studied for clues to the general workings of nature'.[34]

In Garrick was to be found the collision of two performance traditions: one technical, the other historical. He shared with Diderot a broadly Cartesian understanding of the body as a machine activated by spirit, a similarity of basic medical understanding that had been applied to acting for over a century. He also, however, located himself in a genealogy of performing Shakespeare, and it was to this end that his disquisitions upon the art of acting were directed.[35] If 'Diderot thought he had found a perfect acting machine',[36] it was a machine inspired by and devoted to traditions of performing Shakespeare.

In short, Diderot's text is based upon a model which itself owed much to the Shakespearean theatre, and as such it becomes a kind of reading of Shakespearean performance. The absent presence of Shakespeare within his text, a ghost within the Enlightenment machine, can therefore be recalled in a way that once again finds the actor to have been elided within a superordinate discourse.

Goldsmith famously wrote of his friend Garrick in 1774:

> On the stage he was natural, simple, affecting;
> 'Twas only that when he was off, he was acting.[37]

Garrick's success rested on a performance of mimesis that was not restricted to the stage, but overflowed into conventional life also. He blurred conventional distinctions, creating a persona that was able to adopt any variation of identity without remaining fixed to an unfailing self. This condition of mimesis, of performance and of simultaneous presence and absence, is the starting point, conscious or otherwise, for all the actors who appear in the following pages.

IV

Ours is an age in which, thanks to the popularity of his works on film, more people have gained access to Shakespeare in performance than on the page for the first time since his own lifetime.[38] This alone is reason enough for increased attention to be devoted to the conditions of these performances. The testimonies of actors have, as we have seen, been sorely neglected by the academy, even by those sectors focusing on performance analysis, which historically tend to be 'concerned with the effect produced, not with the phenomena accompanying its production', as the journalist and dramatic critic William Archer wrote in his 1888 response to Diderot.[39]

Such testimonies quite predictably make up various kinds of material. The present study focuses on accounts written by predominantly British actors, in most cases specifically for publication. Though recourse is made to interview material, to private correspondence and journals, and to third-party reportage, the emphasis remains on work designated by the actor/writer to enter the public domain. This may take the form of published books, for example Steven Berkoff's *I Am Hamlet*, or articles, such as Harriet Walter's 'The Heroine, the Harpy and the Human Being'.[40] Or it may be found in essays perhaps revised by an editor, as is the case with the *Players of Shakespeare* series, or recorded discussions which have been transcribed and approved by the participants, as can be found in *Clamorous Voices*.

In the case of older accounts, avenues for publication are even more diverse, and include lectures, commentaries, polemics, introductions, speeches, editions of plays, letters, memoirs and acting-copy marginalia. In these instances the opportunity for later revision is considerable; well-known examples include Bram Stoker's editing and even ghost-writing of many of Irving's publications, and the influence of the ambiguous figure of Chris St John (close female friend of Terry and possible lover of her daughter Edy Craig) on those of Ellen Terry.[41]

Even in the case of apparently straightforward modern publications important differences of intent need to be considered. Michael Pennington's *Hamlet: A User's Guide* and Antony Sher's *The Year of the King* are familiar recent examples of actors detailing the application of their craft to a particular play in performance, yet are vastly different in their aims and their genres, as the titles suggest.[42] The former is an analysis of the workings of a play throughout a series of retrospectively recalled productions in which the writer participated. The latter is an account of an individual's rehearsal process compiled from diary entries made during that process.

As a consequence of the often peripatetic and occasional nature of publication, the kinds of material discussed are rarely unified in tone or genre. The linking thread is their subject matter, acting Shakespeare, and the fact of their organised dissemination into the public domain. Few of the actors cited are known as authors independently of their identities as performers – Berkoff, Sher and Frances Kemble are perhaps the only examples of this – though the increasing numbers of university-educated performers working in the theatre in the last three decades has contributed to something of an explosion of sophisticated accounts, penned by knowledgeable and subtle actors-turned-authors. This corpus has yet to be examined in any real detail, and provides an invaluable guide to the strategies of Shakespearean production today. Whereas Worthen glances at select examples of modern writing by actors to form generalisations based on historical acting methodologies, I wish to look more fully at the rhetoric employed by performers in the varying contexts of its production.

The aim of the present study, then, is to allow a hitherto ignored constituency of Shakespeare Studies to be heard. That this is ironically the constituency most central to the continuing existence of such a discourse only reinforces the need for the academy to broaden its remit and expand its resources.

Notes

1 W. Hazlitt, 'On Mr Kean's Richard II', in *A View of the English Stage* (1818), in Duncan Wu (ed.), *The Selected Writings of William Hazlitt*, London: Pickering & Chatto, 1998, 9 vols, vol. 3, p. 52.

2 S. Booth, quoted by Keith Brown, review of *Players of Shakespeare 1*, TLS, 22.8.86.

3 The first specific example of an actor publishing his account of playing Shakespeare is David Garrick's *An Essay on Acting: In which will be considered the Mimical Behaviour of a Certain Fashionable Faulty Actor, to which will be added a Short Criticism of His acting Macbeth*, London: L. Bickerton, 1744. It is not that autobiographical material of an earlier date does not contain such reflections in passing, just that Garrick was the first to isolate such commentary as a separate genre.

4 See T. Hawkes, *Meaning By Shakespeare*, London: Routledge, 1992.

5 For accounts of the position of Shakespeare as cultural commodity see, among many others, S. Bennett, *Performing Nostalgia: Shifting Shakespeare and the Contemporary Past*, London: Routledge, 1996; M. Bristol, *Big-Time Shakespeare*, London: Routledge, 1996; T. Hawkes (ed.), *Alternative Shakespeares 2*, London: Routledge, 1996; B. Hodgdon, *The Shakespeare Trade: Performances and Appropriations*, Philadelphia, Penn., University of Pennsylvania Press, 1998; G. Holderness, *The Shakespeare Myth*, Manchester: University of Manchester Press, 1991; J. Joughin (ed.), *Shakespeare and National Culture*, Manchester: University of Manchester Press, 1997; A. Sinfield, *Faultlines: Cultural Materialism and the Politics of Dissident Reading*, Oxford: Clarendon, 1992 etc.

6 See *The Poetics*, 2 47a. There is famously no equivalent word to mimesis in English, and theorists repeatedly must fall back on a fusion of 'imitation', 'representation', and even 'invention' (strictly; *poesis*). Philip Sidney's phrase 'figuring forth' is as apt, if archaic, a rendering as I have come across. Given this, for the sake of convenience and clarity I have retained the conventional transliteration of the Greek term.

7 See Sidney in Geoffrey Shepherd (ed.), *An Apology for Poetry*, Manchester: Manchester University Press, 1973, especially pp. 100–101; P.B. Shelley, *A Defence of Poetry*, in Reiman and Fraistat (eds), *Shelley's Poetry and Prose*, New York: Norton, 2002; E. Auerbach, *Mimesis*, Princeton, N.J.: Princeton, 1953; M. Foucault, *The Order of Things*, trans. A.M. Sheridan Smith, London: Tavistock, 1970; R. Girard, 'Mimesis and Violence', in James G.Williams (ed.), *The Girard Reader*, London: Crossroads, 1996 etc.

8 W.B. Worthen, *Shakespeare and the Authority of Performance*, Cambridge: Cambridge University Press, 1997, pp. 95–151.

9 Ibid., p. 108.

10 R. Fiennes on Henry VI, in *Players of Shakespeare 3*, R. Jackson and R. Smallwood (eds), Cambridge: Cambridge University Press, 1993, pp. 101–114, p. 113.

11 M. Stafford-Clark, *Letters to George: The Account of a Rehearsal*, London: Nick Hern, 1989, pp. x–xi.

12 H. Irving, 'An Actor's Notes on Shakespeare', in *The Nineteenth Century*, vol. 1, May 1877, pp. 524–30, p. 530.

13 In this he has much in common both with the fetishisation of Shakespeare as actor evident in the work of Donald Foster, and in that of the present-day actor Simon Callow. See, for example, *Being An Actor*, London: Nick Hern, 1983.

14 See H. Bloom, *The Anxiety of Influence*, Oxford: Oxford University Press, 1973.

15 H. Walter, *Macbeth*, ed. Colin Nicholson, *Actors on Shakespeare* series, London: Faber, 2002, p. 1.

16 A. Sher, *The Year of the King*, London: Methuen, 1984, p. 36.

17 See J. Aubrey, *Brief Lives* (*c*. 1667), ed. Richard Barber, Suffolk: Boydell Press, 1975, p. 90.

18 Stevenson in C. Rutter (ed.), *Clamorous Voices*, London: The Women's Press, 1988, p. xiv.

19 Bogdanov in M. Bogdanov and M. Pennington, *The English Shakespeare Company: The Wars of the Roses*, London: Nick Hern, 1990, p. 241.

20 *The Works of William Shakespeare*, ed. Henry Irving and Frank A. Marshall, with notes and introduction to each play by Frank A. Marshall and other Shakespearean scholars, London: Blackie, 1895, 2 vols. The title of the second, and all subsequent editions, is *The Henry Irving Shakespeare*, a title the publishers of the 1922 edition, Gresham, felt deserved special mention as being preferable to the standard one.

21 See Suchet's essays on playing Caliban and Iago in P. Brockbank (ed.), *Players of Shakespeare 1*, Cambridge: Cambridge University Press, 1985 and Jackson and Smallwood (eds), *Players of Shakespeare 2*, Cambridge: Cambridge University Press, 1988, respectively.

22 See Beale's essay on playing Thersites in Jackson and Smallwood (eds), *Players of Shakespeare 3*, Cambridge: Cambridge University Press, 1993.

23 G. McMullan (ed.), *Henry VIII*, Arden, 3rd series, London: Thomas Nelson, 2000, p. 119.

24 F. Robson, Introduction to *The Winter's Tale*, in *Introductions to Shakespeare: Being the Introductions to the Individual Plays in the Folio Society Edition, 1950–76*, London: Michael Joseph, 1978, pp. 225–33, p. 226.

25 Ibid., p. 227.

26 McMullan, *Henry VIII*, p. 118.

27 Robson played Queen Elizabeth I on screen on two occasions: *Fire Over England*, 1936 and *The Sea Hawk*, 1940. This may well have led to an increasing interest in and knowledge of the period, which later informed her stage roles.

28 E. Burns, *Character, Actor and Being on the Early Modern Stage*, London: Macmillan, 1990, p. 190.

29 C. Frey, *Shakespeare Quarterly 38*, spring 1987, p. 115.

30 Ibid., p. 116.

31 M. Redgrave, *The Actor's Ways and Means*, London: Nick Hern, 1995, p. 65.

32 D. Diderot, *The Paradox of the Actor*, in Geoffrey Bremner (ed. and trans.), *Diderot: Selected Writings on Art and Literature*, Harmondsworth: Penguin, 1994, p. 106.

33 See the work of M. Foucault, especially *Madness and Civilisation* (trans. R. Howard), New York: Tavistock, 1965.

34 J. Roach, *The Player's Passion: Studies in the Science of Acting*, Toronto and London: Associated University Presses, 1985, p. 127.

35 See in particular his *Essay on Acting*.

36 Roach, *Player's Passion*, p. 152.

37 O. Goldsmith, *Retaliation*, in Arthur Friedman (ed.), *The Collected Works of Oliver Goldsmith*, Oxford: Clarendon, 1966, vol. 4 of 5, pp. 352–62, p. 357, lines 101–2.

38 See Bristol's *Big-Time Shakespeare*, London: Routledge, 1996 and Robert Weimann's *Author's Pen and Actor's Voice: Playing and Writing in Shakespeare's*

Theatre, Cambridge: Cambridge University Press, 2000, esp. pp. 2–4, for a discussion of this phenomenon.

39 W. Archer, *Masks and Faces*, in Diderot/Archer, *The Paradox of Acting/Masks or Faces?* New York: Hill and Wang, 1957, p. 77.

40 Published by Faber, 1989 and *New Theatre Quarterly*, spring 1993, respectively.

41 See J. Holledge, *Innocent Flowers: Women in the Edwardian Theatre*, London: Virago, 1981 for further information on St John.

42 London: Nick Hern, 1996 and Methuen, 1984 respectively.

Chapter I

Against the grain
Shakespeare and the problem of character

> Suffice it, that one great principle [of continuity] is common to all, a principle which probably is the condition of all consciousness, without which we should feel and imagine only by discontinuous moments, and be plants and animals instead of men.
>
> S. T. Coleridge[1]

> On stage, if the inner line is broken an actor no longer understands what is being said or done and he ceases to have any desires or emotions. The actor and the part, humanly speaking, live by these unbroken lines ... Let those lines be interrupted and life stops. A role must have continuous being.
>
> K. Stanislavsky[2]

> WHORE (to RALPH): And what is this play about?
> RALPH: Well, there's this Nurse ...
>
> M. Norman and T. Stoppard[3]

I

The biased perspective of the actor Ralph Bashford, playing the nurse and in turn played by Jim Carter, in *Shakespeare in Love* is familiar to us all as an exaggerated representation of the stereotypical self-absorption of the actor. Harriet Walter tells her own versions of this anecdote as a preface to her essay in *Players of Shakespeare 3*.[4] This time, the story is based on both an actor playing the doctor in *King Lear* and a scene in François Truffaut's film *Day for Night*,[5] in which successive members of the cast are interviewed by a journalist, each claiming their role as central to the story. Walter goes on from this to claim a grain of truth within the comic hyperbole:

> From the moment we are invited to play a part, a mental process gets underway, intended to bridge the gap between me and her/him. Subjectivity begins to set in and the character becomes the centre of our universe.[6]

Richard McCabe, recalling Autolycus, writes in similar vein:

> The role invades all your waking and sleeping hours like a bad con-
> science and is only stilled by finding solutions that are acceptable to
> both your character's inner life and one's own sense of personal truth.[7]

It is suggested by both cinematic representation and the actors' own
accounts that subjective, introspective constructions of character are the
norm.

I begin my discussion of actors' reflections on Shakespeare by looking at
the collision between twentieth-century, particularly post-Stanislavskyan,
actor training methods and sixteenth/seventeenth-century texts, and inves-
tigating the rhetorical processes by which actors bridge the gap between
the two within their writing. The focus of the discussion in this chapter will
be first on the *Players of Shakespeare* series, probably the most extensive
compendium of actors' accounts of playing Shakespeare available,[8] and
second on what emerge as consistently problematic roles for actors searching for interiority. The most obvious examples of these are 'clown' parts,
but the series also reveals a markedly agonistic relationship with two other
characters in particular: Richard III and Shylock.

The two films mentioned undermine the idea of interiority by suggesting
implicitly that introspection is, in fact, alien to characterisation. In
Shakespeare in Love this is achieved by the casting of the burly, lugubrious
Jim Carter as Ralph, invoking the audience's cultural knowledge of vau-
deville/music-hall traditions of transvestism and the pantomime Dame.
Moreover, those appreciative of the 'in-jokes' which are a speciality of
this film will have noticed that the 'real' nurse in the film – belonging to
Viola's household – is played by Imelda Staunton, Carter's real-life wife.
Thus one actor plays another actor who is portraying a character synonymous with another character played by the first actor's actual partner.
The multiple layers of fictionality, of mimesis, are sufficient for us to feel we
are comfortable and familiar with all the types of 'characterisation' in
evidence without resource to any level of psychology or inner life.

Objections to this line of reasoning could mention the subsidiary and,
more importantly, comic nature of the characterisation here discussed –
neither Carter nor Bashford are called upon to portray complex or highly
emotional situations. I will discuss later the ideologies implicit in this point,
which rest largely on notions of the size of a role and, much more problematically, its generic status within the fiction. Sufficient doubt is cast for
the moment by the second film, mentioned by Harriet Walter.

Truffaut's *La Nuit americaine* is a film about filmmaking, hence the
pseudo-documentary on-set interviews described by Walter. One of the
actors interviewed is portraying the romantic lead of the film-within-a-
film, and is in turn played by Jean-Pierre Léaud. Léaud is a regular cast

member of Truffaut's films, occupying the position of alter ego for the director, to the extent of playing the same character, Antoine Doinel, in a sequence of films based on Truffaut's life begun when the actor was fifteen and ending only at the director's death twenty-five years later.

In *La Nuit americaine*, then, the characterisation is complicated from the beginning by this actor's presence as precisely the type of character we have come to associate on screen with Truffaut/Doinel. Our expectations are then undermined by the appearance of Truffaut himself playing – naturally – the director of the film-within-the-film. It gradually becomes clear from the clips we see that this film-within (entitled *Meet Pamela*)[9] is a bricolage of scenes from almost all the director's previous films, including ones featuring Léaud, which now again feature the same actor, playing an actor portraying characters synonymous with those we know him to have played before. The levels of mimesis here become dizzying, and the approach to characterisation is correspondingly complex, radical and fragmentary, so that the humour of the actors' interview remarks has a double resonance in that they represent precisely the kind of characterisation that this film explodes.

The purpose of this preamble is to establish not only that there is a myriad of ways of approaching character, but to put forward the premise that the introspective manner in which many actors construct character is more often than not fundamentally at odds with how that character is constructed in the script and subsequently reconstructed by the spectator. Part of the humour of both films is the gap between the speakers' understanding of character and that of the spectator, and it is this gap that can be so wittily exploited in film by techniques of montage editing.

Moreover, both these films rely on a spectator's ability to move comfortably between layers of mimesis, understood in subsequent discussions to be consonant with concepts of representation and fictionality. Actor training methods fundamentally equip the performer with mimetic strategies of varying complexity, concerned as they are with representing some idea of 'truth' or 'reality' to an audience through the medium of a persuasive fiction, and in this sense the engagement with a playtext is an engagement with mimesis.

Cinematic form demonstrates clearly how a viewer assembles a coherent and cohesive idea of character from often disconnected or sharply juxtaposed sources of information. In this he or she is assisted by little more than received knowledge and experience of narrative structure, with the continuous presence of the actor's body acting as a peg on which to hang that structure.[10] The causal relationship that is assumed to exist between event and character gives the narrative meaning, even though this relationship is invariably composed in the editing suite, where actors are (particularly in the case of films reliant on special effects) often made to respond to something they didn't know anything about when they filmed the scene.

Reading a narrative on film therefore becomes an attempt to reconcile the temporal dynamic of plot with the supposedly atemporal demands of character. We want the heroine to experience a 'journey'. As N.J. Lowe remarks, 'Our desire for harmony between the two dissonant and incomplete story models makes us vulnerable to sustained and purposeful affective manipulation. It is this that accounts for the power of plot.'[11]

All this, however, is strikingly at odds with the approach to performance expressed by Walter and McCabe, an approach that is summed up neatly by W.B. Worthen: 'Actorly reading is notably trained on questions of character, the integrated, self-present, internalised, psychologically motivated "character" of the dominant mode of modern theatrical representation, stage realism.'[12] Cinematic acting is not stage acting, of course, yet as the Truffaut anecdote and its use by Walter testify, actors rarely modify their rhetoric when working in either medium. Discussing the volumes from which the accounts of McCabe and Walter are drawn, Worthen comments:

> In the *Players of Shakespeare* series, the politics of interpretation emerge in the ways performers understand and represent character. Despite the British theatre's reputation for being less involved in an explicitly Stanislavskian tradition than the American stage, the *Players of Shakespeare* essays are informed by notions of a coherent and internalised characterisation fully consistent with Stanislavskian mimesis.[13]

It is my contention, as it is Worthen's and others', that this approach can be inappropriate and sometimes counter-productive to the performance of Shakespearean drama.[14] Further, I claim in this chapter that a surprising number of essays in these volumes display a thoughtful awareness of this problem, even while sometimes continuing to pay lip-service to post-Stanislavskyan conventions. In short, as in so many areas of Shakespearean criticism, the actors have got there first.

This last factor is important because it is not just actors in performance who tend to be susceptible to a received mythology of characterisation. Scholars and critics, too, still to some extent lack a competent vocabulary with which to analyse the phenomenon of Shakespearean character construction. As Peter Holland comments, 'We are left with an apparent ability to analyse most of the lines spoken, but unable to analyse most of the characters in any one play, assuming somehow that the few characters we can analyse will adequately represent the others.'[15] When Samuel Crowl writes that 'if one had to place their efforts in a critical context, the firm of Bradley, Granville-Barker and Barton would quickly spring to mind',[16] it is only the inclusion of John Barton's name that tells us he is referring to actors and not scholars.[17] Indeed, the reliance of the academy on A.C. Bradley in matters of character criticism still outweighs that of the theatre, which as Worthen and Holland state, prefers Stanislavsky even in the case of Shakespeare. Indeed, so prevalent are appropriations of various aspects of Stanislavsky's work in the rhetoric of actors that it may be helpful to outline briefly the contours of this system of actor training.

Born to an extremely wealthy family in Moscow in 1863, Konstantin Stanislavsky co-founded the Moscow Art Theatre in 1897 and, inspired partly by the work of Anton Chekhov whose plays he premiered and starred in, devoted the remaining forty years of his life to composing a system of actor training, left incomplete at his death in 1938. The result is an assembly of ideas, approaches and exercises published in three main texts: *An Actor Prepares, Building a Character* and *Creating a Role.*[18] This trilogy focuses on four main principles: physical preparation; psychological consistency in characterisation (expressed in the formulation of a through-line of action, or psychological arc, from the character's first to last appearance); close study of text (including breaking it down into a series of motivated actions); and construction, using techniques of emotion memory, of an 'inner life' and of a full backstory to the character's actions. The system is rarely taught in complete sequence, even in drama schools, yet most actors will employ a collage of techniques gleaned from it in approaching a part.

A frequent criticism of the academic community by actors is that scholars are preoccupied with 'examining the most abstruse aspects of scholarly questions in a spirit of audacious inquiry, without realising they are splitting hairs and vivisecting follicles'.[19] Modern scholarship, in other words, is all very well in the lecture room but does not lend itself to performance. This clearly is an over-generalisation. Nevertheless, it is possible that a postmodern emphasis on plurality, intertextuality and historicity is not going to be as appealing a starting point for an actor concerned with making his/her character cohesive and comprehensible as, say, asking 'how many children had Lady Macbeth?' This notorious example of character criticism comes not in fact from Bradley, as is usually supposed, but was coined by F.R. Leavis and taken for the title of L.C. Knights's famous 1930 essay.[20] Ironically, Bradley himself goes to some length to emphasise his distance from such matters, emphatically stating that: 'whether Macbeth had children or (as seems usually to be supposed) had none, is quite immaterial ... I hope this is clear; and nothing else matters.'[21] In contrast, Harriet Walter writes of surveying criticism on Macbeth: 'One footnote I read dismissed the question of Lady Macbeth's child or children as "unprofitable". That editor did not have to play the part'.[22] The issue of children in *Macbeth* was raised by Bradley in a discussion of to whom Macduff addresses his line 'He has no children' (5.1, 217) – a simple matter of stagecraft. It is a question, however, asked and answered with all seriousness by arguably the most distinguished Shakespearean in the entire *Players* series, Derek Jacobi, upon playing Macbeth in Adrian

Noble's 1993 Barbican production. Jacobi remarks that he 'had decided that somewhere in the past of their relationship they had lost a child ... it's something that really needs a programme note: you can't act it, really, though you can think it'.[23] Although Jacobi is unable to act the desolation of losing a child directly because of its absence from the text, such is the importance of making this decision for his characterisation of Macbeth that he feels the audience should be aware of it. It is hard to imagine this pseudo-Bradleyan approach being superseded for this actor at least by an awareness of new historicist thought.

II

The *Players of Shakespeare* volumes are explicitly about the process of characterisation. In the Foreword to the first volume, published in 1985, the editor Philip Brockbank stated his aims:

> to concentrate on the actor's work in creating a Shakespearean character on stage. The aim was not stage history of the traditional kind, nor theatrical reminiscence, but commentary illuminating the role and revealing the actor's professional disciplines.[24]

The performers asked to contribute to the volumes are very much required to respond: 'Well, there's this ...' (fill in the gap) at some length. The aim throughout all four volumes is not to provide a critical account of the productions in which the actors found themselves, nor is it to provide anything other than an implicit commentary on the concept of acting Shakespeare. It is, to paraphrase Philip Brockbank, to record the brief chronicles of a moment in the careers of both an actor and a Shakespearean character. The subjective perspective of the accounts is stressed by all three editors of the series: Brockbank, Robert Smallwood and Russell Jackson. The volumes are a record of performance choices by a series of actors tackling Shakespeare in a major institution whose productions will tend, rightly or wrongly, to be taken as representative of Shakespearean performance in Britain.

Continuing his discussion of the volumes, Worthen remarks:

> Granted, Gregory Doran is one of the few actors to allude directly to a 'Stanislavskian search for detail' ... Nonetheless, throughout *Players of Shakespeare* actors conceive of character as an entity whose 'radix traits' can be discovered in the text and used to motivate a single spine of action, the actor/character's 'journey' through the play.[25]

Doran is an interesting choice of example, not only because his is the only essay on a 'bit-part' (Solanio) in the series, but also because his discussion is devoted to a questioning of the very tendencies of which Worthen holds him to be an examplar. In the section from which Worthen quotes Doran writes:

> The search for supplementary detail can become an obsession when one is playing these parts. In fact, no one even calls Solanio by name. Nevertheless, the Stanislavskian search for detail goes on, the tentative extrapolation of arguable subtextual hints into quintessential radix traits; forgetting the fact that in a play of some 3000 lines, Solanio only has fifty-seven.[26]

The playful sense of absurdity evident here soon becomes a firm denial of such an approach:

> It's easy to become so involved in the search for character that your perspective becomes distorted. Even the attempt to discern a through-line can be deceptive. I don't really think Shakespeare thought in those terms. These characters work from moment to moment; there is little psychological progression discernible.[27]

Far from being an illustration of Stanislavskyan dependency, Doran's essay is a diary of the processes of questioning such a stance. Significantly, it is the experience of playing such a small part ('these parts') that sparks off such a critical response, as Doran becomes aware of the character's functional relationship to the plot more than its supposedly self-contained personality.

Just as interesting as his discussion of Doran is Worthen's choice of exception to the Stanislavskyan rule, Antony Sher. Sher was Shylock to Doran's Solanio in Bill Alexander's 1987 production of *The Merchant of Venice*, and three years earlier he had been cast as the Fool in *King Lear*, his first RSC role. This is the focus of his essay in *Players 2*. In the course of the piece, he relates how during rehearsals the director Adrian Noble sent the cast out to find an animal on which to model an initial characterisation. On a visit to London Zoo, Sher chose a chimp, in the process running into his Lear, Michael Gambon, peering into the gorilla's cage, 'man and beast locked in solemn contemplation of one another'.[28] Sher's chimp later found its way into his physical characterisation of the role.

Worthen seizes on this encounter as an example of an actor for once not using a post-Stanislavskyan methodology to sanction a performance of Shakespeare, instead 'contemplating himself in the other, and the other in himself, the actor's economy of production finally excludes Shakespeare altogether'.[29] There are several components of Sher's rhetoric that unfortunately undermine this alleged radicalism. Not the least is the conventional place of animal study within most drama-school curricula. *The Student Actor's Handbook* instructs us to

visit a zoo or park. Of course, it is more desirable to watch an
animal in his natural habitat ... The animal image ought to parallel your choice of objectives and to reflect what other characters
say about you. Now you must explore ways to translate your
animal into a human being ... You must humanise the entire
process.[30]

The objective of the exercise is not to move the characterisation away
from the human but, perversely, to anthropomorphise the animal and
then psychologise it, finding yourself in the object, rather than the animal in yourself. This is reinforced by the manner in which Sher's acro-
batic idea of the role influences his choice of animal to begin with, a
process evident also in the animal choices of actors playing Richard III,
as will be seen. An extreme example of laying bare such anthropo-
morphic ideologies can be found in Michael Bryant's response to being
dispatched to study the behaviour of badgers while playing Badger in
Nicholas Hytner's production of *The Wind in the Willows*: 'I have made a
discovery about the habits of badgers: their movement and their posture
have an extraordinary resemblance to Michael Bryant.'[31] Moreover, if
participating in the exercise makes the actor unusual, then almost all
drama-school graduates are equally remarkable (not to mention the
gorilla-gazing Gambon). Nor is Sher free of a more overt kind of psychologising within his account; he worries early on about the Fool's
'character', about making himself believable as a court fool, and also
as a Shakespearean actor.

There remains, however, an emphasis within his essay on elements other
than the psychological that is worth commenting on, if not to the degree
that Worthen does. Sher explains his use of the chimp as follows:

> I have dwelt this long on the external image of the performance
> because it seems to me that there is a group of Shakespearean roles
> where it is as desirable for the actor to present a striking physical
> image as it is for him to do justice to the text and the emotions;
> some other roles that are in this group that come to mind include
> Caliban, Ariel, Puck, Thersites and Richard III. [32]

The choice of roles to be collocated here with the Fool is highly significant.
Thersites and Richard III both have strong textual descriptions or references to deformity or physical unusualness. Caliban also fits into this
category, but Ariel and Puck are distinguished in the text not primarily
by physicality (though this often is the case in performance), but by their
lack of humanity. Being 'spirits of another sort', they cannot, it is implied,
be psychologised as thoroughly as other roles and so the default emphasis is
on their bodies.

III

Sher is adjusting his conception of characterisation to fit the type of character he plays – though his account of playing Richard III, despite what he says here, records a famous dependence on psychology, to the extent of taking 'Richard' to a psychoanalyst.[33] Further, his comments on playing Shylock, Leontes and Macbeth (in 1987, 1998 and 1999–2000), are all equally based on an application of Stanislavsky – as he says, 'I do believe in digging deep into yourself to make the emotional moments of a role as truthful as possible ... psychology is an essential part of approaching any role, for me.'[34] The Fool, then, is unique in Sher's repertoire for its apparent relegation of psychologising techniques. Nor is he unusual in this regard. Playing Shakespearean fools and clowns encourages a response in actors significantly different to that of other roles or types of roles, to the extent that there is a tripartite pattern undergone during rehearsal: first, an actor worries about being funny (or not), then they discover that conventional modes of characterisation do not apply, and finally they develop a highly physical characterisation often involving a degree of 'business'.

This, I want to argue, represents a process of rediscovering performance techniques stretching back four centuries.[35] Four of the accounts of portraying clowns in *Players of Shakespeare* locate the character within a particular historical tradition – Edward Petherbridge's piece on Don Armado takes this to such an extreme that he barely finds the space to mention the role itself. Two such accounts are by actors who have carved a niche in taking on fool/clown roles: Geoffrey Hutchings, here talking about playing Lavatch, and Christopher Luscombe, who writes of playing both Gobbo and Moth.

The productions in which these actors found themselves are separated by over a decade, and the actors themselves belong to different generations. There is, however, a common thread – a perceived dread of being cast in such parts. Luscombe sums it up by asking: 'Why are actors so reluctant to take on these particular roles? Whenever I told anyone that I was going to Stratford to play them I always seemed to be greeted with sympathy.'[36] In the next essay in that volume, David Tennant writes as if in response to this question while relating his disappointment on being cast as Touchstone rather than Orlando in *As You Like It*. In his view Orlando is 'not an easy part in itself but at least I could approach it fairly conventionally. I could look at who the character was, what he wanted, what his through-line was and so on.'[37] Tennant's essay is a paradigm of the model described above. Feeling initially a pressure to 'be funny or sink', Tennant approached the role in a manner worthy of a psychoanalyst. Talking of his first impressions of Touchstone he recalls:

The flights of ideas, the energy of thought and the inability to shut up are all traits of manic episodes in a bi-polar mental illness. It is

perhaps an actor's affectation to think of Shakespearean characterisation in this way, but it helped me to make sense of some of
Touchstone's less easily motivated moments.[38]

The slightly defensive tone of this remark perhaps indicates an awareness
already of the inappropriate nature of his approach, but, as Tennant says,
'with something else to play it freed me up to concentrate on what I was
saying'. The use of Stanislavsky, then, becomes a prop, providing Dutch (or
Russian?) courage in the face of a daunting performance challenge, made
all the worse by what Tennant perceives as a tradition of playing fools: 'Of
course the only way to exorcise these ghosts is to do your own version of this
part ... to approach it as you would a new part in a new play, but I could
feel the finger of history tapping on my inexperienced shoulder.'[39]

Making the part his own, making it a subjective experience to the point
of playing schizophrenia, is a rebuttal to the past. Stanislavskyan acting
becomes a defence against the historical power of Shakespearean performance. As the rehearsals progressed, and it became clearer that a clini-
cally unstable Touchstone was not really the way to go, Tennant
discovered another protective device:

> I started trying to throw everything at it. Touchstone became a spin-
> ning top chucking off silly voices, silly walks, even acrobatics to try
> and inject some life ... Of course what I was doing was running scared
> of the words and not trusting Shakespeare.[40]

Finally, the most successful weapon against the difficulties of the role was
the playwright himself, the Shakespearean name appropriated as a defence
against Shakespearean character. Such a move is also found in Julian
Glover's essay on playing Friar Lawrence in Adrian Noble's 1995 RST
Romeo and Juliet. Working from an admittedly disadvantageous start – he
describes his initial view of the Friar as 'a bumbling, boring old twerp who
gets it all wrong and screws up everybody's lives'[41] – he eventually comes
to believe, echoing Ralph Bashford, that the play should be renamed 'The
tragedy of the Good Brother'. Instrumental in this fittingly Damascene
conversion is Glover's recourse to the authority of the Word, of which he
remarks that, when in doubt, 'with Shakespeare I go to the First Folio.
This version is not the Bible, but can be a great source of inspiration if you
know the sort of clues to look out for.'[42] What is interesting here is that,
despite apparently dismissing the Folio's definitive status, Glover still
retains a theological frame for his remarks, a tendency reinforced by his
confessed reliance on advice from Patrick Tucker of the Original
Shakespeare Company.

Such quasi-religious terminology is encouraged, according to Kathryn
Hunter, by the training process, in her case undergone at RADA: 'There

wasn't a method as such, except a very large word, which was Truth. It's like reading the New Testament: The Kingdom of God is within you.'[43] Though Hunter later came to reject such rhetoric, her analogy is apt. Text, author and politics are subordinated to a universalist discourse of theological subjectivity in which all variables and conditions are subordinated to a post-humanist idea of Logos. As Denis Salter has written in a discussion of Method acting in relation to post-colonialism:

> Method acting takes it for granted that ideology and the social order that it interpellates do not exist. 'I act, therefore I am': beyond this self-referential and self-generating, deliberately apolitical proposition, Method acting has refused to let the postcolonial actor go.[44]

And it is not just the postcolonial performer who is caught up in such solipsistic operations. For David Tennant also, invoking the author-god and 'trusting Shakespeare' did the trick, and he was able to find a solution: 'I found the only was to deal with Touchstone's apparent contradictions ... was to stop striving for the logical through-line and to play each moment as it arrives. After all, the evolution of any human relationship is far from linear.'[45] In a reversal of the usual process, Shakespearean authority here sanctions a deviation from conventional twentieth-century performance practice rather than a greater reliance upon it. The principal reason for this, I suggest, can be found within the typology of the role itself. David Wiles makes the point that

> We do not find the term 'clown' in colloquial usage [in the period]. We may safely conclude, therefore, that in a theatre-related context the term 'the clown' refers always to the resident clown or fool in a professional company.[46]

Within the dramatis personae of a play, then, the signifier 'clown' refers to a type of role, rather than a coherent character, a tendency that can be extended, as I shall argue, to other types, such as 'King', or 'Queen'.[47] Moreover, in the case of 'clown' it is a type with a known player: either Will Kemp or Robert Armin. Kemp and Armin occupy a place in the history of acting that Burbage, significantly, does not. They are acknowledged to have defined the roles that make them famous, and are at liberty to redefine that role in performance – Hamlet's rebuke to the clown-actor is often interpreted apocryphally to refer to Kemp.

Three of the actors describing playing the fool mention either Kemp or Armin. Their modern-day counterparts within *Players*, Luscombe and Hutchings, are very conscious of their place in a tradition of fools. Hutchings goes to the length of identifying three varieties of them:

simpletons, servants and jesters, recalling Robert Armin's own considerably more sophisticated typology of folly, summarised on the title page of his *Foole Upon Foole*:

> A flat foole and a fatt foole,
> A leane foole and a cleane foole,
> A merry foole and a very foole.[48]

Despite such apparent return to typological characterisation, or perhaps because of his lack of Arminesque flair for taxonomy, Hutchings eventually resorts to exactly the kind of psychologising the roles usually deny:

> Having created the character, discovered his attitudes to life, found the logic behind his thinking, his motivations and drives, it doesn't seem to me difficult to make the humour work, particularly with such a superb writer as Shakespeare.[49]

Hutchings here mixes a rhetoric of originality ('created') with one of exploration ('discovered', 'found') and reverence (the 'superb writer'), in such a way as to display clearly the theological operations of Stanislavskyan acting authority – and revelation sanctioning a self-authoring act.

As had Sher, Hutchings decided to play his clown as disabled, in this case a hunchback. Though this is the somewhat paradoxical result of over-psychologising a part, there is a bizarre resonance with the stage history of the part, which Wiles claims stems from Armin's characterisation of Lavatch as deformed, playing on the actor's own unusual physique.[50] Tennant's schizophrenic Touchstone also has unlooked-for echoes in the character's linguistic position in the play, which is simultaneously intensely present in references to his jester's motley, and nominally absent – 'Touchstone' is the name adopted in Arden by a character whose actual name is never revealed. Moreover, as Wiles remarks, it is a name perhaps pointing to Armin's previous occupation as goldsmith within his probable first role for the King's Men. Physical and verbal hints of Armin's performances within the text are picked up on and psychologised by the actors, rather than seen as the vaguest of indications of a possible historical playing style.

Hutchings also has in common with Tennant an interest in accents. Interestingly, both actors made the choice not to play the role in RP, but to revert to their native accents – Dorset and Aberdeen respectively. Tennant's decision was all the more striking in a production that had three Irish actors as Rosalind, Orlando and Duke Senior, all playing in RP.[51] This brings the characterisation closer to the 'personality role' that most actors identify the fool as belonging to, but it also raises the issue of class, as accents on the traditional Shakespearan stage almost always carry connotations of lower-class status and/or humour, often limiting casting choices. Barrie Rutter cites this tendency as the principal motivation for forming Northern Broadsides: 'I was kept in the basement of Shakesepare and only given the comic bits. I have a slow-burning revenge against people who have told me I can never play kings because I don't have R.P.'[52] Similarly Jane Horrocks maintains, with some justification, that if she'd remained with the company with her Lancashire accent she'd still be playing 'weird little crippled people'.[53]

Wiles explains this as partly the result of shifting meanings of the term 'clown', which originated as an affected and pejorative word describing someone of lower rank. It was also used in a strictly technical sense in early Elizabethan theatre. By the late 1590s:

> The social-pejorative meaning and the technical-theatrical meaning were disconnected. In the decade that followed ... two distinct meanings of the term became acceptable. When Touchstone in 1599–1600 jests upon his encounter with a 'clown', he puns upon the now twofold meaning of the word.[54]

When M.M. Mahood comments that 'one criterion we tend to apply without being aware of it is social status; traditionally a bit part is thought of as a plebeian character',[55] she could just as easily be speaking of clown/fool roles. This perception of the roles is reinforced by their tendency to be written in prose, as both Simon Russell Beale and Richard McCabe testify. Beale recounts a particularly apt anecdote on this subject as he recalls advice given to him by Joe Melia:

> He said to me that so long as I was saying something funny, so long as I used a recognisably comic rhythm, I would get a response regardless of whether the majority of the audience immediately understood the words. He called it 'adopting a confident vernacular tone'.[56]

Luscombe, in contrast to Hutchings and Tennant, but in the spirit of Joe Melia, began his characterisation having accepted that 'meticulous psychological realism is not enough'. He goes on to comment:

> It's often suggested that Shakespeare's clowns rely on 'personality performances', where the perceived idiosyncrasies of the actor are more important than detailed characterisation. Will Kemp, who created so many of these roles, began his career as the Earl of Leicester's fool, and one can only assume that his solo work informed his acting style.[57]

He comes closer to the probable technique of Kemp when he goes on to say that his own generation 'has seen comics such as Frankie Howerd as

Bottom – or was it Bottom as Frankie Howerd? That blurring of the edges seems to me to be part of an honourable tradition.'[58] As an inheritor of the Kemp tradition, he finds it easier to avoid psychology than Hutchings's and Tennant's Arminian roles, though in this he is helped by Gobbo and Moth's specific social situations, giving them specific contexts and broadly realistic relationships, as opposed to the extra-social fools of Armin. The closeness of the fool to the fiction determines the degree of mimetic flexibility; fools that exist on the boundaries of the play world are troubling for actors concerned with the representation of internalised mimetic truth, and one way of compensating for this appears to be a recourse to the authority of the fool tradition itself.

In *Shakespeare in Love*, we first meet Will Kemp backstage at Whitehall, the clown standing with one leg on a box, his elbow on his knee, holding a skull. The scene of course plays on the familiar nineteenth-century iconography of the part of Hamlet, and is reinforced by Kemp's first line: 'When will you write me a tragedy, Will? I could do it.' The joke plays on the convention that comic performers aspire to be serious, respected, tragic actors, if only someone would give them the chance to escape the restrictions of comedy. Clowns and fools, as Luscombe reminds us, are considered less impressive roles than heroes, a fact compounded by the mistaken tendency to see comedy as being natural and instinctive, and tragedy as requiring a form of genius and intellectual energy. As Leigh Hunt wrote:

> It appears to me that a great tragedian is a finer genius than a great comedian. Passions are more difficult of conception than habits; tragedy is wholly occupied with passions ... in comic characters we generally recognise the manners and peculiarities of some person with whom we are acquainted, or who is at least known to the world; but of the deeper tragic passions we have only read or heard.[59]

This is undoubtedly connected to the social status of the characters and to the extra-textual nature of so much of the clown's act.

All these factors are present in Richard McCabe's essay on playing Autolycus, who possesses the typical fool attributes: he 'talks directly to the audience, offers an alternative view of the action of the play, and is almost completely in prose'. He continues by identifying the character as 'an Armin fool', before outlining the Armin 'type': 'The advent of Armin heralded a darker, more intellectually complex character, with Touchstone probably the first of the Armin fools.'[60] McCabe uses this characteristic to justify an extremely Stanislavskyan interpretation of the part, complete with backstory tortuously worked out and presented to the audience. McCabe decided that Autolycus had been a city trader, sacked for embezzlement and insider dealing. He had a mock newspaper made up with a prominent photo of himself in an Armani suit being hauled off to gaol under the headline 'Servant Guilty'. In this way, by producing the newspaper on the line "but now I am out of service", I was able to give the audience a past history and a reason for my present situation'.[61]

Autolycus thus ceases to be a 'self-contained entity' and acquires a journey. McCabe chose also to use a selection of accents, but rather than an attempt to imply exterior character they came to denote realism, becoming a vehicle for making the character's con tricks more credible, as he adopted a different one each time the Clown – or Young Shepherd, as he was called in this production – is cozened. The change of name for this character, increasingly common in production (but resolutely refused in editions of the play),[62] demonstrates clearly the tendency towards realistic logic – there is an Old Shepherd, and therefore his son must be the Young Shepherd.

McCabe concludes with a remark quoted earlier, that his intention is to find solutions that are acceptable to both 'your character's inner life and one's own sense of personal truth'. In the case of Autolycus, these things are effectively identical and are perceived as transcending the text. McCabe makes little reference to the authority of Shakespeare or even the playwright's relationship to the text. For him, character is transcendent and to be located as much within the actor as within the text. It is therefore appropriate that his unconventional approach to a clown role is ultimately sanctioned more by reference to an actor, the 'intellectually complex' Armin, than to an author.

In contrast, a valuable indication of just how technical, planned and precise a comic performance can be is provided by Donald Sinden's essay on Malvolio, which is a paradigm of external characterisation. He explains: 'He has a small, tight, mean mouth, the corners of which turn down. He is thin – too thin – from his years of austerity ... The eyebrows, the mouth, the wrinkles – every one of them vertical, and that is what I must be – vertical.'[63] He then literally charts his performance, plotting his position on a graph of the stage and assessing the success of his characterisation according to audience response. This takes the form of a 'laugh-ometer', in which moves and delivery are planned according to the size of the laugh they are intended to garner. It is difficult to ascertain to what extent this scheme has been retrospectively applied, though it has probably been continually modified throughout the course of the run, acquiring a sense of unity it most likely lacked during the process of experiment. The result is a performance as choreographed as a piece of dance, in which every line, indeed almost every moment on stage, was worked out and tested in detail.

The most interesting consequence of this approach is the establishment of a kind of performance subjectivity just as individual as that of Philip Voss's ultra-Stanislavskyan performance of Menenius, in which he speaks of following his 'point of concentration' in rehearsal to the point of undermining the performances of his fellow cast members.[64] Sinden recalls his character-isation from Malvolio's point of view, calling other characters by name and replicating Malvolio's misapprehensions, to the extent of possibly confusing a reader who does not know *Twelfth Night* well. Yet he never ceases to provide a full account of his technical decisions. He explains this as follows:

> I am now 100% Malvolio, but in a comedy I, the actor, must remain 100% myself, standing outside my character, my ears on stalks, listening for the very slightest sound from the audience, controlling them, so that I am able to steer a cue ... If on any night Malvolio takes over, the precision, the immaculate timing, the control suffer. If the actor takes over, the performance becomes technical and the audience is always aware of it.[65]

This kind of precision is echoed by an actor who is ostensibly very different in approach, Simon Russell Beale, who remarked that his performance of Ariel was '99% conscious' of the audience and 'therefore if you ask me: "What do you do on that particular line on that particular scene?", I can tell you'.[66] The performance is defined by the audience response: in an empty theatre there is a real sense that Sinden's Malvolio would not exist. Peter Holland has remarked that

> At times ... it has seemed that consideration of the audience at all has been completely absent, that character study is still based on an assumption that the theatrical must be suppressed in favour of the fictional, and that Shakespeare only wrote plays through the misfortune of being born too early to have written novels.[67]

Sinden's approach is entirely theatrical and owes little or nothing to novelistic or psychological methods of constructing character. In both this essay and in an interview during his performance of King Lear, he sums up his methodology in the same words:

> Ellen Terry said the best line that's ever been said about acting. Two sentences in which every word is of monumental importance. She said: 'To act, you must make the thing written your own. You must steal the words, steal the thought, and convey the stolen treasure to others with great art.'[68]

Sinden's authority, importantly, is an actor, not a playwright. Moreover, though Terry's words initially recall the possessive perspective of Ralph Bashford, they are significantly modified by the inclusion of the audience, and by the acknowledgement of theft. In other words, performance becomes transitive, it automatically has an addressee. More interesting, though, is the characterisation of actor as thief. In *The Dialogic Imagination* Mikhail Bakhtin comments

> Language, for the individual consciousness, lies on the borderline between oneself and the other. The word in language is half someone else's. It becomes 'one's own' only when the speaker populates it with his own intention ... when he appropriates the word, adopting it to his own semantic and expressive intention. Prior to this moment the word exists in other people's mouths.[69]

Terry's advice, and Sinden's application of it, implicitly recognise the borderline state of all language and appropriates that position in order to define the stage self. This theft is then reconfigured as a gift in order for the transaction with the audience to be complete. Bakhtin continues:

> Not all words for just anyone submit equally to this appropriation, to this seizure and transformation into private property: many words stubbornly resist, others remain alien, sound foreign in the mouth of the one who appropriated them and who now speaks them ... it is as if they put themselves in quotation marks against the will of the speaker.[70]

The experience of performing – or hearing – a famous Shakespearean speech is markedly similar to this, as is the frequent occasion on which a small or medium-sized character will suddenly break his or her idiom to perform a complex or poetic speech. The authority of the words is not successfully stolen and remains with the playwright or, in the case of the clowns, perhaps the performer whose patter has been partly transcribed.

For Sinden, then, characterisation is a liminal phenomenon, existing on the fringe of contact between performer, text and spectator. It exists only in interaction, rather than in the fictitious fabric of a completed psychology. Sinden, through recourse to the authority of performance rather than of authorship, predicates his characterisation on the play-acting of those he is addressing, which as his account makes clear includes the audience as much as, and perhaps more than, his onstage addressees. This radical conception of characterisation as liminal performance is echoed by Simon Russell Beale's discussion of Thersites, in which he remarks that 'the element of theatricality, of performance, as opposed to the detailed realisation of character, seems to be of paramount importance'.[71]

Beale begins his account of playing Thersites with a thoughtful linking of characterisation with linguistic style:

> Too little has been written about the performance of Shakespeare's prose as opposed to the performance of his verse – probably because the added comic and therefore idiosyncratic ingredient is rather

difficult to define, because analyses of the clowns rely so heavily on their being seen and cannot be fully discussed apart from particular performances. So, for an actor, constructing a Shakespearean clown is a leap in the dark.[72]

Beale is one of the few actors who reads criticism voraciously and approaches a part with an academic frame of mind, believing that 'an intellectual journey is emotionally exciting ... There doesn't seem to be another way to do these great Shakespearean roles – I just hope the result isn't academic. I love the construction of an argument.'[73] To have this frame removed is to undermine an authority, throwing him back on to the authority of the playwright. Consequently, he is much more aware than other actors in the *Players* series of a direct engagement with Shakespeare.

Early on in rehearsal, combating phase one of Shakespearean-clown-syndrome – Can I be funny? – Beale discovers that 'to my enormous relief and delight I found that once I had started working, Thersites was genuinely, fluidly funny and, even better, psychologically complex'.[74] A familiar sequence then sets in, culminating in Beale formulating a series of intentions and objectives, motivations and explanations for Thersites' behaviour, including a physical handicap that prevented him from fighting. Beale thus reached a point similar to that characterising the performances of Sher or McCabe, before he began questioning his work:

It [Thersites' handicap] is a sentimental argument, but it developed to provide a firm psychological basis for Thersites' consistently reductive analyses. It was also the argument that was the first to be challenged by the demands of audiences over the period of playing.[75]

Attending to the response of the audience, he slowly began to alter the characterisation:

I began to care less about why Thersites is the sort of man he is than about the fact that he is a brilliant performer – to care less about causes than symptoms, as it were. This simpler approach had two effects: it allowed Thersites to become less human and more diabolical, and it pushed the play into much darker, more destructive areas. What I lost was a whole set of complex reasons behind Thersites' actions.[76]

The interaction with the audience the role of clown allowed him slowly erased the psychology of the role, replacing it with a liminal, borderline characterisation similar to that of Sinden:

What is certain is that I realised that Thersites is a movable feast, that his function in the play was determined as much by audience response and by my own state of mind at the time of playing as it was by the work I did in rehearsal.[77]

Beale's choice of words here is particularly apt, his phrase 'a movable feast' containing an implication of the carnivalesque that is highly appropriate for the suppurating Thersites. His recognition that his own mood affected his performance more than is customary is a further link to the traditions of clown performance, incorporating the actor's own surface emotions rather as a stand-up comic might do.

The position of the clown in the play, on the frontier of internal action but aware of the audience, has been theorised by Robert Weimann as a platea position as opposed to the locus of the play itself. As he explains, 'unlike the locus, which could assume an illusionary character, the platea provided an entirely non-representational and unlocalised setting'.[78] Yet in the case of Thersites, who has a role within the action of the main plot, such an opposition cannot be maintained. Nor can it be said that the character moves from one such position to another. An ironic detachment is maintained in dialogue with other characters, and the servant Thersites remains when the audience is addressed. Rather there is in evidence a dual position where a character occupies the two zones simultaneously, as clown and as Clown, as it were, function (role) and character (expression) co-existing at the same time.

The complexities of address that this position necessitates prompt Beale perceptively to state that 'it is the responsibility of the actor playing him to make sure that Thersites' views do not imperceptibly come to appear as those of Shakespeare. He must not become the voice of the playwright.'[79] The clown's privileges do not extend to surrogate authorial expression, as the confusion of 'role' with the functions of an implied narrator often leads spectators familiar with nineteenth-century novelistic realism and with cinema to suppose. It is this strict understanding of Thersites' role, rather than his character, that allows Beale to not only evade the pitfalls of imposed psychology but also to avoid a reliance on an appropriated authorial mandate. In terms of mimesis, then, Beale refuses to imitate a notion of reality, instead allowing his performance to be dictated by its individual circumstances. To an incomplete degree, the performance is anti-mimetic.

IV

Clowns and fools allow the workings of their inscription to be laid comparatively bare. Consequently their subversive capabilities within the playworld are limited, as their modes of attack are known. There is no harm in a licensed fool. Matters become considerably more complex, however, when aspects of the clown's role are buried within seemingly conventional characterisation. As Lesley Wade Soule writes:

Not being fully mimetic himself, the clown is less effectively anti mimetic. Nor can he achieve the critical irony of the anti-mimetic actor, who can subvert from within, seeming to disappear behind the impersonation and then emerging unexpectedly with a parodic gesture or subversive comment.[80]

Recalling Sher and the chimp, Simon Russell Beale when embarking on playing Richard III commented:

At drama school they used to send us out to study an animal at London Zoo and you had to be that animal in class for two hours. Subliminally, that's almost always how I work. And the great thing about Richard is that you have so many to chose from. Tony Sher chose spider. I chose toad.[81]

Given that Beale was a student at the time Sher was researching the Fool, it's a wonder they didn't run in to each other at the zoo – two prospective hunchbacks staring at the wildlife. In another interview, Beale remarks that he hasn't 'the physical dexterity to play him as a spider, as Tony Sher did. I'm the "bunchbacked toad". I think Richard III is the best clown Shakespeare ever wrote.'[82]

Beale's next Shakespearean role after Thersites, again in a production directed by Sam Mendes at Stratford, was Richard. Beale here draws attention to exactly that facet of the role that Soule calls 'the anti-mimetic character', one that subverts the established fictional frame of the play-world. That Richard has many of the features of the Vice as well as of more contemporary Clown roles is a commonplace, and was echoed directly in David Troughton's jester costume in the 1995 RSC production he discusses in *Players 4*. The other Richard in the series is that of Anton Lesser, who played the role in Adrian Noble's edited version of the first tetralogy, *The Plantagenets*, in 1987. Perhaps the most famous Richard of the last two decades was Antony Sher in Bill Alexander's 1984 production, written about at length in Sher's *The Year of the King*.

As Beale informs us, Sher's choice of animal for the role was the 'bottled spider', illustrated in several sketches reproduced in his book. He was not the first to start from this decision. John Barrymore in 1920 too modelled his performance on the 'bottled spider', inspired by a real one observed in the Bronx Zoo: 'the personification of a crawling power'.[83] More than most Shakespearean roles, Richard seems to engender repetition in per-formance choices – mimesis of previous performances rather than an actual original. In this it continues the likeness to the Clown, a role that also maintains a certain pattern of 'business'.

Olivier, referring to his celebrated stage and film success in the part, remarked that 'one thing that may lead an actor to be successful in a part

... is to try to be unlike someone else in it'.[84] Consequently, one of his impulses was to go against the interpretation of Donald Wolfit, who had produced his own successful production shortly before Olivier embarked on the role. Similar pressures were felt by Antony Sher, who recounts even dreaming of Olivier:

> Again that shadow falls across the landscape and I dart around trying to find some light of my own. My Richard is still in its infancy, barely that, it is still struggling to take form, uncertain even whether to take form. And there's this fully formed, famously formed, infamous child murderer leaning over the cradle.[85]

The imagery here is of course highly appropriate: the figure of Olivier merging with that of Richard and attempting to smother a mirror image. Sher is grappling with the notoriety and fame of a role in a manner entirely suitable for a play that, in its original incarnation, would have played upon the fame of the central character in Elizabethan England. As Burns remarks; 'Individuated figures, named and known as themselves, tend to reflect on the conditions of their fame – the action tends to be developed out of such considerations, and the player's action ... is used to present it as character.'[86] In other words, character is created in definition to the persona of the named figure as extant before the play is written, just as Sher and others define their approaches against the previous work of celebrated actors. The processes of authorial and performance constructions of character echo and inform each other.

Within the play, Richard is a child killer who has a spectacularly bad relationship with his own mother, a factor picked up on by almost all players of the role. Sher, after repeated consultations with his psychoanalyst, concludes that Richard's problem stems from 'an absence of love. Caused by a hating mother. This is what I will base my performance on. But I will have to be quite secretive about it because it sounds so corny – his mother didn't love him.'[87] David Troughton similarly decides that 'here was the perfect psychological reason for his twisted outlook on life, for his difficulty in framing any meaningful, loving relationships ... the complete absence of any motherly love'.[88] Received notions of a classical Oedipus Complex are thus imported into performance decisions.

Interestingly, in his introduction to the Oxford edition of the play, John Jowett theorises that Richard himself blames his mother for the way he is – including the breach birth that left him disfigured – but that there comes a point when this excuse is no longer tenable, even to Richard:

> Richard fended off any responsibility for his own accounts for as long as he could blame himself on his ontological beginnings, and hence on his mother. Her rejection of him signifies not only that humanity as a

whole has turned against him, but also that he must take new account of himself.[89]

In short, Shakespeare's Richard pre-empts that of Sher and Troughton by deliberately appropriating this line of reasoning in order to evade accountability. Psychology becomes evasion. Despite Worthen's claims, Sher never shrugged off the psychological overtones of his approach. Troughton, however, did – in large measure because of the extremely metatheatrical nature of the production in which he found himself.

The idea of Richard as 'metaphorical jester' led to an even stronger emphasis being placed on his relationship with the audience. Sher had previously noted the intimacy of this connection, referring to the audience as 'a convention of trainee Richard IIIs'. Troughton takes this further, through an imaginative use of the concept of conscience: 'Richard had already displayed an awareness of conscience and had made clear that the audience was a theatrical extension of his own self, with whom he could converse at any point in the play.'[90] Troughton brings the audience into Richard's head, understanding the construction of the play as one man's point of view, but rejects a psychological way of doing this, instead achieving it through the much more appropriate device of conscience. As Jowett comments, 'Richard has attempted to fabricate himself as an autonomous being, but his recognition of conscience is a discovery that he has done so within a larger scheme of creation.'[91] Troughton's interpretation here was based on Richard's lines on the eve of battle, which he understood as representing the theatrical audience:

> My conscience hath a thousand several tongues,
> And every tongue brings in a several tale,
> And every tale condemns me for a villain. (5.4, 172–74)

Revealing the complex significance of this scene further, Troughton played the Q1 version of line 162: 'Richard loves Richard; that is, I and I' rather than Q2's 'I am I', explaining that 'the first Richard in the sentence is the audience and the second is himself, the man. Two separate identities forming one complete person creating "I and I".'[92]

The emphasis placed by Troughton on this speech in particular as key to the role is echoed five years later in Jowett's edition, which retains the Q2 reading: 'The entire play's vantage point is that of Richard on the eve of battle ... By the end, the carefully patterned repetitions, implausible in themselves, might be understood as a retrospective narrative of self.'[93] And Troughton concludes that, 'unable to live with the two separate identities within himself, Richard dies at the hands of his conscience rather than at the point of a sword'.[94] This is an interpretation that unwittingly echoes the remarks of Montaigne: 'So wonderful is the power of conscience; it makes us betray, accuse, and fight against ourselves, and for want of out-side testimony, witness against ourselves.'[95]

Richard's self-induced death was emphasised in the production, in which Richard dies under the weight of Richmond's words, spoken from a balcony full of ghosts, and his own deformity. For once, actor and scholar are in harmony. Troughton's Richard becomes integral to the whole play, his interpretation inseparable from that of the production as a whole. Meredith Anne Skura draws links between Richard's division of self and the Chorus in *Henry V* requesting the audience to 'into a thousand parts divide one man, and make imaginary puissance':

> The Chorus doesn't ask the audience, as one might expect after hear-ing that there are not enough actors, to multiply one actor to represent many soldiers, but rather to divide him, as Richard had felt divided. The imagination moves both inward and outward, from mental space to theatrical space ... with the actor's body as the pivot, divided into a thousand parts. It is as if one plenitude created another, the multi-tudinous inner world conditional upon the multitude thronging to see it externalised on the peopled stage.[96]

By employing the trope of conscience, Troughton exactly replicates this move, making the physical space represent Richard's mind and, more importantly, making Richard's mental world a subdivision of that of the theatrical space. Moreover, conscience acquires a tangible reality for Troughton in the grotesque shape of Richard's hump.

Despite following Sher in once again beginning by discovering a realistic medical explanation for the deformity, in this case a breach-birth-related hip dislocation leading to constant pain, a limp and a curved spine, Troughton dropped all notions of naturalism once he had found a suitable way to walk. Instead, the hump became a symbol of Richard's mental state, not unlike Christian's famous burden in Bunyan's *The Pilgrim's Progress*. Troughton talks of several ways in which this could be used, including the intriguing idea of losing the deformity altogether in solilo-quy, which 'made the point that there were two Richards in the play – the one he presents to the audience and the other to the court'.[97]

Though this idea was eventually discarded, the concept of altering the severity of the disability at certain times was retained: 'This allowed me to use my body in extraordinary ways, "adding colours to the chameleon" and changing "shapes with Proteus". Various degrees of deformity could be attained for different scenes to suit different moods.'[98] This is once again consonant with Jowett's insightful discussion of the hunchback as 'a hall-mark of acting as a process of transformation' and 'a metatheatrical function in its own right'.[99] Such a viewpoint was taken to the extreme in Troughton's interpretation, the disability initially seeming (as with his conscience) to be under Richard's volition, part of his performance, before later becoming the cause of his downfall. Thus what at first seems a triumph of self-formation is gradually understood to be an inescapably predetermined deformation. As Jowett comments, as if on Troughton's performance:

> The complex texture of the dramatic role depends on the interplay between Richard as reportraiture and Richard as a figure of immediacy, energy and presence. Deformity gives a physical immediacy to the historical person and to the Vice that precede him alike. At the same time deformity is the defining bodily characteristic of the play-world's here and now.[100]

Troughton's emphasis on the most external aspect of the characterisation of this part, and his understanding and exploitation of its metatheatrical capabilities, produces a characterisation that is not only on the border of audience and actor (as represented by the jester's costume), but is also constructed in the gap between history and performance, and presence and absence. Mimesis here is no longer limited to the representation of a constructed interiority, but extends to an awareness of the self-referential nature of the play and of the history it refashions.

There is one sense in which Troughton's performance could not locate itself historically, and that was the absence of the context provided by the *Henry VI* trilogy. In 1987 Anton Lesser played Richard Gloucester throughout the three plays in which the character appears, and noted that 'an advantage of doing the whole cycle was that you saw the emergence of the figure from history – in the same way that Hitler didn't just turn up out of the blue in 1939'.[101] It is a problem encountered by Antony Sher, again focusing on the extent of the physical disability:

> Discuss the crutches in the light of what the young Richard has to do in *Henry VI*. Is the problem relevant? Does an actor playing Antony in *Antony and Cleopatra* have to cross-check his performance against the same character in Julius Caesar?[102]

If an actor is playing all the parts in the same season, the answer seems to be a resounding 'yes'. Lesser's Henry, Ralph Fiennes, reflected that 'what was wonderful about playing the Henry VI trilogy was the nature of the journey the characters make'.[103] Penny Downie, playing Margaret, reinforced this, saying that for her 'it became very much a single character over three plays'.[104] Lesser himself sums up the collective opinion by remarking that he 'had to build a real person, not a two-dimensional figure of evil, but a person whose seeds I found in *1 Henry VI*'.[105] Here, the actor takes psychological consistency to the point of analysing a play in which his character does not even appear.

Interestingly, the most recent RSC productions of both tetralogies in 2000–2001, which have surprising similarities to Noble's *Plantagenets* in the staging of *Henry VI*,[106] have produced greater disparity among the casts as to this sense of a 'journey'. Fiona Bell playing Margaret and Aidan McArdle playing Richard have both expressed their sense of through-lines in the characterisation. However, Will Houston as Henry V and, significantly, David Troughton as Bolingbroke are less enamoured of the idea, preferring to play their characters as discontinuous, Houston referring to Hal and Henry V as 'two entirely different parts'.[107]

Lesser's characterisation of Richard is less focused on his relationship with the audience than with other Shakespearean texts, authority residing comfortably once more with the playwright. Despite this, there is one moment of doubt within his rhetoric, concerning lines 157–8 in Richard's soliloquy at the end of act one. The soliloquy sets out Richard's plans, including the seduction of Lady Anne, which Richard tells us he will carry out 'for another secret close intent'. As Lesser remarks, 'and they say soliloquies are for characters to tell the truth to the audience!'[108]

Lesser here touches on an important point. Only the imposition of a pseudo-fourth-wall technique, in which it is assumed that the character is unaware of the spectator, requires the soliloquy to be inward-looking and confessional. No such restriction existed on the Renaissance stage, where both actor and character were fully aware of the audience. As Richard's words make clear, the purpose of the soliloquy is to reveal intention, not truth about an inner self. It is therefore up to the character how much of that intention he or she decides to disclose, and to whom – a meta-theatrically present audience or a projection of various thought processes.

Richard further emphasises the same point in conversation with the Princes:

Nor more can you distinguish of a man
Than of his outward show, which God He knows
Seldom or never jumpeth with the heart. (3.1, 9–11)

This is somewhat ironic spoken by the deformed Duke, but nevertheless a Renaissance commonplace.[109] It is echoed more famously, of course, by Hamlet:

For they are actions that a man might play:
But I have that within which passeth show;
These but the trappings and the suits of woe. (1.2, 84–6)

This admission of the incapability of inferring inner truths necessitated a dramatic form that included manifold devices for the expression of intention, but that above all retained the Aristotelean emphasis on *praxis* and *mythos* as opposed to the post-Romantic, and particularly post-Stanislavskyan emphasis on *ethos* or, later, on subtext. The metaphor of an inner 'journey' originates with the Protestant, eschatological preoccupation with Grace evident in religious autobiography of the mid-seventeenth century. It is certainly not a preoccupation of Renaissance drama. Modern actors too often assume the exact opposite, that what matters is what happens when the character is not on stage. As Holland says:

> The character's 'journey' through the play ... depends for the actor on a notion of a findable and playable inner consistency. How the actor gets from one scene of onstage presence to another is located in the offstage fictive continuities of the character.[110]

Indeed, in *An Actor Prepares*, Stanislavsky wrote that the playwright 'omits much of what happens offstage ... we have to fill out what he leaves unsaid. Otherwise we would have only scraps and bits to offer out of the life of the persons we portray ... we must create for our parts unbroken lines.'[111] In short, 'actors worry where their characters go when they are not visible to the audience'.[112] Justifying a decision made about Macbeth's intention, Harriet Walter states 'it must have happened offstage'.[113] Paraphrasing Antony Sher, Michael Goldfarb in an interview with the actor conducted when Sher was playing Shylock in *The Merchant of Venice*, writes:

> Unlike Richard III who is on stage [for] most of the play and goes through his emotional transitions before the audience, Shylock is off-stage for much of the performance and most of his emotional changes take place in the dressing room.[114]

Bringing the 'offstage' and non-textual life of a character on stage, demonstrating to the audience aspects of that character they would not expect to find in a reading of the play, is a preoccupation that reaches the point of obsession with Shylock.

V

In his essay on the role in *Players 1*, Patrick Stewart encapsulates the actor's problem with this role:

> Shylock appears in five scenes. Each scene has a quite distinctive quality. One approach would be to blend these qualities in such a way as to present a regular and consistent picture at all appearances. On the other hand, the particular characteristics of each scene can be isolated and individually played without reference to other scenes.

This approach relies on the conviction that it will not be until the moment of his final exit that the last piece will be added to the puzzle that is Shylock, and the picture completed and truly consistent.[115]

Once again, consistency is all, and either approach is emphatically tele-ological, a factor no doubt influenced by Shylock's final moments taking the form of a conviction at trial. The character becomes inextricably bound up with notions of legality, in addition to the more obvious features of commerce and trade. Stewart's comments here put the weight of his interpretation not just on the trial scene, but upon Shylock's exit, his final move from stage presence to absence following his defeated 'I am content'. This moment has become a celebrated means of establishing a completing gesture to an actor's characterisation: Irving ended the play with Shylock's mournful exit, an option considered also by Sher;[116] Olivier from the corridors behind the stage delivered a blood-curdling cry the echoes of which, according to Bulman, resonated in the mind of the spectator throughout the final act.[117]

Stewart's interpretation was not sympathetic. He felt the line 'I am content' illustrated Shylock's absolute dependency on wealth above all other considerations. For him, the character was obsessional:

A man in whose life there is an imbalance, an obsession with the retention and acquisition of wealth which is so fixated that it displaces the love and paternal feelings of father for daughter. It transcends race and religion and is felt to be as important as life itself.[118]

This view was supported early in rehearsal when Stewart was pleased to find that the director John Barton's brief 'was very simple – he [Shylock] must be a monster'. Stewart's approach pursued this line with, as he admits, only one exception – Shylock's grief at the loss of Leah's ring. 'That word shatters our image of this man Shylock ... Shakespeare doesn't need to write a pre-history of him – those two lines say it all.'[119]

Yet this moment was not enough to shatter Stewart's and Barton's view of the character, whom they saw as mean, to the point of storing fag-ends in his shabby waistcoat, and obsessively mercantile. Tubal's report on Jessica's extravagances included his own bill for residence at 'the Genoa Hilton', a moment that, among others, was felt by Arnold Wesker to be unreservedly anti-Semitic: 'Canny old Tubal presents him with a bill. Ho! Ho! The audience laughed again to be reminded that not only do Jews suck dry Christian blood, they suck dry each other's as well!'[120] The moment was present in both Stewart's performance in 1979, in which he pocketed the bill without paying, and in Barton's restaging of the same production with David Suchet two years later, when Suchet paid up instantly.[121]

Although working within the same basic framework, Suchet's Shylock was a very different performance – an ostentatious, polished and assured man of business modelled on the Rothschilds. In approaching the role Suchet devoted much of his time to a close textual analysis, discovering not only the contrast between scenes, but also the contradictions within them, and even within speeches. On 'Hath not a Jew eyes?' he comments: 'In the big speech there are real contradictions. Earlier he has said he will not eat with you, drink with you, pray with you. We know he's kosher. Yet here he says "fed with the same food". Well, he's not, in fact.'[122] Suchet then allows this discrepancy to inform the playing of the trial scene, in which he observes that 'Shakespeare is also very clever with the pound of flesh without blood because kosher meat is meat without blood.'[123] Suchet therefore locates Shylock's conflict in a sense of his religion; in the trial scene the near-parodic portrayal of Jewish vengeance is countered by an excessively parodic enacting of Jewish ritual.

This careful technique of microscopic textual analysis is evident also in Suchet's two essays for the *Players* series, on Caliban and Iago.[124] After reading vast quantities of scholarship on Iago, he concluded that 'almost everyone who has ever written about Iago or played Iago is always in search of one thing: motivation'.[125] Iago thus becomes a paradigm for the search for inner psychological consistency. Suchet discovers that no one has found a satisfactory explanation of Iago's actions; instead 'we get a series of labels', ranging from latent homosexual through Machiavel to 'the devil's emissary'. Suchet dismisses all of these (though he allowed the 'ambiguity of latent homosexuality' to filter through at points in his performance) as evidently wrong because they allow 'the actor to play the role almost irrespective of his Othello'.[126]

Eventually Suchet decided to base his performance on Iago's role, rather than his character: his place in the play's *mythos* rather than his independent existence as *ethos*. He thus investigated 'not how to play Iago, but why Shakespeare wrote him ... why does Shakespeare need him?'[127] Suchet found his answer in Emilia's speech in act three:

> But Jealous souls will not be answer'd so;
> They are not ever jealous for the cause,
> But jealous for they're jealous. (3.4, 159–61)

Iago, in other words, 'represents Jealousy, is Jealousy', and Suchet's performance was of a man riddled and obsessed with that one thing who found or invented reasons 'to make those deeds allowable ... even though they are not valid justifications'.[128] As with Beale's performances, Suchet finds a solution in a kind of anti-mimesis.

Suchet's Shylock was similarly a man obsessed with one aim, vengeance, while at the same time haunted by his religion. In contrast,

Stewart claimed to have played down the cultural differences of the role:

> I was anxious to minimise the impression of Shylock's Jewishness. Whenever I had seen either a very ethnic or detailedly Jewish Shylock I felt that something was lost. Jewishness could become a smoke-screen which might conceal both the particular and the universal in the role. See him as a Jew first and foremost and he is in danger of becoming only a symbol.[129]

Yet he also claimed the character's desire for his bond was 'symbolic', and although he does not say of what, he presumably means this in a religious sense. The perverse decision to establish a villainous continuity in the character by excising his most conspicuous identifying feature allows commercial extremism to be played as dominant, with Judaism brought in here and there for comedy value or to justify awkward contradictions. In this production, Portia was justified in inquiring: 'Which is the merchant here, and which the Jew?' (4.1, 170).

Stewart is unique among accounts of playing the role to proffer a Shylock ostensibly largely without Jewishness. Yet this approach finally emphasises the character's cultural status even as it apparently subordinates it. Obsession with wealth becomes a religion in itself, one identified with Judaism through bits of business such as the moment with Tubal. Shylock regains a stereotypical identity, endowed by an audience susceptible to a degree of possibly unconscious anti-Semitism. By playing a particular through-line, then, Stewart manipulates the history of the role in order to allow the audience to perceive another such line. The teleological dependency of his characterisation upon the moment of Shylock's defeat reduces the role to that single, final moment.

Katherine Eisaman Maus has written of the importance of jurisprudence to an understanding of Elizabethan/Jacobean theatre, commenting that 'English courts made no rules about the admissibility of evidence, no qualitative distinction among kinds of proof, until well into the seventeenth century. The power to convince the jury was all that mattered.'[130] In short, the emphasis was on rhetoric in the courts as it was in the theatre. In the case of *The Merchant of Venice*, such an emphasis helps us to understand how Stewart's decision goes against the grain of the part's careful construction, which echoes what Maus calls 'the effect of the English [legal] system, [which] was to displace the focus of public attention from the processes of punishment to the processes of gathering and interpreting evidence'.[131]

In other words, the effect of legal rhetoric was not teleological, but metonymic, privileging the parts of the argument over the end result. In *De Oratore*, Cicero sets out the five component parts of rhetoric: *Inventio,*

Dispositio, Elocutio, Memoria and *Actio*.[132] Unsurprisingly, given the prominence of the teaching of rhetoric in the sixteenth-century schoolroom, such Ciceronean composition finds a structural place within *The Merchant of Venice*. Though there is no direct equivalence between these categories and Shylock's five appearances in the play, it is interesting to note that his first and last appearances correlate exactly with the Ciceronian headings of *Inventio* and *Actio*. In particular, the first meeting of Bassanio, Antonio and Shylock proceeds through the points of *Inventio* with almost formal precision. According to Aristotle these points are: *Ethos* – establishing good character ('Antonio is a good man'); *Pathos* – manipulating the audience into the right frame of mind ('I would be friends with you and have your love'); and *Logos* – proving, or seeming to prove, the case (the parable of Jacob and Laban).[133]

By using the parts of rhetoric so explicitly, Shylock establishes a model of character that is above all legal. His punning on 'good' twins this with the commercial meaning of security, able to repay the debt. As an alien living a precarious existence within strictly enforced boundaries, Shylock's concept of character is necessarily so defined. As John Drakakis writes, 'whereas among the Christian Venetians subjectivity is negotiable, and permeable, the Jew's behaviour and his identity are constrained by Law'.[134]

Such a legalistic understanding of self must necessarily be metonymic, concerned with details, parts and moments. As Maus has demonstrated, this was also the natural condition of the Shakespearean stage: 'English Renaissance theatrical method is . . . radically synecdochic, endlessly referring the spectators to events, objects, situations, landscapes that cannot be shown them.'[135] Shylock's otherness, and particularly the received image of his Jewishness, exacerbate this phenomenon.[136] In 1562 Bishop John Jewell wrote:

> *Chrysostome* compareth the state of the Jewes unto a candle: and the state of the Christians, to the Brightness of the Sunne. Againe he likeneth the Jewes to the first draught, or plat of an image, set out only in bare lines: and the Christians unto the same image lively filled up with all due proportion, and resemblance and furniture of colours.[137]

The Jew is an unfinished draught, requiring the Christian to complete it. Moreover, the Jew is also a bare plot, form without content, needful of Christian detail to flesh it out, as it were. Shylock is depicted as lacking, and what he lacks is Christianity, given to him at the final moments of the trial. He becomes, in both senses of the word, content.

Shylock's character is constructed according to a model that continually refers not just to a selfhood concealed beneath 'outward show', but one that is present elsewhere, off stage. Such is the urge to show offstage business in this play that Irving inserted for Shylock a sixth scene, placed just before the interval in order to provide him with a suitably grand exit. In this scene we see Shylock return home after Jessica has fled, and knock just once, poignantly, on his door. Later Shylocks expanded this moment of gentleness to more melodramatic proportions, with Tree discovering Jessica's absence, crumbling to the ground and covering his head with a convenient pile of ashes.[138]

These insertions have much to do with the need to be centre stage and to transform a supporting character into a lead role, but they also connect with perceptions of the Jew as other. Irving spoke at length of his inspiration for the role:

> I saw a Jew once, in Tunis, tear his hair and raiment, fling himself in the sand, and writhe in a rage, about a question of money – beside himself with passion. I saw him again, self-possessed and fawning; and again, expressing real gratitude for a trifling money courtesy. He was never undignified until he tore his hair and flung himself down, and then he was picturesque.[139]

Apocryphal as the story possibly is, it is interesting for its simultaneous profession of admiration and difference. This Jew is fascinating because of his exoticism and because of his displacement to the appropriately othered location of Tunis.

Over a century later, Antony Sher played a Shylock remarkably similar to the Jew of Irving's 'picturesque' encounter. A Levantine, dressed in the garb of a Turkish peddler, his accent was thick, toying with caricature. Bulman remarks that this Shylock recalled 'unassimilated Shylocks of earlier times, from Macklin to Kean'.[140] Sher himself reflected that 'there is something about the way in which Shylock is moved to exact extreme penalties by the extent of the barbarism he endures which seems to me to have applications to South Africa and the Middle East'.[141] Consequently his Shylock evoked not just Jews but other 'semitic peoples: Arabs, Palestinians, Iranians', with deliberate overtones of clichés of Middle Eastern terrorism. Bulman reads Sher's performance as a response to the strategies of previous Shylocks inspired by the actor's own cultural differences:

> Just as he had in his celebrated performance of Richard III, for which Olivier's performance had provided a similar obstacle, Sher sought to overturn the tradition of 'English' characterisation and to play Shylock afresh ... He conceived of characters from an alien perspective, in light of cultural models different from those traditionally offered to British actors.[142]

As Irving's Tunisian shows, however, perhaps these cultural models were less distinct than Bulman supposes. Significantly, Shylock was the first role in which Sher professed a strict Stanislavskyan system of emotional recall, as opposed to the loosely psychoanalytic approach he had used for Richard: 'Emotional recall is something I've never used before in my work. I didn't know how to. It's such a private thing I didn't know it could be taught.'[143] Reviews of the production made much of Sher's own Judaism in a way that they had failed to do with David Suchet six years previously, implying that the characterisation to a degree was born from Sher's personality and that Shylock was an extension of the actor. At face value, the actor's own rhetoric supports this, but is complicated by the fact that the emotional recall played not on Sher's religion but on his nationality: 'We didn't want our production to be about anti-Semitism only but about racism more generally. Curiously, although I was born Jewish, *The Merchant of Venice* has always said more to me as a South African.'[144] Sher, at this point still a South African exile, appropriates the displaced within himself to sanction the authority of his performance. His Judaism is not different enough, does not carry the cultural otherness today that it did four hundred years ago. Therefore, other facets of his identity – his birth nationality and, interestingly, his homosexuality – are conscripted into service as signifiers for oppressed otherness. Presenting character becomes a mimesis of the othered elements of his own personality.

This move to make the play more generally political included bringing out the racism of Portia's remarks to Morocco, echoed by the pertinent casting of black actors as servants, and making several characters homosexual to mirror the homoeroticism of the Antonio/Bassanio relationship, including the Salads, with Gregory Doran as Solanio. As Bulman remarks:

> In Alexander's production, therefore, alienation is not limited to the Jews. It infects the whole society – a society whose notions of class, whose rules of conduct in sex as in business, even whose religion, alienates men from one another and, worse, from themselves.[145]

One consequence of this was the alienation of the player of a much larger role in the play: Deborah Findlay as Portia. In her essay in *Players 3* she writes:

> I was asked to hit my servants, be calculating about money, beady about Antonio. All these things came from a misunderstanding of her true worth. They were all rejected when I realised that her place is above and beyond this pettiness and that because she is rich and has all the natural confidence that wealth can give she is not necessarily a 'bad thing.'[146]

Feeling hemmed in by the male politics explored by Alexander and Sher, Findlay increasingly formulated an isolated and defensive Portia, even transforming the comments about Morocco into an example of feminism in action: 'We felt that Morocco would treat a wife as his property . . . This may have been seen as reacting against his colour but it is much more to do with being treated as a sexual object – an interesting conundrum: who is the oppressor?'[147] The latter is a question that is arguably addressed by the scene itself, rather than the openly racist Portia. For Findlay, the casket scenes demonstrate a patriarchal society at work, and Morocco is part of this system. Alexander's political brief ignored the unpleasant misogyny of the text, downplaying the sexist innuendo of act five, which Findlay rightly perceived as 'another trial scene'. Reacting against this, Findlay in turn ignored the racial and class prejudice of her character, finally concluding that Portia 'addresses herself to the philosophical problem of how we should lead our lives'.

If Sher's Shylock echoes nineteenth-century players of the role, Findlay's comments are strikingly reminiscent of those of Ellen Terry, who wrote: 'Portia is the fruit of the Renaissance, the child of a period of beautiful clothes, beautiful cities, beautiful houses, beautiful ideas. She speaks the beautiful language of inspired poetry. Wreck that beauty and the part goes to pieces.'[148] Terry is here responding indirectly to Irving's decision to cut many of Portia's lines, including of course the whole of act five, very much making the part 'fall to pieces'.

Interestingly, the Portia of John Barton's second production of the play, Sinead Cusack, also experienced tensions in rehearsal, and again this was in connection with directorial imposition. Barton was very sure about aspects of blocking – including having Cusack roped to a post in the casket scene – and costume, deciding that ' "I think that Portia misses her father so much she wears his coat." Indeed, he lent me his bearskin and I used to . . . play it in John's mouldy old coat.'[149]

The implicit identification of director with father encapsulated their relationship, which often involved Cusack quietly rebelling; she 'lost' her rope somewhere between Stratford and London. Interestingly, reviews of the production, though favourable,[150] were also quick to spot tensions at play: 'For all its charm and intelligence, Miss Cusack's Portia comes over as a directed performance.'[151] This prescience was echoed in John Peter's comments on Findlay's Portia six years later: 'I honestly can't decide whether this is an abysmal performance or wilfully misdirected: one way or another it misses the ironical treatment of romantic feeling which is the counterpoint of Bassanio's greed.'[152] Findlay herself couldn't agree more, attributing the responsibility for the lack of emphasis on the Portia/Bassanio relationship to the dominance in her production of Alexander's and Sher's pro-Shylock bias. She writes that 'the play is termed a comedy.

One has to consider this in the playing of it. Too often it is seen as the tragedy of Shylock.'[153]

Weighting towards the predicament of a particular character can alter the genre of the play. Sinden indicates the potential for this when he talks of Malvolio being a tragic character, and actors playing Jaques often echo these sentiments,[154] yet only with Shylock does the preoccupation with one character destabalise the generic status of the play. Much of the reasoning for this can be seen as residing with attitudes towards Shylock's final moments, and particularly, I would argue, with his enforced conversion. As Suchet points out, four hundred years ago such an act would have been seen as generous: Shylock's soul has been saved, and this most Christian of actions fits neatly into the comedic structure of reconciliation. Suchet's performance reflected this: 'My Shylock recognises that he has had a lucky escape and that the accommodation is a fair one. When he leaves the stage he knows full well that he still has a life ahead of him.'[155]

Antony Sher claims the disproportionate balancing of the play is due to it assuming the weight of 'post-Holocaust history', yet a brief glance at nineteenth-century performance history shows that, if anything, productions justified the alternative title *The Jew of Venice* more at that time than at any other period in its history. Irving's cuts altered the genre of the play in a manner that Alexander's stopped short of doing, and the emphasis placed by leading actors on playing the role was huge. Nowhere is this more evident than in the letters of Edwin Booth, who wrote to Howard Furness, editor of the Variorum Shakespeare, about the role: 'Shylock haunts me like a nightmare: I can't mount the animal – for such I consider Shylock to be.'[156]

This comment is all the more remarkable for the fact that Booth was not even playing the part at the time. He was merely responding to a query put to him by his friend Furness. Two years later, he wrote to him again:

> The Jew came to me last evening, just as I was leaving Pittsburg, and stayed with me all night on the sleeping car, whence sleep was banished, and I think I've got him by the beard, or *nose*, I know not which; but I'll hang on to him a while, and see what he'll do for me. I'll have his pound of flesh if I can get it off his old bones.[157]

Not the least noteworthy aspect of these letters is the extraordinarily erotic tenor of the anti-Semitism therein expressed. Understanding a role is reconfigured in terms of sexual dominance, even rape. Shylock appears at night, almost in a the form of a dream, Booth's unconscious working overtime and manifesting 'The Jew' as a spectre of his repressed fears.[158]

Booth's comments and Irving's redefinition of the role illustrate the manner in which the legalistic, rhetorical conception of character represented by Shylock held a fascination for actors wishing to make their mark long before Stanislavsky. Moreover, it is a role that lead to a remarkably pre-Freudian psychologising of the character, the play reshaped to foreground a consistent, sympathetic but fascinating Shylock. Edward Burns links the increased naturalism of Macklin and Garrick, first displayed in the roles of Shylock and Richard III respectively, to the development of the novel: 'Rather than seeing "character" in the modern sense as a "novelistic" importation into other art-forms, one might recognise here Fielding's reliance on the theatrical and the visual to pose the question of character and nature.'[159] Equally, it was this artistic inter-reliance that refined notions of continuity and causality in the performative construction of a role, reaching its peak a century before Stanislavsky,[160] a period which saw 'the cluster of first usages of "egotism" and its cognates ... the period we designate "Romantic"'.[161] As Coleridge wrote in the epithet with which I began this chapter, 'Suffice it, that one great principle [of continuity] is common to all, a principle which probably is the condition of all consciousness, without which we should feel and imagine only by discontinuous Moments'.[162]

Over two centuries earlier Montaigne had written an account of human action that could almost be taken as a blueprint for Shakespearean characterisation:

> I have often thought that even good authors are wrong in obstinately attributing to us a steadfast and consistent character. They hit upon a general feature in a man and arrange and interpret all his actions in accordance with this fanciful conception; and if they are unable to twist them sufficiently, set them down to dissimulation ... I find nothing more difficult to believe than man's consistency.[163]

It is important to recognise the basis of Montaigne's understanding of character in morality and ethics, factors that play a considerably reduced role in Coleridge's Romantic consciousness. Nevertheless, there is an extent to which both authors can be seen as writing about 'personality', as Montaigne's terminology is by no means exclusively religious, just as that of Coleridge is not restricted to the appropriation of more scientific discourses.

An approach that acknowledged Renaissance perspectives on selfhood would recognise that

> Naturalistic techniques are not appropriate to Shakespeare. The plays aim for a distillation of life, not an imitation of it. Naturalism, or theatrical behaviourism as it may more properly be labelled, is a formula, guaranteed to rob words of their value, to limit the actor's means of expression and deny those who people the plays their essential humanity.[164]

In writing thus, Ian McDiarmid is exceptional, clearly voicing doubts more vaguely expressed by others in the *Players* series. He continues by remarking that he had 'long thought that the phrase "creating a character" was an unhelpful one and not really what acting is about ... the central dynamic is to be found in the collision of the contradictions'.[165] This collision for McDiarmid takes place explicitly in conjunction with the audience. As with Sinden, Beale and particularly Troughton, McDiarmid consciously defines his approach to the role through its relation to the audience, he adopts a form of liminal performance. To continue with the Aristotelian terminology used earlier, this represents a concern with *praxis* and *mythos*, action and plot, rather than *ethos*, which is increasingly shared by Shakespeare through his career.

In an interesting echo of the fragmentation of conscience spoken of by Richard, Shylock too in a moment of crisis resorts to the same trope of multiplied division. In his case, the move is applied to money. On Bassanio's offer of six thousand ducats – twice Antonio's debt – to let the merchant go, Shylock replies:

> If every ducat in six thousand ducats
> Were in six parts, and every part a ducat,
> I would not draw them. I have my bond.[166]

In other words, for 36,000 ducats, he would not relent. This is precisely the sum offered to Bassanio by Portia on Antonio's behalf, and of which her husband has clearly decided to keep the most part for himself:

> Pay him six thousand and deface the bond
> Double six thousand, and then treble that. (3.4, 298–9)

As Holland makes clear, the actual value of these sums is important.[167] Accordingly, he calculates that in today's terms Antonio's debt is roughly £270,000, and Bassanio offers him twice that – £540,000 to forego execution. But most significantly of all, Portia actually offers – and Shylock actually refuses – a sum in excess of £5 million. For such an apparent miser, and for a man whose existence depends on money, this refusal is significant. Like Leah's turquoise, Shylock's revenge is priceless.

Money in this scene, like conscience on the eve before Bosworth, transforms its significance entirely. One man whom we had thought conscience-free suddenly and devastatingly rediscovers it; another man whose life is defined by money suddenly and crucially dismisses vast sums. Identity is reconfigured in extreme situations, and supposedly continuous character is subordinated to the function of that role at that moment. McDiarmid writes that 'when they [Leah's ring, Jessica] are stolen by the Christians, I conjectured, it was as if his identity and his heart had been removed at one stroke.'[168] In McDiarmid's view, this moment is Shylock's dissection by the Christians, in which he loses his own flesh and blood just as bloodlessly as Portia exhorts his revenge to be.

When first offered the role, McDiarmid had been concerned that the central problem, as he saw it, 'was not so much to divest myself of the paranoias, echoes, traditions of previous productions and performances, but rather how I might find a way to persuade an audience to do this'.[169] His solution was to play the moment absolutely, rejecting an 'over-generalised understanding of Stanislavsky' and any attempt to locate the 'psychology of the personality', instead defining the role, rather than the character, in relation to the people – cast, audience – with whom he must interact.

VI

G.H. Lewes described the actor as 'a spectator of his own tumult; and though moved by it, can yet so master it as to select from it only those elements which suit his purpose. We are all spectators of ourselves.'[170] Such conscious control of the performer's role, as opposed to the inhabitation of character, is neither less skilful nor less profound than 'being' the person represented. In his work with the Wooster Group in New York the actor Willem Dafoe developed a method of achieving this that is remarkably close to the processes talked of by Sinden, Beale, Troughton and McDiarmid: 'When we make a theatre piece, we accommodate what [the performers] are good at or how they [are] read. They have functions, so it's not like we treat each other as actors and there has to be this transformation.'[171] The performance exists at the level of clown platea; the actors never think of themselves as a character inside a fiction. More than this, however, Dafoe is able to apply this methodology to a conventionally written play that on the surface requires a traditional approach to characterisation, without ever resorting to anything approaching psychology:

> The more I perform, the more my relationship to the audience becomes totally abstract ... Even when I have a character, I'm always curious to see how I'm read, what people think I am, who I am, and then you lay the action on top of that, so you're confronting yourself in these circumstances. It's open-ended. I'm not presenting anything; I'm feeling my way through. If you were very conscious of acting a character, somewhere you would close it down, you'd present it, you'd finish it. In this stuff, you never know.[172]

The absence of presentation is the principal difference between Dafoe's work and that of the more radical of the *Players of Shakespeare* essayists, and it is also the factor differentiating him from a radical Brechtian approach. Philip Auslander comments:

For Dafoe, performance is essentially a task, an activity: the persona he creates is the product of his own relation to the 'paces' he puts himself through in the course of an evening. While unconscious of the audience, he is hyper-conscious of creating a public image. The multiple, divided consciousness produced by doing something with the knowledge that it is being observed, while simultaneously observing oneself doing it, yields a complex confrontation with self.[173]

Dafoe creates his performance in relation to a sequence of spectatorship, a peformative identity created in a form of Lacanian fragmentation of self, the actor very much becoming 'the observ'd of all observers'. When playing John Proctor in Miller's *The Crucible*, Dafoe remarked:

> There's a double thing happening. I'm saying the text, but I'm always wondering what my relationship to the text is. Me personally, not the character, because I don't know about the character. If someone asked me about John Proctor, the character, I wouldn't be able to tell them a thing.[174]

The actor's presence on stage is defined in relation to a series of variables: audience, cast, stage, costume, lighting, sound, text, received knowledge of the play, the actor's own body, and so on. In the gap between these things a sense of self is temporarily constructed by the spectator, but, crucially, not by the actor. There is no central subjectivity projected onto the stage and, which is the Wooster Group's aim, the performance becomes a site for a Derridean free play of signification. Interpretative authority resides no longer in the text or the playwright, nor in the performers themselves, but is continually redefined by the audience. The actor becomes the site for a liminal performance, existing on the boundaries of his relationship with the audience. Significantly, precisely this lack of interpretative control caused Miller to ban this production of his play because of the Wooster Group's decision to perform only one segment of it, repeated three times, the second time as if on LSD. When interpretative control is absent, today's theatre is still able to impose a form of legislative authority.

Dafoe's emphasis is on *praxis*, action, and avoids any attention at all to *ethos*, except as a marginal interest in how the audience construct it from his actions. In this he is startlingly Elizabethan, locating his position in the fiction as a participant in the *mythos* of a piece, rather than as a transcendent selfhood. As Goldman says, 'a character, in a play, is something an actor does'.[175] Ultimately, this relocates the mimetic act, moving away from an essentialist imitation of personality and towards a more conditional representation of action. Perhaps Soule's category of anti-mimetic character could be reconsidered, instead thought of as a mimesis of a different model; less interior and ahistorical, more provisional and public.

More than this, Dafoe is moving away from a consideration of a determined model for the mimetic act and begins to refuse conventional processes; for him, mimesis is a spectator sport, the actor needs no involvement
with it.

VII

The *Players of Shakespeare* volumes demonstrate that, contrary to Worthen's
generalisations, many actors do think of performance in terms other than
those dictated by Stanislavsky or by a broadly post-Romantic sensibility.
The through-line from Coleridge to twenty-first-century performance is
itself fractured, and the authority of the Shakespearean word is as often
questioned and problematised as it is revered or appropriated.

What lags behind the discoveries of those of actors are those of directors
and of the theatrical establishment. When Sher, playing the Fool, had the
idea of using the two halves of an eggshell over his eyes on the line 'Nuncle,
give me an egg ... ' (*King Lear*, 1.4, 155–63), he found that although
Adrian Noble 'was taken with the dual image of blindness and prophecy,
he wasn't content to let me use an egg in the production until I came up
with the explanation that the Fool had stolen one for his tea'.[176] Similarly,
Geoffrey Hutchings had to fit his Lavatch into Trevor Nunn's Chekhovian
vision of *All's Well that Ends Well*, and twelve years earlier Donald Sinden
was pleased to find a bit of comic business was explained for him by Nunn
as being 'justified subtextually'. Given the large proportion of productions
in the *Players* series directed by Noble, Nunn, or Barton, it is unsurprising
that conflicts over issues of subtext arise with the regularity they do.[177]

Worthen is undoubtedly correct to characterise the position of the director as

> a distinctive crisis in modern theatrical performance, one of legitimacy
> ... the function of the director is to manage the conceptual, rhetorical
> or ideological relationship between the dramatic text – as 'literature',
> inscribed with the values of coherence and transcendence – and
> theatre.[178]

This translation of 'literature' into 'theatre' represents a fundamental
alteration in theatre ideologies over the last four centuries. Whereas
Elizabethan performances would have been supervised by the theatre
manager, the playwright or sometimes the principal actor, today a forma-
lised leader has been introduced. Worthen goes on to remark that 'what
intervenes between texts and performances ... is labour',[179] and it is here
that we begin to find a clue as to the actual role of the director. This is to
supervise the production of a commodity, the transformation of raw material into a finished item, to shape the text along its grain until it has been

crafted into the required dimensions and given an otherwise absent direction.

Behind this process lurks a fear of unbridled signification that can also, as we have seen, be found in the approach of post-Stanislavsky acting. There has to be a journey, a direction to the work. Furthermore, this must be consistent and explicable, the performance susceptible to a form of pseudo-biblical exegesis. The director is very much the agent of this, occupying a priest-like role in the interpretation of the Word to the capitalist congregation.[180]

The text of course always retains a life of its own, playing freely in the interpretation of every individual who reads or watches it. The methodologies of companies such as the Wooster Group and the liberating and experimental approaches of directors such as Steven Pimlott, Sam Mendes, Deborah Warner and others demonstrate clearly that alternatives to systems of Stanislavskyan Shakespeare do exist. The accounts contained within the volumes of *Players of Shakespeare* testify time and again that actors are prepared to take these alternatives when given the opportunity and indeed have often anticipated such decisions in their own thinking.

Despite, or possibly even because of, their linear, cohesive structure – characters presented in the folio order of the plays in which they appear, the emphasis on the actors' journeys – each volume of the series is strikingly similar to a performance, with a dozen or so actors strutting and fretting their brief span upon the stage. Each role is exclusive, central, cancelling out all the others and engaging with all other past interpretations for the duration of the account, before being both supplemented and supplanted by the next. In this they follow also the model of inheritance of the roles themselves from other actors, and also the positioning of those actors within a tradition of performance. Reading the actors talking of Richard III and Shylock, it has become clear that their acts of interpretation and mimesis are based as much on those of their precursors in the parts as they are on the text; Sher's troubled dreams are filled with the menacing profile of Olivier, rather than a historical king or even a Midlands playwright. This obsession with inheritance, with a kind of Bloomian anxiety of influence or paternity, is a central factor in many actors' approaches to, and reflections on, the performance of Shakespeare. It is this preoccupation that is the subject of Chapters 2 and 3.

Notes

1 S.T. Coleridge, Lecture, 1807, in A. Taylor (ed.), *Coleridge's Writings*, vol. 2, 'On Humanity', p. 33, London: St Martin's Press, 3 vols, ongoing.
2 K. Stanislavsky, *An Actor Prepares*, trans. E.R. Hapgood, London: Theatre Arts, 1936, p. 254.

3 M. Norman and T. Stoppard, screenplay for *Shakespeare in Love*, New York and London: Faber, 1999, p. 106.
4 *Players of Shakespeare 3*, ed. Jackson and Smallwood, Cambridge: Cambridge University Press, 1993. Henceforth, reference to the *Players of Shakespeare* series will take the form of the abbreviated title *Players*, used to refer to the whole series, followed by a number when referring to an individual volume.
5 In French, *La Nuit americaine*, Films du Carosse, 1973.
6 H. Walter on playing Imogen, *Players 3*, pp. 201–20, p. 201.
7 R. McCabe on Autolycus, in Smallwood (ed.), *Players of Shakespeare 4*, Cambridge: Cambridge University Press, 1998, pp. 60–71, p. 65.
8 The series as it exists at the time of writing, 2003, comprises fifty-one individual accounts given by forty-nine actors, thirty-four of them male, playing forty-six characters in forty-four productions of twenty-seven plays with twenty-three directors and designers over, with two exceptions, a period of seventeen years. Of the eleven plays not yet covered, *A Midsummer Night's Dream* and *1 Henry IV* are perhaps the texts most notable by their absence, though that will probably be remedied in the forthcoming *Players 5*. See the appendix for more details.
9 This film-within-the-film was actually made in 1990 by Truffaut's friend Louis Malle, as *Damage*.
10 On the ways in which narratives are read and understood see, for example, S. Chatman, *Story and Discourse*, Ithaca, NY: Cornell University Press, 1978; R. Barthes, 'Introduction to the Structural Analysis of Narratives', in Stephen Heath (trans. and ed.), *Image, Music, Text*, London: Fontana, 1977; R. C. Holub, *Reception Theory: A Critical Introduction*, London: Methuen, 1984; Malcolm Coulthard, *Advances in Spoken Discourse Analysis*, London: Routledge, 1992 etc.
11 N.J. Lowe, *The Classical Plot and the Invention of Western Narrative*, Cambridge: Cambridge University Press, 2000.
12 W.B. Worthen, *Shakespeare and the Authority of Performance*, Cambridge: Cambridge University Press, 1997, p. 127.
13 Ibid.
14 For other, more or less extensive, commentaries on this issue see D. Wiles, *Shakespeare's Clown: Actor and Text in the Elizabethan Playhouse*, Cambridge: Cambridge University Press, 1987; L.W. Soule, *Actor as Anti-Character*, Westport, Conn.: Greenwood, 2000; E. Burns, *Character, Acting and Being on the Pre-Modern Stage*, London: Macmillan, 1990; A. Sinfield, *Faultlines: Cultural Materialism and the Politics of Dissident Reading*, Oxford: Oxford University Press, 1992 etc.
15 P. Holland, 'The Resources of Characterisation in Othello', in *Shakespeare Survey 41*, Cambridge: Cambridge University Press, 1989, pp. 119–34, p. 120.
16 S. Crowl, review of *Players 3*, *Shakespeare Bulletin 13*, no. 1, winter 1995, p. 46.
17 The state of character criticism has improved since Holland's article, but the exceptions still tend to prove the rule. See especially Burns and Maus, notes 12 above and 98 below).
18 *An Actor Prepares, Building a Character and Creating a Role*, all translated by Elizabeth Hapgood and published by Theatre Arts in 1937, 1950 and 1961 respectively.
19 C. Marowitz, *Recycling Shakespeare*, New York: Applause, 1991, p. 73.

20 See J.R. Brown, introduction to the third edition of Bradley's *Shakespearean Tragedy*, Harmondsworth: Penguin, 1992, p. xxx.

21 A.C. Bradley, *Shakespearean Tragedy*, London: Macmillan, 1905, 3rd edn Harmondsworth: Penguin 1992, p. 464.

22 H. Walter, *Macbeth, Actors on Shakespeare* series, ed. C. Nicholson, London: Faber, 2002, pp. 27–8.

23 D. Jacobi on Macbeth, *Players 4*, pp. 193–210, p. 201.

24 Brockbank (ed.), *Players of Shakespeare 1*, Cambridge: Cambridge University Press, 1985, p. ix.

25 Worthen, *Authority*, pp. 127–8.

26 G. Doran on Solanio, *Players 3*, pp. 68–77, pp. 71–2.

27 Ibid., p. 72.

28 A. Sher on The Fool, in Jackson and Smallwood (eds), *Players of Shakespeare 2*, Cambridge: Cambridge University Press, 1988, pp. 151–67, p. 154.

29 Worthen, *Authority*, p. 152.

30 L.J. Dezseran, *The Student Actor's Handbook*, London: Mayfield, 1975, pp. 97–8.

31 Quoted in R. Eyre, *Utopia and Other Places*, London: Vintage, 1993, p. 103.

32 Sher, *Players 2*, p. 157.

33 This account, *The Year of the King*, London: Methuen, 1984, was written before Sher's article on the Fool, though it concerns a role he played in the season after *King Lear*. Sher's dependency on psychoanalysis in his rehearsal techniques can perhaps be seen as being parodied in the decision to cast him as the prototype analyst in *Shakespeare in Love*.

34 Sher in C. Zucker, *In the Company of Actors*, London: A&C Black, 1999, p. 173, p. 178.

35 For analyses of Renaissance acting methods see J.R. Brown, *Shakespeare's Plays in Performance*, New York: Applause, 1993; E. Burns, *Character, Actor and Being on the Early Modern Stage*, London: Macmillan, 1990; and esp. A. Gurr: *The Shakespearean Stage, 1574–1642*, Cambridge: Cambridge University Press, 1980; *The Shakespeare Playing Companies*, Oxford: Clarendon, 1996; *Staging in Shakespeare's Theatres*, with M. Ichikawa, Oxford: Oxford University Press, 2000 etc.

36 Luscombe on Gobbo/Moth, *Players 4*, pp. 18–30, p. 18.

37 Tennant on Touchstone, *Players 4*, pp. 30–45, p. 31.

38 Ibid., p. 35.

39 Ibid., p. 36.

40 Ibid., p. 39.

41 Glover, *Players 4*, pp. 165–177, p. 166.

42 Ibid., p. 166.

43 K. Hunter in D. Tushingham (ed.), *Live 2: Not What I am, The Experience of Performing*, London: Methuen, 1995, p. 71.

44 D. Salter, 'Acting Shakespeare in Postcolonial Space', in J. Bulman (ed.), *Shakespeare: Theory and Performance*, London: Routledge, 1995, pp. 113–133, p. 128.

45 Tennant, *Players 4*, p. 40.

46 D. Wiles, *Shakespeare's Clown: Actor and Text in the Elizabethan Playhouse*, Cambridge: Cambridge University Press, 1987.

47 This manner of thinking in terms of 'roles' rather than 'characters' is reflected also in the change of terminology used by the Arden III series in listing what Oxford call 'The Persons of the Play'. Instead of '*Dramatis Personae*' (Arden II), or 'The Characters of the Play' (Penguin), Arden now prefers simply 'List of Roles'.

48 Robert Armin, *Foole Upon Foole, or Six Sortes of Sottes* and *A Nest of Ninnies* in J.P. Feather (ed.), *The Collected Works of Robert Armin*, 2 vols, New York and London: Johnson Reprint Corporation, 1972, vol. 1.

49 Geoffrey Hutchings on Lavatch, *Players 1*, pp. 77–91, p. 89.

50 See Wiles, *Shakespeare's Clown*, p. 148.

51 In a talk at The Shakespeare Institute, 16.05.96, Niamh Cusack, playing Rosalind, claimed her native Irish accent was less conducive to voice projection than RP.

52 B. Rutter, quoted by D. Shellard in *British Theatre Since the War*, New Haven, Conn.: Yale, 1999, p. 217.

53 J. Horrocks, in Tushingham (ed.), *Live 2: Not What I am*, London: Methuen, 1995, p. 68.

54 Wiles, *Shakespeare's Clown*, p. 72.

55 M.M. Mahood, *Playing Bit-Parts in Shakespeare*, London: Routledge, 1992, reprinted 1998, p. 34.

56 S.R. Beale on Thersites, *Players 3*, pp. 160–74, p. 161.

57 Luscombe on Gobbo and Moth, *Players 4*, p. 21.

58 Ibid.

59 L. Hunt, in *These Were Actors: Extracts from a Newspaper Cutting Book, 1811–1833*, selected and annotated by J. Agate, London: Hutchinson & Co., 1946, p. 17.

60 McCabe on Autolycus, *Players 4*, p. 61.

61 Ibid., p. 64.

62 See, for example, Orgel's 1996 Oxford edition of *The Winter's Tale*.

63 Sinden on Malvolio, *Players 1*, pp. 41–67, pp. 46–7.

64 P. Voss on Menenius, *Players 4*, pp. 152–65, p. 163.

65 Sinden, *Players 1*, pp. 46–7.

66 Beale, in *Live 2*, p. 62.

67 Holland, 'Othello', p. 121.

68 'Playing King Lear: Donald Sinden talks to J.W.R. Meadowcroft', *Shakespeare Survey 33*, 1980, pp. 81–9, p. 86.

69 M. Bakhtin, *The Dialogic Imagination*, Austin, Tex.: University of Texas, 1981, reprinted in *The Bakhtin Reader*, ed. P. Morris, London: Edward Arnold, 1994, p. 77.

70 Ibid.

71 Beale, *Players 3*, p. 160.

72 Ibid., p. 161.

73 Beale, interviewed by Clare Bayley, *Independent on Sunday*, 23.7.95.

74 Beale, *Players 3*, p. 161.

75 Ibid., p. 164.

76 Ibid., p. 165.

77 Ibid., p. 162.

78 R. Weimann, *Shakespeare and the Popular Tradition in Theatre*, Oxford: Oxford University Press, 1978, p. 79.

79 Beale, *Players 3*, p. 162.

80 L.W. Soule, *Actor as Anti-Character*, Westport, Conn.: Greenwood, 2000, p. 9.
81 Beale, interviewed by Jenny Gilbert, *Independent on Sunday*, 14.3.93.
82 Beale, interviewed by Peter Lewis, *Sunday Times*, 2.8.92.
83 J. Barrymore, *Confessions of an Actor*, New York, 1926, p. 99.
84 Olivier, interview, in T. Cole and H. Chinoy (eds), *Actors on Acting*, New York: Crown, 1970, 3rd ed. pp. 410–17, p. 410.
85 Sher, *The Year of the King*, London: Methuen, 1984, p. 38.
86 Burns, *Character, Acting and Being on the Pre-Modern Stage*, London: Macmillan, 1990, p. 92.
87 Sher, *King*, p. 130.
88 Troughton on Richard III, *Players 4*, pp. 71–101, p. 87.
89 Jowett, Introduction to *Richard III*, Oxford: Oxford University Press, 2000, p. 69.
90 Troughton, *Players 4*, p. 95.
91 Jowett, *Richard III*, p. 69.
92 Troughton, *Players 4*, p. 95.
93 Jowett, *Richard III*, p. 67.
94 Troughton, *Players 4*, p. 97.
95 M. de Montaigne, 'Of Conscience', in *The Complete Essays*, trans. M.A. Screech, Harmondsworth: Penguin, 1991, pp. 411–17, p. 412.
96 M.A. Skura, *Shakespeare the Actor and the Purposes of Playing*, Chicago, Ill.: University of Chicago Press, 1993, p. 234.
97 Troughton, *Players 4*, p. 75.
98 Ibid.
99 Jowett, *Richard III*, pp. 33–4.
100 Ibid., p. 34.
101 A. Lesser on Richard Gloucester, *Players 3*, p. 142.
102 Sher, *King*, p. 123.
103 R. Fiennes on Henry VI, *Players 3*, pp. 99–113, p. 113.
104 P. Downie on Queen Margaret, *Players 3*, pp. 114–140, p. 114.
105 Lesser, *Players 3*, p. 141.
106 Similarities include ending *3 Henry VI* with the first word of *Richard III*, 'Now', and the linking of Joan and Margaret, on which Downie commented, 'Our intention was to show Margaret in a sense taking over where Joan had left off, a new Frenchwoman to be a scourge to the English', *Players 3*, p. 117 and who are doubled in the 2000 RSC *Henries* directed by Michael Boyd.
107 Bell and McArdle in conversation at the Swan Theatre, 15.01.2001, and Houston and Troughton during talks given at the Shakespeare Institute, summer 2000.
108 Lesser, *Players 3*, p. 151.
109 The genealogy of this concept goes back to St Augustine, who in *On Faith in Things Unseen* wrote: 'Perhaps you will say that you see the will of another through his deeds? then you will see acts and hear words, but of your friends' will, you shall believe that which cannot be seen or heard', quoted by K.E. Maus, *Inwardness and Theatre in the English Renaissance*, Chicago, Ill.: University of Chicago Press, 1995, p. 10. Augustine in turn was referencing 1 Samuel 16:7: 'For man looketh on the outward appearance, but the Lord beholdeth the heart.'
110 Holland, 'Film Editing', in Ioppolo (ed.), *Shakespeare Performed*, London: Associated University Presses, 2000, pp. 273–299, p. 292.

111 Stanislavsky, *An Actor Prepares*, p. 257.
112 Holland, 'Film Editing', p. 292.
113 H. Walter, *Macbeth, Actors on Shakespeare* series, ed. C. Nicholson, London: Faber, 2002, p. 36.
114 Sher interviewed by Michael Goldfarb, *The Guardian*, 16.4.87.
115 P. Stewart as Shylock, *Players 1*, pp. 11–29, p. 19.
116 Sher, *King*, p. 136.
117 J. Bulman, *The Merchant of Venice*, Shakespeare in Performance, Manchester: Manchester University Press, 1991, p. 91.
118 Stewart, *Players 1*, p. 16.
119 Ibid., p. 23.
120 A. Wesker, *The Merchant*, London: Methuen, 1983, p. iii.
121 See *Playing Shakespeare* video, BBC 1979 and accompanying book: J. Barton, *Playing Shakespeare*, London: Methuen, 1984, for example p. 170.
122 Suchet in J. Cook, *Shakespeare's Players*, London: Harrap 1983, p. 84.
123 Ibid., p. 6.
124 Suchet on Caliban, *Players 1*, pp. 167–179. Suchet on Iago, *Players 2*, pp. 179–99.
125 Suchet, *Players 2*, p. 181.
126 Ibid.
127 Ibid., p. 182.
128 Ibid.
129 Stewart, *Players 1*, p. 18.
130 Maus, *Inwardness and Theatre*, p. 104.
131 Ibid., p. 107.
132 Cicero, *De Oratore*, vol. 1, 2 vols with trans. by E.W. Sutton and intro. by H. Rackham, in *Cicero*, Cambridge, Mass.: Harvard, 1967, 28 vols, vol. 8, i.xxxi. pp. 142–3.
133 Aristotle in G.A. Kennedy (ed. and trans.), *On Rhetoric: A Theory of Civic Discourse*, Oxford: Oxford University Press, 1991.
134 J. Drakakis, "*Jew*: Shylock is my name": Speech Prefixes in *The Merchant of Venice* as Symptoms of the Early Modern', in H. Grady (ed.), *Shakespeare and Modernity: Early Modern to Millennium*, London and New York: Routledge, 2000, pp. 105–121, p. 19.
135 Maus, *Inwardness and Theatre*, p. 32.
136 For an account of the position of Jews in Renaissance England see the work of D.S. Katz, in particular *The Jews in the History of England 1485–1850*, Oxford: Oxford University Press, 1994 and *Philo-semitism and the readmission of the Jews to England 1603–1655*, Oxford: Oxford University Press, p. 1982.
137 J. Jewell, *A Replie unto M. Harding's Answer*, London, 1611, Sg.Gg1v. I am grateful to Adrian Streete for bringing this quotation to my attention.
138 See Bulman, *The Merchant of Venice*, for further description of performance traditions.
139 Irving, *Impressions of America*, London, 1884, p. 161.
140 Bulman, *The Merchant of Venice*, p. 119.
141 Sher, in *Drama 4*, 1987, pp. 27–30, p. 28.
142 Bulman, *The Merchant of Venice*, p. 120.
143 Sher, interview with Goldfarb.
144 Sher, *Drama 4*, p. 28.
145 Bulman, *The Merchant of Venice*, p. 131.
146 D. Findlay on Portia, *Players 3*, pp. 52–68, p. 56.

147 Ibid., p. 59.
148 E. Terry, *Four Lectures on Shakespeare*, ed. Christopher St John, London: Hopkinson, 1932, p. 116.
149 S. Cusack on Portia, *Players 1*, pp. 29–41, p. 33.
150 M. Billington in The Guardian, 23.4.81 wrote 'It ... is a production that glistens with intelligence and heart and that solves the play's usual intractable problems at a stroke.'
151 R. Cushman, *The Observer*, 26.4.81.
152 J. Peter, *Sunday Times*, 3.5.87.
153 Findlay, *Players 3*, p. 67.
154 See, for example, Alan Rickman's essay on Jaques in *Players 2*.
155 Suchet, 'Talking about playing Shylock – A Personal Essay by David Suchet', in Gamini and Fenella Salgado (eds), *The Merchant of Venice*, Harlow: Longman, 1986, p. xviii.
156 Letter to Furness, 9.9.1885, in E. Booth Grossman, *Edwin Booth: Recollections by his Daughter*, New York, 1894, p. 173.
157 Letter to Furness, 31.1.1887.
158 Such intent psychosis, evident also in public responses to Irving's performance of Shylock, may also have left a trace in the novel written by Irving's acting manager: *Dracula*.
159 Burns, *Character, Acting and Being on the Pre-Modern Stage*, p. 192.
160 For neoclassical and Romantic criticism of Shakespeare, see esp. vols 5 and 6 in B. Vickers, *Shakespeare: The Critical Heritage*, London: Routledge, 1979, 6 vols. Also of interest with regard to the earlier period are Joshua Reynolds's records of his conversations with Johnson and Garrick on these issues: F.W. Hilles (ed.), *Portraits by Sir Joshua Reynolds*, New York: McGraw-Hill, 1952.
161 S. Bygrave, *Coleridge and the Self*, London: Macmillan, 1986, p. 3.
162 Coleridge, Lecture, 1807, in Taylor (ed.), *Coleridge's Writings*, vol. 2, 'On Humanity', p. 33, London: St Martin's Press, 3 vols, ongoing.
163 Montaigne, 'Of the Inconsistency of our Actions', in *The Complete Essays*, ed. Screech, bk II, pp. 373–81, p. 378.
164 I. McDiarmid on Shylock, *Players 2*, pp. 45–55, p. 47.
165 Ibid., p. 47.
166 Shakespeare, *The Merchant of Venice*, in Wells and Taylor, *Complete Works*, 4.1, pp. 83–5.
167 Holland, '*The Merchant of Venice* and the Value of Money', in *Cahiers Elisabéthains 60* (October 2001), pp. 13–31. References to Holland's reckoning are to p. 29.
168 McDiarmid, *Players 2*, p. 48.
169 Ibid., p. 45.
170 G.H. Lewes, *On Actors and the Art of Acting*, Leipzig; Bernhard Tauchnitz, 1875, p. 113.
171 W. Dafoe, 'Task and Vision', in P. Auslander, *From Acting to Performance*, London: Routledge, 1997, p. 307.
172 Ibid., p. 308.
173 Ibid., p. 307.
174 Ibid., p. 308–9.
175 M. Goldman, 'Characterising Coriolanus', in *Shakespeare Survey 34*, Cambridge: Cambridge University Press, 1981, pp. 73–84, p. 77.
176 Sher, *Players 2*, p. 162.

177 Throughout the series, which covers almost thirty years of selected RSC history, aside from these men only John Caird has directed more than two productions mentioned. Noble has directed ten.

178 Worthen, *Authority*, p. 41.

179 Ibid., p. 21.

180 For an elaboration on the connections between religion and performance/ audience relations, see, for example, R. Williams, *Culture*, London: Fontana, 1981, ch. 6.

Chapter 2

Aged customs

Negotiating traditions of Shakespearean performance

The word 'imitation' seems to be used as a slur upon the actor alone. The painter and the sculptor go to Italy to study the old masters, and are praised for their good copies. They are not censured for imitation, and why may not the actor also have his preceptor, his model? Why should he be denounced for following the footsteps of his old master? Why should he alone be required to depart from tradition?

E. Booth[1]

'They should neither do a mean action, nor be clever at acting a mean or otherwise disgraceful part on the stage for fear of catching the infection in real life ... since then we care for our charges and want them to be men of worth, we will not allow them to take the parts of women, young or old (for they are men) ... Nor should they get into the habit of imitating actions or words of madmen.'

Plato[2]

[Brian] Cox: What about Coriolanus again?
[Ian] McKellen: God, I'm too old!
Cox: Olivier played him when he was your age.
McKellen: Mm. It's an idea ...

Quoted by B. Cox[3]

I

Sir Henry Irving received his knighthood in July 1895. He was the first actor to have the honour bestowed upon him, though he had refused it twelve years earlier when proposed by his friend and Prime Minister, William Gladstone.[4] As with so many other aspects of Irving's career, this was a fact not lost upon Lord Olivier, of whom it is said that his desire for a peerage resulted to some extent from a need to go one better than the man who had died two years before Olivier's birth. In *On Acting* he recalls in his early thirties seeing an actor perform an impression of Irving, only to declare:

I vowed to eradicate all knowledge of the Old Man [Irving] from the public's memory forever. I was determined to become the Old Man myself. Let them impersonate me fifty years after my death. I was determined to become the greatest actor of all time.[5]

Greatness is here configured in terms of legacy and memory rather than ability, reinforced by Olivier's intended appropriation of the title 'Old Man', famous not just as the soubriquet of Irving, but as the popular name for Gladstone, the 'Grand Old Man' of British politics. Performance and politics are here unconsciously merged in a tradition of aspiration and emulation that crosses the boundaries of individual discourse. The knighthood conferred on Irving represents a significant moment in the history of performance in England, a moment when the figure of the actor becomes a figure of the establishment, when a 'very pleased' Queen Victoria admits her favoured tragedian to the rarefied circle of the British aristocracy. Irving recalled:

The room in which The Queen received us was a small one, and I had to walk but a few steps forward and kneel. The Queen extended her hand, which I kissed, and her Majesty touched me on each shoulder with the sword and said 'Rise, Sir Henry', and I rose. Then departing from her usual custom, she added 'It gives me great pleasure, sir'. I bowed and then withdrew from the room with my face to her Majesty.[6]

Excluded from the Socratic Republic and the Academy of Plato, the actor is welcomed into the British Empire through virtue of the Lyceum of Irving.

The well-known and much-cited Book III of *The Republic* does not, of course, banish all poets. Provided their subject matter is appropriate, lyric poets are permitted to remain, and epic writers are excluded only after some debate and because of their tendency to dramatic representation. It is only in the – possibly appended – argument of book ten that Socrates denounces all poets universally.[7] The major formal quality that leads Socrates to banish dramatic poets is, famously, mimesis. In book three this notion is defined closely in terms of the poet representing himself as that which he is not – in short, acting, as the initial epigraph demonstrates. Mimesis at this stage does not mean a generic imitation of reality that includes metaphor and simile and so prohibits all poetry – this extension of the concept emerges in book ten. What is excluded is dramatic representation and role-playing, whether in embedded speech or point of view in epic or, more damningly, drama.

Dramatic mimesis is dangerous because, in Plato's view, 'it is unsuitable for our state, because there one man does one job and does not play two or a multiplicity of roles'.[8] What is alarming in this consequence of mimesis is the pluralisation and fragmentation of the subject produced by performance, a fear of a decentring of a stable identity that will spread through the ranks of the spectators. The mimetic act of the performer is in turn imitated by the spectator, producing a snowballing anarchic event that threatens to overturn society.

Such a construction of the relation of actor to society in terms of mimesis is evident also in the figure of Irving, this time in an interesting inversion of Platonic banishment as he is celebrated as a pillar of the establishment. Irving's mimetic relationship to the elite of Victorian society is evident not only in his affectionate nickname but also in his patriarchal dominance of the Lyceum Theatre and in his self-image as a great gentleman of the arts – an image that famously infuriated George Bernard Shaw.[9] Rather than embody Plato's problematic as the model for mimesis, Irving reverses this structure and becomes the imitator himself, thus acquiring acceptance into society.

A further dimension to the rhetoric of mimesis is identified by Edwin Booth in the quotation above. This is the relationship of the actor to his or her predecessors, 'preceptors', as Booth calls them. He isolates acting as the only profession in which imitation of a master is not encouraged, indeed is denounced as a denial of the 'truth' of performance. The tradition, evident in the sister arts of painting and music, of an open or covert apprenticeship system, is considered inappropriate for theatre. Booth, a member of a celebrated acting family, is highly conscious of the inevitable debt any performer, particularly of Shakespeare, owes to their predecessor in the role.

Booth, then, identifies on the one hand a tradition of mimesis apparently denied to acting, and on the other the need for a mimesis of the tradition contained within other art forms, especially painting. The connection, especially evident in the nineteenth century, between theatre and fine art will be returned to later in this discussion. For the purposes of argument at this stage, I wish to identify three key ways in which mimesis can be understood in the rhetoric of actors. The first is the relationship, as old as Plato, of the performer to the society in which he/she is based. The second is the position of the actor within the traditions of his/her profession, encapsulated humorously by Brian Cox's anecdote relating a discussion with Sir Ian McKellen as to what role the latter could play in tandem with Cox's 1991 King Lear.[10] The third is evident within the context of playing a particular role, and the heritage contained within this task. All of these factors, endemic to acting in general, are intensified and possibly even manufactured by the influence of the Shakespearean name. In short, whereas the previous chapter looked at the relationship of the actor to traditions of performance technique, this chapter investigates the rhetorical structures by which actors characterise their connection to the larger patterns of socio-historical positioning.

The third aspect of this discussion – the mnemonic structures and traditions of playing a specific role – will be addressed more closely in Chapter 3, which deals with *Hamlet*. All three concerns are seen, however, to thread through the arguments in both ensuing chapters, which essentially focus on the same themes. In my argument I take as my starting point René Girard's construction of the mimetic act as one of rivalry, in which the imitator mimics the model because he/she wishes to appropriate that which the model possesses, prompting the model to redouble their appropriative act – so effectively mimicking their imitator – and so 'each becomes the imitator of his own imitator and model of his own model'.[11] Girard's strict binaries will then be complicated both by reference to alternative theories of mimesis and by the subtle ways in which actors themselves continually renegotiate and redefine their mimetic activities.

According to Girard's model, Olivier's attempts to become a second Irving serve as much to reinforce Irving's reputation as to enhance his own. His status as the Old Man only recalls memories of the previous Old Man. In a more active way, the relationship between John Gielgud and Olivier in which both men refer to each other as 'different sides of the same coin' is also embodied in a rhetoric of reciprocal mimetic conflict. A similar language of imitation and deviation can again be located firmly in the relationship between Gielgud and Richard Burton during their production of *Hamlet* in 1964, an analysis of which forms part of the Chapter 3.

Girard describes this pattern of reciprocal mimetic conflict, as we have seen, in terms of mutual desire for a common object. The common object of desire for all the actors under discussion is of course Shakespeare, a writer whose intense exploitation of the manifold opportunities offered by the concept of mimesis would surely have placed him in the front rank of those exiled by Plato.

The multiple subjectivities of the dissembling actor are in the nineteenth century themselves appropriated by actors to construct a public identity, a persona. Irving is possibly the greatest exponent of this, manipulating both the conventions of the late Victorian aristocrat and the mystical name of Shakespeare to create a prominent social role for himself. In the 1890 edition of *The Complete Works* that bore his name, Irving's introduction was entitled *The Great Englishman*. In the context of *The Henry Irving Shakespeare*, to whom exactly this description refers is somewhat elided. Irving spent much of his career publicising the respectability of his profession, in harmony with one of the great concerns of the age. The agent for this upward mobility was Shakespeare. In a speech given at the unveiling of the American Fountain in Stratford-upon-Avon[12] he proclaimed: 'It is the lasting honour of the actor's calling that the Poet Of All Time was a player, and that he achieved immortality by writing for the stage.'[13]

Thus the Victorian celebration of Shakespearean deification is appropriated for the cause of Irving's own reputation and public image.[14] By identifying Shakespeare as an actor first and a playwright second, Irving sets himself up in Shakespeare's image not by virtue of literary talent, but as one great actor following another, even as that other great actor reincarnated. Given that, in common with most contemporary commentators of the bard, he also believed that 'his spell is woven from the truth and simplicity of nature herself',[15] Irving becomes a kind of poet-surrogate, a mimetic presenter of truth to be compared with the greatest poets of the age. In this way the profession of acting is lifted to the position of an art form within his discourse, a social position that renders it only fitting that its leading figure be later knighted.

Irving's innovation lies in the manner in which he used his rhetoric to guarantee a social, even political position that spills over the boundaries of his profession. The idolatry of actors was nothing new in the nineteenth century, but as individuals they were transient idols in the public eye, worshipped only so long as they were active. Even the great Siddons, revered after her death for over a century, entered a form of personal obscurity after retirement even though her public persona lived on. Irving, conversely, entered into a form of professional obscurity from the late 1890s after the loss of the Lyceum, but remained a celebrated social figure until his death.[16] His appropriation of a representation of Shakespeare as one 'People's William' reinforced his social equality with the other.

By supplementing the Shakespearean reputation with his own, Irving is engaged in a task which Derrida, problematising the rigid Girardian model, would say has as its aim the displacement and supplanting of the mimetic model.[17] To a marked extent, this endeavour was successful. His Shakespeare productions at the Lyceum were often cut to ribbons, restructured and had new dialogue introduced, and these textual supplements (when they were acknowledged) were often taken as improvements. Historically there is nothing new in this treatment of Shakespeare, yet Irving's changes were significantly different in kind. He claimed to reproduce them on a smaller scale in his *Complete Works*, stating that it was necessary for the public to read the plays as they were seen, subordinating the word to stage action, writing in his introduction, 'surely the end of all plays is to be acted, and not simply to be read in the study',[18] a justification which appears remarkably modern today.

What is in evidence here is a double operation familiar to critics of modern editorial activity, one of maintaining fidelity to the sacrosanct word while often cutting these same texts extensively, supplementing in order to supplant, imitating to displace. It is an impression reinforced by the fact that the judicious trimming evident in the edition bears little relation to the more extensive cutting found in prompt copies of his productions. Such tendencies were not lost on his severest critic, George Bernard Shaw, who remarked:

> He took no interest in the drama as such: a play was to him a length of stuff necessary to his appearance on the stage, but so entirely subordinate to that consummation that it could be cut to his measure like a roll of cloth.[19]

At the same time, Shaw was aware of Irving's historicist appropriations, commenting that 'From the public point of view he never looked back, from my point of view he never looked forward ... he was more old-fashioned than the oldest of his predecessors, and apparently more illiterate than the most ignorant of them.'[20] Shaw's attack on Irving's illiteracy is particularly vicious in the context of the latter's *Complete Works*, in which Irving is in fact positioning himself in another tradition, that of the practitioner as editor – it was of course the actors Heminges and Condell who were responsible for the first complete edition of Shakespeare's works. In a sense, then, Irving is merely reinstating an established line of influence.

II

Irving's mimetic appropriation of history in order to construct a venerated, mystic public persona in many ways makes him the quintessential Victorian, along with Tennyson and the Pre-Raphaelites. Shaw's remarks, while accurate in essence, owed their vitriol to a further kind of mimetic rivalry, one that was violent in its expression. Shaw resented both Irving's dominance of the theatre and, more particularly, his dominance of Ellen Terry, with whom Shaw had a 'paper courtship' lasting thirty years. These two objects of rivalry were unsurprisingly merged in Shaw's writing, the one often representative of the other, his general opinion being that 'Irving, wasting his possibilities in costly bardicide, was wasting Ellen Terry as well.'[21] More specifically, Shaw resented Irving's patriarchal role in the Lyceum, writing:

> As to Miss Ellen Terry, it was the old story, a born actress of real women's parts condemned to play a figure as a mere artist's model in costume plays which, from the woman's point of view, are foolish flatteries written by gentlemen for gentlemen ... what a theatre for a woman of genius to be attached to.[22]

According to Shaw, Terry's position had barely altered from her time as an actual artist's model for the Pre-Raphaelites,[23] except that Irving's construction of her was not so openly objectifying. The position of women on the Victorian stage was a problematic one, rarely stable and frequently paradoxical. The principal theatres were undoubtedly patriarchal in their dominance by the actor-manager, often with a 'wife' real – or, as with Terry, surrogate – as lieutenant and star actor. In her autobiography Madge Kendal writes of her theatrical relationship with her husband, the actor-manager W.H. Kendal, in no uncertain terms: 'When I write *I*, I mean *We*, and when I write *We*, I mean *He*.'[24]

The professional identity of the female actor was on one level therefore inextricably bound up with that of her 'husband', who, in Irving's case, reinforced his paternalism through appropriation of Shakespearean authority. On the other hand, the fame that these actors enjoyed in their own names gave them a certain freedom (both financial and rhetorical) and social standing experienced by women in few other walks of life. Yet often this success was based on perpetuating, willingly or not, a stereotype of feminine passivity. An example of this was the career of Terry, frustrating not only for Shaw but for Ellen herself. As Kerry Powell comments:

> Whereas Florence Nightingale and others had seen the stage as providing women with the liberation from Victorian femininity, some of the most successful actresses underwrote the very conventions of passivity and private feeling that made other women yearn for the freedom of theatrical life.[25]

Terry herself backed this up in a resigned letter to Shaw in 1896, in which she acknowledges that 'with justice you might scream out against a woman of my age playing the parts I do. I only do it to please H.I. and because I "draw"'.[26] The simplified and fantasised picture of femininity presented on the Victorian stage helped to reinforce such ideologies in the home, the angel in the house most often found in the flesh on the stages of theatres like the Lyceum. Life, if not directly imitative of art, was certainly repeatedly confirmed by it in its ideological construction.

Terry's ability to 'draw' was emphatically based on a certain presentation of femininity as passive and beautiful. Continually frustrated by Irving in her desire to play stronger Shakespearean heroines, in particular Rosalind, she was limited almost always to 'foolish flatteries written by gentlemen for gentlemen'.[27] On the flyleaf of one of her editions of Shakespeare she wrote tellingly, ' "one man in his time plays many parts" (and so does a woman!)'.[28] Yet her Lyceum experience was one of repression, in which the greatest performance was perhaps that of her stage marriage to Irving, itself as much an embodiment of the values of Irving's rhetoric as anything she did on stage.

Her frustration found a fascinating outlet in her notes, made in the margins of her scripts, and in occasional letters. When playing Ophelia she labelled the character 'a kitten', 'Nothing, on a stick!',[29] and less facetiously said 'her brain, her soul and her body are all pathetically weak'.[30] What is evident here is not just a dislike of a role, but an intense resentment of being continually required to portray such 'nothingness', of always presenting the victim. Famously, her attempt to alter even the traditional costume of Ophelia, from white to black, was thwarted.[31] The received character of Ophelia came to encapsulate this seemingly endless stream of passive victims – a kind of archetype for them all, sanctioned by the authority of Shakespeare.

Her portrayal of Ophelia led to one particularly interesting observation, which resulted from a visit to an asylum for research purposes:

> Like all Ophelias before (and after) me, I went to the madhouse to study wits astray. I was disheartened at first. There was no beauty, no nature, no pity, in most of the lunatics. Strange as it may sound, they were too theatrical to teach me anything. Then, just as I was going away, I noticed a young girl gazing at the wall. I went between her and the wall to see her face. It was quite vacant, but the body expressed that she was waiting, waiting. Suddenly she threw up her hands and sped across the room like a swallow. I never forgot it. She was very thin, very pathetic, very young, and the movement was as poignant as it was beautiful.[32]

Terry found madness too theatrical, too removed from nature. The unnaturalness of the scene before her made it unsuitable for Terry's usual mimetic processes to operate. It is as if the inhabitants of the asylum pre-empt their representation on stage by creating a form of performance that is already complete. Terry cannot imitate, because the condition of the inmates is already a distorted copy, a pale imitation of the accepted view of nature. They no longer participate in the received mimetic order, occupying a position akin to the stage, one of the 'already imitated'. In Dympna Callaghan's terminology, they are the presentations of an exhibition, the 'thing-in-itself', rather than the representations of mimesis.[33] Terry becomes spectator, a model for imitation rather than an imitator, and it is only by finding someone who escapes human, social mimesis entirely by using a bird as a model that she is able to find a useful subject for her research. The girl becomes an original by virtue of her mimicry of animals rather than humans, and Terry is able to define herself as imitator again. The endowment of originality through mimesis of a non-human model can be seen also in Antony Sher's more compromised reliance on the chimp, as discussed in Chapter 1.

The madhouse, like the stage, already exists outside of a conventional social order. Such parity of semiotic status is familiar in anti-theatricalist discourse back to Plato, who makes a point of forbidding, in particular, the mimesis of madness. Marginalised in so many ways from nineteenth-century society, women on the stage often find a voice in the equally marginalised discourse of insanity. Already displaced from themselves, the inmates of the asylum visited by Terry represent the ends of her task, not the initiation. They already are her performance, and Terry needs to join them by, as Girard has commented, imitating not themselves, but the object of their imitation. The swallow-girl is of use because Terry can recognise and imitate what she imitates. As Powell comments:

> From beginning to end the Victorian period was able to tolerate the actress, with her unique powers of speech and action, by confining her within rhetorical structures of madness, disease, prostitution, deformation and inhumanity. Seen as sick, depraved, and exotic, these independent women could not easily present a serious threat to the social order which, in normal circumstances would have rendered them, as women, idle and silent.[34]

Excluded from the mainstream mimetic order, the actor had two choices: represent the conventional construction of passive femininity or find another voice through joining another mimetic order, that of madness. Harriet Walter theorises that perhaps 'it was to protect themselves from madness that they tailored their ambitions to fit the possibilities or impossibilities of the male-dominated world'.[35]

In true Hamlettian fashion, the insane language of the stage keeps at bay the hysterical discourse of a patriarchal society. Discourses of insanity, as Michel Foucault has shown, escape the normal semiotic system and provoke a freer play of signification that makes them dangerous and therefore powerful. Within the confines of stage madness, however, this danger is mediated by mimesis, though the empowerment of liberated expression is retained.

III

One of the most famous embodiments of female madness on the nineteenth-century stage was that of Lady Macbeth. The subject of legendary performances throughout the century, she is also the most frequently analysed in print by the actors who played her. This tradition, both of performance and written reflection, begins with Sarah Siddons. Her *Remarks on the Character of Lady Macbeth* was in all likelihood written after her retirement from the stage in 1817, and was published posthumously in Campbell's 1834 biography of the actor. In it, she begins by espousing a largely received impression of the character, stating that 'in this astonishing creature one sees a woman in whose bosom the passion of ambition has almost obliterated all the characteristics of human nature'.[36]

Unsexed, Lady Macbeth becomes unnatural. But the account becomes quickly more interesting. The character is endowed with a purely supportive role, 'she devotes herself entirely to the effort of supporting him',[37] that later allows her influence to become corruptive. She charms Macbeth like a second Eve:

Such a combination [of qualities] only, respectable in energy and strength of mind, and captivating in feminine loveliness, could have composed a charm of such potency as to fascinate the mind of a hero so dauntless, a character so amiable, so honourable, as Macbeth.[38]

These qualities are itemised quite clearly. According to her notion, her beauty 'is of that character which I believe is generally allowed to be most captivating to the other sex – fair, feminine, nay, perhaps even fragile'.[39] Interestingly, this view of Macbeth as virtuous and largely blameless, brought low by his conniving 'fiend' of a wife, is not shared by Siddons's brother, John Philip Kemble, who played the role several times with her. In an article written to defend Macbeth against charges of cowardice, he presents a well-balanced portrait of a flawed hero, both 'hateful' and 'courageous', a 'tyrant' with 'dignity'.[40]

Siddons's view of Lady Macbeth is problematised even more by the fact that her description is in conflict with several contemporary accounts of her performance of the role. Evidence of this disparity is given within the *Remarks* by the physical description of the character given by Siddons, a description entirely at odds with her own physique, in both colouring and build. The contradiction does not end there. As Manvell comments in his biography, 'from the first the impression she created in the audience was far from that presented in her account – she inspired sheer awe and terror'.[41] The vast difference between Siddons' account and her portrayal is, however, dismissed by Ellen Terry:

If there was such a difference, as this note indicates, between the great actress's theory and practice, it would not surprise me ... It is not always possible for us players to portray characters on the stage exactly as we see them in imagination.[42]

It is also possible, of course, that Siddons's views changed after retirement and, no longer bothered by the necessity of performance herself, she carried out a purely imaginative reconstruction of the character. The *Remarks*, after all, is an analysis of a character, not of a performance. There is no reason for the actor to be constrained by her own performative self.[43] Moreover, the disparity is troubling only if we impose a system of retrospective mimetic consistency upon Siddons. There is no real necessity to posit absolute coherence between a mental construct of character and its representation on stage. The gap here between multiple constructions of the signified merely demonstrates the instability of the theatrical sign, a continual deconstruction of the textual subject in performance.

The performance of Lady Macbeth by Terry at the end of the century interestingly inverts the relationship with the role established by Siddons.

In a letter to Clement Scott she recounts the sending of a particularly symbolic gift on the eve of her first performance:

> Was it not nice of an actress she sent me Mrs Siddons' shoes ... I wish I could have 'stood in 'em'! She played Lady M. (her Lady M. not Shakespeare's & if I could, I wo have done hers, for Shakespeare's Lady M. was a fool to it.)[44]

Terry's performance was famously gentle and passive, closer to Siddons's description of the character than her performance, and at odds with Terry's own desire to unlock 'my powers of being bad' and to 'be damned charming'. But here the difference is explained by Terry herself, following an indication given in the above letter. Terry wanted to play Siddons, stand in her shoes, not those of Lady Macbeth. The imprint left by Siddons is still considerable, as Harriet Walter explains, 'even after I have played her, the archetype remains – a towering Siddons-like shadow, impervious to my interpretation'.[45] For Terry, Siddons, rather than the queen, was the challenge; the tradition of performance, rather than canonical dominance, was the greater influence. In a letter to William Winter, the American critic, she wrote:

> Everyone seems to think Mrs Macbeth is a Monstrousness & I can only see that she's a woman – a mistaken woman – & weak – not a Dove – of course not – but first of all A WIFE.[46]

This jumble of thoughts was clarified further in her diary: 'Those who don't like me in it [the role of Lady Macbeth] are those who don't want, and don't like, to read it fresh from Shakespeare, and who hold by the "fiend" reading of the character.'[47]

An intermediate reading of the character is provided, appropriately, by an actor who was coached by her Aunt Siddons and who lived to see Terry's performance, Fanny Kemble:

> There is no such thing as [a monster] in all Shakespeare's plays. That she is godless, and ruthless in the pursuit of the objects of her ambition, does not make her such. She is energetic, decisive and daring. Many men have been so; she is that unusual and unamiable (but not unnatural) creature, a masculine woman, in the only real significance of that much misapplied epithet.[48]

Agreeing with Terry in the character's humanity, and with Siddons in her attraction, she goes against the grain of performance interpretation by considering the character masculine, making the role into a kind of transvestite performance. Forced to play the femininity, however, Terry is once again denied the empowerment that may have challenged or subverted Irving's patriarchal rule.

Much as Terry would have loved to play the part as Siddons – emphasised by her reference to the role as 'Mrs' Macbeth – she interpreted the text the same way Siddons did in her analysis. Only perhaps in John Singer Sargent's portrait of her in the role does the performance within the performance emerge, Ellen Terry playing Sarah Siddons as Lady Macbeth, a repressed play-within-the-play that illustrates aptly the *mise en abyme* of theatrical performance of such a canonical role. She said of the portrait that it encapsulated 'all I meant to do ... but I never achieved what he painted'.[49] Siddons's career held similar allure for the star of the Lyceum, who expressed many times a desire to be at Covent Garden eighty years previously. Terry's mimetic model was Siddons, the great tragedian par excellence, just as, later, Olivier's would be Irving. In this way the mimetic tradition of acting runs parallel to that of interpretation, with each new performance establishing a *mise en abyme* of imitation within imitation; an intertextual and reciprocal mimesis.

IV

The mimetic status of the Victorian actor extended further than her relationship to society and to earlier performers; it also, unsurprisingly, encompassed her relationship to character. In a letter dated 1902, Terry wrote:

> Be sure that the red roses you gave to 'Portia' so long ago made her-me a little better ... I've gotten over the wishing I were Portia ... I nowadays think that 'in another & a better world than this' (!) I may (?) open my eyes & say 'Oh Bottom how art thou translated!!!' & find no E.T. left! But some creature begotten of Portia Beatrice Imogen Rosalind Volumnia Cordelia Hamlet Cesar Silvius!!![50]

The identification with character is here so strong, even long after the performance is over, that a fascinating slippage of self occurs throughout the letter. It is not uncommon for actors immersed in a role to use personal pronouns interchangeably – descriptions of the character often move from 'her' to 'me' as the actor recalls decisions made 'in character'. With Terry, however, the case is significantly different. She is not recalling an experience on stage or a decision of characterisation made in rehearsal. She is writing of a personal experience as Ellen Terry, one connected to playing Portia, but not involved in playing the role. The slippage occurs, as it were, in reverse. There is no slippage from character to self, as usually happens in performance discourse, but rather from self to character. It is as if Portia is playing the role of Ellen Terry, Victorian actor and public figure. The mimetic order is reversed, as Portia imitates Terry. Bernard

Shaw commented upon an aspect of this phenomenon when he wrote that 'spectators ... did not want Ellen Terry to be Olivia Primrose, they wanted Olivia Primrose to be Ellen Terry'.[51]

Terry's letter reveals both the artifice of the Terry persona and her unhappiness with being imprisoned within it; her desire to find 'no E.T. left' is very much a consummation devoutly to be wished. Later in life she commented that the task of the actor was to 'learn how to translate the character into herself, how to make its thoughts her thoughts, its words her words'.[52] Her letter indicates the reverse of this, the translation of self into character, the abdication of selfhood and complete assimilation with the other, a process of self-erasure that indicates a profound desire for the most drastic shift of subjectivity away from the late nineteenth-century Terry towards the 'fruit of the Renaissance, the child of a period of beautiful clothes, beautiful cities, beautiful houses, beautiful ideas. She [Portia] speaks the beautiful language of inspired poetry.'[53]

This yearning to be Portia, some perfect idea of unattainable renaissance otherness, is consonant with her involvement with the Pre-Raphaelite Brotherhood and with a general Victorian nostalgic identification with a golden past. It is also uniquely her own, and tied to her position as a dominant cultural figure condemned to portray passive and subordinate women. Sue-Ellen Case observes:

> One of the results of the representation of woman as other in the male gaze is that she also becomes an other to herself. Within the patriarchal system of signs, women do not have the cultural mechanisms of meaning to construct themselves as the subject rather than the object of performance. A wedge is created between the sign 'woman' and real women that insinuates alienation into the very participation of women in theatrical representation or within the system of communication in the dominant culture.[54]

Very much in the position of subject socially and culturally, Terry found herself owing this social subjectivity to constantly being in a position of artistic and professional objectification. First as artist's model and then as actor, Terry became a signifier for a certain kind of Victorian 'womanhood'. Her individual subjectivity was defined by precisely that form of objectification that prevented her from fully realising an artistic voice. She very much becomes other to herself. It comes as no surprise therefore that submergence into the subjectivity of character provides her with that temporarily liberated identity she was unable to achieve in reality.

In terms of mimesis, Terry does not, in her attitude to character, construct herself in a model of mimetic rivalry. Instead, she realises a system of what Girard labels 'mimetic antagonism', which is 'ultimately unitive, or rather reunitive, since it provides the antagonists with an object they can really share, in the sense that they can rush against it in order to destroy it or drive it away'.[55] Terry sees herself at one with Portia, and with the ever-unplayed Rosalind, and with Siddons because these 'roles' give her the opportunity to construct an otherwise impossible subjectivity in the face of social repression. In the letter above she does not so much identify with the other as with the same, moving away from the other she felt her artificial identity in fact constituted. Alienated from the self constructed by her profession and social position, she realised an alternative identity in the roles she played.

Portia, Rosalind and Siddons all made a stand against patriarchy, but they did so by becoming, for a time, masculine. All became transvestite performers – Siddons in several Shakespearean roles, most famously Hamlet. This transvestite self was something Terry experienced in her first Shakespearean part, Mamillius, and later as Puck, but never again, not even in the looser sense described by Fanny Kemble, except in her surrogate self Portia. In this she was surprisingly unusual. Most celebrated nineteenth-century female actors, from Siddons, through Vestris, Duse and Cushman to Sarah Bernhardt, played prominent male roles. Charlotte Cushman's performance of Romeo in 1855 prompted a favourable response from the *Illustrated London News*: 'For force and passion it exceeds that of any male performer, and yet avoids exaggeration.'[56]

Siddons's Hamlet was well received, and Bernhardt's is now near-legendary, though it was not without its detractors at the time. Max Beerbohm thought that 'Sarah ought not to have supposed that Hamlet's weakness set him in any possible relation to her own feminine mind and body.'[57] Yet in this view he was surprisingly alone, and surprisingly unfortunate in his choice of vehicle for this view. Bernhardt, uniquely – as far as I can find – among transvestite performers of Hamlet in the nineteenth century emphasised the role's masculinity, remarking that she saw 'a character who is manly and resolute'. The criticism of female performance of male roles otherwise avoided Hamlet. Typical of this is William Archer's review of an all-female *As You Like It* at the Prince of Wales Theatre in 1874, in which the players wore beards: 'The next time I want to see a bearded lady, I shall seek her in the proper habitat – the caravan.'[58] The obfuscation of femininity that results from wearing a beard is too much. Women attempting to be wholly masculine violated gender boundaries in a way that playing the feminised Hamlet did not.

V

At first glance, Bernhardt's performance seems to be a triumph of optimism over nature. As a fifty-five-year-old Frenchwoman with no fluency in English playing Hamlet in London, Bernhardt by today's standards was far from typecast in the role. Yet even forty years later John Gielgud could admiringly refer to the famous moment of Bernhardt's hesitancy over killing Claudius at prayer, sword raised over her head, like 'a great interrogation mark', without any apparent feeling that the casting was inappropriate.[59] Bernhardt herself commented that 'what people are determined to see in Hamlet is a feminised, hesitating, bemused creature. What I see, however, is a person who is manly and resolute, but nonetheless thoughtful.'[60]

In this characterisation, Bernhardt was indeed being radical, but not in the mere fact of cross-gendered casting. It had become a tradition in itself for *Hamlet* to be acted with a female lead in the nineteenth century. One of the earliest such leads was Siddons herself, who played the part no less than five times over a twenty-seven-year-period, beginning in 1775,[61] a length of experience of the role unmatched by an actor of any gender since except Macready. The Romantic emphasis on Hamlet's weakness, vacillation and volubility lead to a sub-tradition of seeing the Prince as feminised, even feminine. This was exploited further by Bernhardt's linking the play with two others, *Lorenzaccio* and *L'Aiglion*, in what she called her *Hamlet Cycle* of 1896.[62] It was in this spirit that Edwin Booth wrote that he 'always endeavoured to make prominent the femininity of Hamlet's character'.[63] An extreme version of this emerged with Edward Vining's 1881 book, *The Mystery of Hamlet*, which claimed that Hamlet was in fact a woman, in love with Horatio, who in turn was enjoying an affair with Ophelia.[64] Steven Berkoff echoes this when he postulates a homoerotic attraction between Hamlet and his confidant which even overlaps into his offstage relationship with the actor playing the role – 'something too much of this?'[65]

Artistically, the melancholy, graceful, feminine Dane with skull carefully wrapped in a handkerchief is hard to avoid. Delacroix's version was painted from a female model, Mme Pierre,[66] and the idea took hold with particular strength in France where the *travesti* tradition of cross-gendered playing was still hugely popular. The female form became a convenient signifier for the feminine in Hamlet.

It was not by simply being a woman in the part that Bernhardt was courting controversy, however, but by explicitly claiming such emphatic masculinity for her interpretation. In doing this, she was laying claim to yet another tradition. As Taranow comments:

> As part of the feminising tradition, Bernhardt performed her Hamlet in travesty; not, however, as a man with a feminine soul, but as a boyish young man with a masculine soul; not as the vacillating procrastinator of romanticism, but as the determined and purposeful avenger of the Elizabethan theatre.[67]

Her interpretation was predicated on her understanding of Elizabethan/Jacobean revenge drama, ironically without taking account of how the play itself subverts this tradition. In Granville Barker's terms, she played Thomas Kyd's hero rather than Shakespeare's.[68] Yet this does not satisfy the question of how such a physically inappropriate performer played not only Hamlet but Shylock, while her contemporary Julia Glover played both Hamlet and Falstaff. The beginnings of an answer can be found in Bernhardt's comments on her performance. In an interview with *The New York Herald*, she expostulated: 'There is no absurdity [of casting] ... The question is, does the actor produce the illusion? Does she make the audience forget the actor in the character? If she does, where is the absurdity?'[69] Bernhardt here is close to T.S. Eliot's famous 'extinction of personality', coined in his discussion of precisely this issue of tradition and the individual. Bernhardt continues:

> It is not sufficient to look the man, to move like a man and to speak like a man. The actress must think and feel like a man, to receive impressions as a man, and to exert that innate something which, for want of a better word, we call magnetism.[70]

The method by which she accomplishes this in particular anticipates Eliot:

> An actor ... must in a way forget himself, and divest himself of his proper attributes in order to assume those of his part. He must forget the emotion of the moment, the joy or the sorrow born of the events of the day ... to be worthy of the name an actor must be capable of a continuous dissection of personality.[71]

Bernhardt asserted the impossibility of a dual performance identity. To play a role convincingly, the actor must 'lose his ego during the time he remains on stage'. Prefiguring this, as early as 1759 the actor and playwright Charles Wilkes wrote that

> To do justice to his character he [the actor] must not only strongly impress it upon his own mind, but make a temporary renunciation of himself and all his connections in common life, and for a few hours consign all his private joys and griefs to oblivion; forget, if possible his own identity.[72]

And in 1817 an anonymous pamphlet proclaimed:

> It would be no gratification to see a real king or countryman upon the stage ... the charm lies in seeing a man who is neither one nor the other, adapting his mind and features to such a personation; and the more distant we know his real character to be from that he is assuming, the greater is his merit.[73]

The actor's self is abdicated in favour of that of the character. Perhaps the clearest example of the art of forgetting the actor – both by the audience and the actor himself – is provided by Hazlitt in his review of Kean's Othello, in which he writes: 'Othello was tall, but that is nothing; he was black, but that is nothing. But he was not fierce, and that is everything.'[74] What counted was the essence of the character – 'that within which passeth show' – rather than the trappings and suits of appearance. 'Naturalism', a word invoked readily by Bernhardt, was here a matter of internal, rather than external, veracity, involving fidelity to the authorial creation.

In the case of Bernhardt this truth ostensibly should be compromised by her connection to yet another nineteenth-century tradition of playing Shakespeare – that of the visiting international star, who performed the role in their first language in a resident company speaking in the language of the host nation. In London Bernhardt played Hamlet in French in a company speaking English. Notions of textual fidelity were therefore inevitably compromised by the translation.[75] Yet even here, the authority of the Shakespearean word retains its transcendence in what was after all a common occurrence. G.H. Lewes was of the opinion that 'no sooner are you moved, than you forget the foreigner in the emotion'.[76] An umbilical connection exists between the word and the auditor, mediated by the oracular figure of the great actor, who acts as midwife to emotional truth and beauty. Lewes does go so far as to be sceptical of the effects generated by a foreign actor out of context:

> There is a mistake generally made respecting foreign actors ... [that] of supposing an actor to be fresh and original, because he has not the conventionalisms with which we are familiar on our own stage. He has the conventionalisms of his own. The traditions of the French, German and Italian theatres thus appears to our unfamiliar eyes as the invention of the actors.[77]

Tradition here is configured as coded, contextual and culturally specific, rather than as univocal and universal in the manner of Shakespeare. It is a critical perspective significantly absent in discussions of Shakespeare, even though the alterations in meaning effected by translation are arguably greater than those evinced by alternative performance styles.

Lewes's own scepticism as to the status of acting as an art form allows him to be cautious as to the effects an actor may produce:

> It is thought a hardship that great actors in quitting the stage can leave no monument more solid than a name. The painter leaves behind him pictures to attest his power; the author leaves behind him books; the actor leaves only a tradition. The curtain falls – the artist is annihilated. Succeeding generations may be told of his genius;

none can test it. All this I take to be a most misplaced sorrow. With the best wishes in the world I cannot bring myself to place the actor on a level with the painter or the author.[78]

In one stroke Lewes here illustrates both the actor's vulnerability to decay and, by extension, other historical and cultural forces, and also his/her need for a tradition to bolster the ephemeral nature of performance. It is the permanence of art and writing that endows it with universality and the transience of performance that is to blame for its indebtedness to a cultural moment. Equally, as with the inheritance of a family name, a tradition and a genealogy endows the profession with a degree of heritage and permanence. There is a link here with Booth's indignation at the actor's lack of artistic privileges – imitation of a master, a place within a tradition, is earned only by an act of accepted authorial creation, which in turn produces an artefact of permanence. The actor's dependency upon the words of the dramatist, combined with the transience of performance, denies his position within the pantheon of great art, instead locating him as the spectre at a feast of genius. As Chapter 3 will demonstrate, the actor's position is frequently that of the Ghost of Hamlet's father, simultaneously imploring 'Remember me' while rewriting the history of that memory. Lewes continues, somewhat acerbically: 'Shakespeare is a good raft whereon to float securely down the stream of time; fasten yourself to that and your immortality is safe.'[79]

This is a prescient understanding of the rhetorical operations of many actors, editors and scholars over the years, but it is important to recall that Lewes understands Shakespeare as a fixed and stable artefact rather than a culturally shifting and ideologically appropriated process of signification. This is not to deny Lewes's appreciation of ideologies surrounding Shakespeare – he was in fact shrewdly aware of many such operations – but rather to locate the critic in his own moment.

Late Victorian theatre in particular privileged the authority of the transcendent Shakespearean word to such an extent that, provided she was seen as having accessed the *logos* correctly, there was little obstacle to Bernhardt playing the role of Hamlet. In a sense she became a different kind of translator, one who undertook to provide a form of exegesis of the hallowed text that spoke directly to the soul of the spectator, regardless of the actual language. As Hazlitt famously wrote seventy years earlier:

Hamlet is a name; his speeches and sayings but the idle coinage of the poet's brain. What then, are they not real? They are as real as our own thoughts. Their reality is in the reader's mind. It is we who are Hamlet. This play has a prophetic truth which is above that of history.[80]

An interesting recent paraphrase of this perspective has been provided by Peter Brook:

> It's not Shakespeare's view of the world, it's something that actually resembles reality. A sign of this is that any single word, line, character or event has not only a large number of interpretations, but an unlimited number. Which is the characteristic of reality. What he wrote is not an interpretation; it is the thing itself.[81]

Brook is here claiming for Shakespeare the creation of a sign system so rich it becomes a state of reality in itself, unlimited and never-ending. Hazlitt, in contrast, is claiming for the dramatist, and for Hamlet in particular, a universality that defines the spectator in relation to the artefact, and also, intriguingly, locates much of the responsibility for that in the mind of the spectator. For Hazlitt the overwhelming power of the play swamps historical circumstance and occupies the mind of the reader, creating their reality for that moment. We become brainwashed by the Bard. Yet this is in Hazlitt's densely packed rhetoric a reciprocal operation, rather like an act of faith. Unlike Brook's parallel Shakespearean universe, in Hazlitt the spectator has a role to play – Hamlet is always a dialogue, brought to life and then subsisting in the mind, in the manner of the man created by the dreaming magus in Borges's fable *The Circular Ruins*.

The complex nature of Hazlitt's understanding of the process of Shakespearean signification does not, however, include the processes of performance, which he saw as limiting and restricting the imaginative process of reading. 'We do not like', he remarked, 'to see our Author's plays acted.'[82] Yet there was for Hazlitt one principal exception to this rule. Though he famously championed Kean, it was an earlier figure that for him epitomised performative perfection – Sarah Siddons. This was in part because Hazlitt only saw Siddons in later life, when her glory had by all accounts faded, and he was perhaps as a consequence more than usually susceptible to popular mythologising about her earlier career. In 1818 he wrote:

> She raised Tragedy to the skies, or brought it down from thence ... She was Tragedy personified. She was the stateliest ornament of the public mind. She was not only the idol of the people ... she was not less than a goddess, or than a prophetess inspired by the gods.[83]

Siddons alone, as Reynolds's portrait makes clear, transcended the ephemeral condition of performance, idolised because of her gender into an inspirational muse. Her mystical persona, actively encouraged by Siddons herself, gave her a position as icon that spanned several art forms, rather than a reputation for excellence in one particular field. Such philogynistic discourse also surrounds Terry, though to a lesser extent, and in both cases it is their performance of femininity that allows them to be so deified.

Siddons' iconic position, like that of Terry, is inextricably connected to her physical presence; she was the 'stateliest ornament' of the stage, and her gestures and facial expressions – like those of Bernhardt recalled by Gielgud – are the stuff of legend. In her youth, before attaining her position of 'Tragic Muse', Siddons was objectified in a far more lurid manner, with commentators focusing on the size of her breasts where later they would eulogise her statuesque beauty.

The operations of objectification and deification of gender are revealed in discourse surrounding Siddons as being remarkably similar, as is revealed in the series of anecdotes detailing Siddons's sitting for *The Tragic Muse*. Siddons's own account of devising her pose for the work, reported by Campbell, was that Reynolds asked her to 'ascend her undisputed throne and graciously bestow upon me some good idea of the Tragic Muse',[84] which Siddons obligingly did. In fact, the pose comes from Michelangelo's Sistine Chapel Isaiah, a reference which none of the anecdotes, including Reynolds's own, acknowledges. In all these accounts, Siddons herself becomes a character in a narrative, rather than an agent, with the tellers emphasising Reynolds' position as actor within the scenario. She is as objectified in anecdote as she is in formal account, and even her moment of greatest iconographic power divests her of agency, as in Reynolds's recollection that Siddons slumped down, exhausted, and he told her not to move.

As Shearer West has demonstrated, the influence of painting and sculpture upon the stage was such that the essence of character was deemed to reside as much in a received catalogue of gestures, expressions and deportment as in what we might today call interpretation: 'By the age of Siddons and Kemble, the actor was not just a performer, but he or she was also an object of aesthetic concern and was scrutinised by a public with a growing knowledge of painting and sculpture.'[85] Interiority was conveyed, in Lewes's term, 'symbolically', in a litany of physical signs often imported from fine art or from various subdivisions of medicine and anatomy.[86] As the century progressed, the relationship between the two disciplines became ever closer. This relationship, importantly, did not pursue external verisimilitude, but a signifying system by which interiority could be made visible – in Hazlitt's terms, Othello's 'fierceness', but not his race. The architect of much of this development, ironically at the expense of her agency, was Siddons herself, who took pains to be identified as an *objet d'art* in her own right. In *The Tragic Muse*, no longer is an actor painted in role, as was the case with Garrick and Kemble, but has become an abstraction of art itself.

A natural extension of this was the signifying systems of costume. From our perspective Bernhardt may have been radical in terms of the combination of her identity and that of Hamlet, but she was deeply conservative in her choice of costume – black tights and doublet, with the (by that time) conventional black plumed hat. Deviation from this combination, like Terry's re-clothing of Ophelia, was scandalous. Once again, the Hamlettian uniform owed much to fine art, in particular the paintings of Delacroix, with gradual amendments and additions occurring in performance throughout the century. Costume, in particular Hamlet's 'suits of woe', became, ironically, an inviolable signifier of 'that within'. Mimesis was constructed in terms of costume, gesture, and a tradition of action and precedent stretching back in theory to Burbage, as will be discussed in Chapter 3.

VI

In wearing his inky cloak, Hamlet is making an obvious statement not only about his emotional state but also about his political and intellectual positioning – he chooses to ally himself with the dead king rather than the live one, identifying himself rather as son to a ghostly Hamlet than to the more corporeal Claudius. As long as Hamlet continues to wear black, these decisions are proclaimed to the world, hence the king's need to get his adoptive son a change of clothes. Similarly, the nineteenth-century actor figured his or her allegiance to the spectral tradition of past Hamlets through the same nighted colour, making physically present those past performances within the current one.

The actor playing Hamlet is caught always in the dilemma of desiring both to imitate the father and to break with this tradition, just as Hamlet must imitate either the chivalric model of his biological father or the subterfuge of his political father. He resolves this dilemma by combining both elements – the final act features both a duel, recalling Old Hamlet's single combat with Old Fortinbras, which occurred on the day of Hamlet's birth, and poison.[87] Similarly, each new player of the role both imitates his or her father and poisons their memory. The strict regulation of costume in the nineteenth century physicalises and makes visible these choices. Bernhardt, in this sense, was giving a highly traditional, and therefore approved, performance. As Ann Rosalind Jones and Peter Stallybrass write, 'the transmission of clothes figures the formation and dissolution of identity, the ways in which the subject is possessed and dispossessed, touched and haunted by the materials it inhabits'.[88] Clothing becomes a signifier not only for performance interpretation – the relation of this Hamlet to the rest of the cast – but also the actor's position in the tradition of production – the relation of this Hamlet to previous casts.

The figure of the transvestite actor within all this is therefore appropriately ambivalent. On the one hand, Bernhardt's gender performance could be overlooked at the time, so firmly did she locate herself within accepted traditions of the role. On the other, this does not negate her gender, rather it elides it. The celebrated transvestite performer Vesta Tilley commented:

> It may be because I appeared on stage as a young man that a big percentage of my admirers were women. Girls of all ages would wait in crowds to see me, and each post brought me piles of letters varying from impassioned declarations of undying love to a request for a piece of ribbon I had worn.[89]

On the late nineteenth-century stage, homoerotic and even homosexual responses were not contained by traditions of costume but rather exacerbated, though Tilley was never a classical actor in the mould of Terry or Bernhardt. Marjorie Garber has argued that

> 'man' and 'woman' are already constructed within drama; within what is often recognised as great drama, or great theatre, the imaginative possibilities of a critique of gender in and through representation are already encoded as a system of signification.[90]

The nineteenth-century theatre, in its emphasis upon the femininity of Hamlet, in a sense already recognised this and, moreover, performed its ramifications. Garber's comment that transvestite theatre is in fact the norm from which we have deviated can be applied to the performances of women a century or more ago, as much as to the Renaissance stage.

A woman playing Hamlet, therefore, only served to emphasise what was already there in the text, drawing out a central theme which, many spectators would argue, told against the evils of inaction. There was therefore both an artistic and moral justification for the tradition of cross-dressing, as well as a purely theatrical one. It was a tradition that, with the important exception of Bernhardt, diminished in frequency as the century progressed and the naturalism of Ibsen and others became the dominant mode of stage mimesis. By the latter part of the century Krafft-Ebing had diagnosed the desire evident in some women to cross-dress on stage as a 'homosexual instinct', itself the consequence of a 'functional degeneration' in the individual.[91] Women could be, and were, incarcerated in asylums for such behaviour.

Transvestism itself became a form of madness, particularly on the stage where, as Powell remarks, women performers were already 'virtually mad by default, and necessarily the objects of medical concern'.[92] The kind of emotion and instability expressed by female characters on stage would often be sufficient to put them in an asylum off stage, as they demonstrate 'the want of that restraint over the passions without which the female character is lost'.[93] The female actor was categorised, even only by implication, as madwoman, and framed in institutionalised rhetoric that undermined the potential power of stage representation. As with Plato's republic, madness, as expressed through transvestism and above all mimesis, is dangerous and should be excluded.

The similarity of the attitudes of dominant contemporary ideologies towards art with that of *The Republic* is illustrated aptly in a passage written by Terry's son, Edward Gordon Craig, albeit in 1914:

> In the theatre we wander aimlessly along, continually labouring without laws to guide us, content to allow mimicry and imitation to usurp the place of art. So that those of us wishing to see a stronger and more natural plant growing up in the place of, or beside, this too artificial and effeminate modern product must, I think, turn their thoughts in the direction that I have indicated – I think they must help us to search for the laws.[94]

The twin, pathological, dangers of mimesis and effeminacy are linked and indistinguishable, and it is when talking of women that Craig's discourse becomes almost hysterical: 'Woman – beautiful, noble, and intelligent, as she often is in daily life – is a constant threat to the existence of art in the theatre.'[95] Such a paranoid response also effectively excludes his sister, the designer and producer Edy Craig, as well as his mother.

The same threatening, mimetic effeminacy can be located in Plato, from Socrates' initial prohibition of the Cronos myth, with its castration complex, through to the final linking of transvestism, madness and mimesis at the end of book three. In his reading of Plato, Lacou-Labarthe comments that 'what is threatening in mimesis is feminization, instability, hysteria'.[96] It is this conceptual feminisation of mimesis that undermines the strict masculine aggression of Girard's theories, carrying out an act that is based neither completely on rivalry nor antagonism. As disenfranchised members of the society mimicked in their craft, Siddons and Terry adopt personae that are constructed from a series of mimetic models, but which seek neither to displace nor supplant them, taken as they are from an eclectic gallery of fictional, conceptual and theatrical figures. As Lacou-Labarthe writes, the mimetic poet 'presents himself as what is not, exposes himself as other than he is, and depropriates himself'.[97] More than this, Terry in particular carries out what he calls 'enunciative depropriation',[98] a fragmentation of her own identity through the mimetic act that in her case results from her adulation of aspects of Shakespearean character.

Terry's relationship with the sanctified reputation of Shakespeare was one of worship – true bardolatry. In her uneasy attempts to transform Terry into a feminist, Nina Auerbach writes that 'she prayed to no man she knew, but she did bow before the great dead: Shakespeare exuded a holiness, an absolute authority, she conceded to no living man'.[99] While this claim of utter independence is not quite the case – Terry conceded a great deal, both to Irving and to Shaw – the relationship to Shakespeare is accurately depicted. In her Memoirs she eulogised the playwright as 'my friend, my sorrow's cure, my teacher, my companion, the very eyes of me'.[100]

Any insight she may bring to her roles is due therefore to Shakespeare, and when she later describes her inspiration during performance as 'divine', 'this gracious dew from heaven', this can be seen as referring as much to the Bard as to the Lord. Her praise of Shakespeare was total, Terry establishing herself in an alternative system of patriarchy in order to tolerate Irving's. It is this worship that prevents her from emancipating her characterisations as much as Auerbach would like. When the *New York Times* commented that 'one had the queer impression that she who is speaking was herself one of Shakespeare's women',[101] the review was almost certainly consonant with Terry's own desire – she became a vehicle for the divine word, a prophetess of Shakespearean scripture. This voluntary passivity in the face of the Bard itself mimics her involuntary passivity in the face of the Bard-surrogate, Irving. Her long-time correspondent Shaw recognised this in her and, unsurprisingly, attempted at length to depose his hated rival in Terry's mind as he did in that of many others. In a letter written in 1896 he instructed her: 'Don't deceive yourself: what you have to do on Tuesday is to be a mother to Shakespear – to cover his foolishnesses and barrennesses, and to make the most of his little scattered glimpses of divinity.'[102]

As much as Shaw wanted to replace other patriarchs with himself in Terry's affections, his advice was in essence sound. Siddons had very much made herself a 'mother' to Shakespeare, appropriating his name and characters to sanction her own 'inflexible' identity, and so employing a patriarch to establish a performance matriarchy at Covent Garden. In doing so she was merely imitating a typically masculine theatrical operation carried out by Garrick and others and evident also in the actions of Irving. But, perhaps because of the proprietary operations of Irving, Terry rejected this option, preferring in her way to venerate the past as a method of inhabiting the present. Seeing this, Shaw warned that

> If you cannot believe in the greatness of your own age and time and inheritance, you will fall into the most horrible confusion of mind and contrariety of spirit, like a noble little child looking up to foolish, mean, selfish parents.[103]

In many ways Shaw's diagnosis was accurate. In her worship of the past Terry conceded to a patriarchal structure in exactly the fashion that Auerbach claims she avoids, imitating while yearning to be those figures of Shakespearean fiction that for her almost assumed the status of actual historical personages. Her life was constantly structured as artefact, whether in the visual or performance arts, and she continually preferred this unreal existence to the shabby disappointments of modernity.

In this way Terry's performances overflowed the boundaries of the proscenium arch, creating an entirely mimetic, pluralised existence – whether as artist's muse for various Pre-Raphaelite artists or object of literary desire for Bernard Shaw. She became, like Sybil Vane in Wilde's *The Picture of Dorian Gray*, a figure for whom the conventional hierarchy of illusion and reality was reversed, until, for Wilde's character, love for Dorian destroys through sincerity her powers of artifice. Sybil exclaims, 'it was only in the theatre that I lived ... I was Rosalind one night, and Portia the other. The joy of Beatrice was my joy, and the sorrows of Cordelia were mine also.'[104] This could easily be Terry speaking.

Such mimetic delusion, so feared by Plato and so essential to actors such as Terry, finding a form of subjectivity through objectification, was the topic of a lecture given at Columbia University in 1863 by arguably the most perceptive and articulate actor on the nineteenth-century stage – Fanny Kemble. Kemble's acting career was sporadic, spectacular and largely unwanted. Daughter of Charles Kemble, niece of John Philip and Sarah Siddons, Fanny took to the stage aged twenty in 1829 to help save the fortunes of a flagging Covent Garden, a task she accomplished with alacrity. By 1832 she had retired to marry southern American plantation owner Pierce Butler, and had begun a twenty-year fight against both immediate patriarchy and ubiquitous slavery, a struggle partly resolved by her eventual divorce in the momentous year of 1848. Her journals reveal a keen intelligence and unusual political sophistication entirely lacking in both her aunt Siddons and Ellen Terry. In this lecture Kemble outlines the relationship between the theatre and reality, or as she terms it, the 'dramatic and the theatrical':

> That which is dramatic in human nature is the passionate, emotional, humorous element, the simplest portion of our composition, after our mean instincts, to which it is closely allied; and this has no relation whatever, beyond its momentary excitement and gratification, to that which imitates it, and is its theatrical reproduction. The dramatic is the real, of which the theatrical is the false.[105]

The terminology used here by Kemble is particularly interesting. The connection between the 'dramatic' and the 'theatrical' is established implicitly in the close semantic relationship between the two words, while the notion of imitation as reproduction comes close to prefiguring Julia Kristeva in its identification of mimesis with the female reproductive act.

In Kemble, a highly developed sense of the mimetic nature of the dramatic precluded, to a large extent, any need for the theatrical in her life. Feeling her own situation in America to be a faint copy of that of the slaves on her husband's plantation only emphasised her pre-existing empathy for those worse off in society. Her commentary in her journals on the passage of the 1831 Reform Bill is exceptionally prescient, predicting future discontent after the working class learn how they have been cheated. In extreme contrast we have Ellen Terry's understanding of class relations:

> A contemporary of Shakespeare's writes that 'those who are illustrious by long descent reveal their nobility beyond possibility of mistake. They have in them a simplicity, a naïve goodwill, a delicate good feeling that separates them from arrogant assumptions or false noblesse.' Of such is Rosalind. She shows these qualities of the well-bred at all times.[106]

Such arrogant assumptions of her own were predictably underscored by her analysis of *Coriolanus*, where she intoned, 'those words "was ever feather so lightly blown to and fro as this multitude" are surely true of the mob at all times in all countries'.[107]

The disparity between the two is all the more extraordinary when the distance of time is considered – almost eighty years before Terry's remarks, and eighteen years before Marx, Kemble was writing

> I cannot conceive what government will do next, for though trade is prosperous, great poverty and discontent exist among large classes of the people, and as soon as these needy people find out that Reform is not really immediate, they will seek something else which it may be difficult to give them.[108]

This 'something else', it is strongly implied, will be revolution. The difference between the two becomes all the more pertinent in the light of the increased professionalisation of the acting trade during the period. By the time of Irving's knighthood, his profession had been unionised in the form of the Actors' Association.[109] It had therefore been strongly reorganised upon class lines, with Terry's fickle 'mob' forming a constituent part of her own profession. The theatre on the one hand displayed the ostentatious wealth and celebrity of patriarchs and stars such as Irving and Terry, while on the other the casual employment and poverty-line wages more openly associated with manual labour and an urban proletariat. Once again, the theatre operated in a mimetic relationship with dominant social ideologies and with the works it celebrated. Terry becomes in this instance very much a Volumnia in relation to her own craft, a matriarch employing the discourse of patriarchy to find a voice. Her own son, with whom she had an

alienated yet suitably obsessive relationship, was himself a Coriolanus figure in the English theatre, contemptuously defecting to Italy, where he first
conceived of the performative proletariat as marionettes.

VII

Women on the nineteenth-century stage established themselves in a sophisticated system of mimesis that had profound repercussions upon themselves
as gendered performers in an increasingly commodified profession. Within
this complex model, gender became the superordinate factor, reinforced by
the political and social dominance of patriarchy. The parallel operations of
artistic authority symbolised by the deified Shakespearean name served
simultaneously to support these structures through intervening figures such
as Irving, while deconstructing them through the provision of a form of
empowering subjectivity in the shape of characterisation and the appropriation of an objectified otherness. It is in their mimetic relationship with
Shakespeare that these actors were most able to articulate the complex
dynamics of performance on a patriarchal stage. The position of the actor
in this society therefore on one level mimicked that of the performer in *The
Republic*, while on another demonstrated the possibility of its subversion.
This multifaceted model set the scene for the position of the actor in the
following century, and also therefore in the theatre of today.

The mimetic traditions of the two great matriarchal acting dynasties of
the nineteenth century – the Siddons/Kembles and the Terrys – continued
into the twentieth, with descendants locked into the same imitative traditions as those of the Shakespearean plays which so constructed their identities. The Terrys continued their influence on modern theatre in the
twentieth century not only through Ellen's son, Edward Gordon Craig,
but also through her great-nephew, John Gielgud. One of the pre-eminent
theatrical figures of the last seventy years, Gielgud rapidly established
himself in the late 1920s and 1930s as the dominant Shakespearean, culminating in two productions as the 'definitive' English Hamlet of his
generation. The position of Gielgud as object and agent of mimesis will
be discussed further in Chapter 3.

Dynastic inheritance was not limited to English families, as the career of
the author of the quotation with which this chapter began demonstrates.
Edwin Booth, the American Hamlet of his generation, is particularly useful
as an exemplar of the issues of mimesis so far discussed in this chapter, in
connection with Hamlet, who is the focus of the next. Booth had inherited
the role from his father, Junius Brutus Booth, who commented when
Edwin was nineteen: 'You look like Hamlet. Why didn't you play that
part for your benefit?'[110] By the time he was thirty, dominance of the
American stage was assured through his electric performances, which
owed much to imitation of his idol (and colleague of his father) Kean,

who had outclassed Junius during his earlier career in England. *The New York Evening Post* could write that 'we today live in the era of Booth, and Booth, to the majority of us, is Hamlet. The Hamlets of the past are to us really no more than the unimagined Hamlets of the future.'[111] Booth negated memory and the past, such was his contemporary presence. Theatrical transience here becomes an indicator of greatness, rather than inadequacy, and freedom from a mimetic model is hailed as a constituent part of that power.

Booth, however, was highly conscious of the past, not only in his adulation of Kean but in his reverence for the shade of his father, whose own image was used in the closet scene. Booth credited this familial positioning as the reason for the powerful continuity in his performance,[112] leading to a record 100 nights at New York's Winter Garden in 1864–5, the same year Henry Irving, five years his junior, made his debut on the English stage.[113]

Booth's position, in appropriately Hamlettian fashion, was defined closely not only in relation to his father but also to his brother. As Thompson and Taylor have written:

> Hamlet is significantly concerned with sibling relationships, and especially relationships between brothers, and ... the Freudian and post-Freudian mode of reading the play as a paradigmatic representation of the Oedipus complex has resulted in a general neglect or distortion of this element.[114]

Exactly one week after Booth finished his hundred nights of deliberation as to whether or not he should 'kill a king', his younger brother John Wilkes, also an actor, entered another theatre and shot Abraham Lincoln. Remarkably, it was only nine months before Edwin returned to the stage as Hamlet, to rapturous acclaim.

Booth's own family history not only became a distorted echo of his most famous role – his first wife committed suicide – it also came to inform perception of his 'right' to play Hamlet. The incredibly public nature of his personal tragedies underlined his supposed understanding of his role. The imitation of tradition, profession and role became total in the case of Booth, forming a reciprocal system of mimetic *mise en abyme* that explodes any fixed, Girardian models of the mimetic process. When the correspondent of the *Evening Post* wrote that Booth 'is Hamlet', his comment acquired a resonance that exceeded the essentialism of Hazlitt through the irresistible figural similitude of the events in the actor's life. Biography and circumstance came to shape performance reputation.

The sense of resonance between role and actor, biography and characterisation, continued, though usually in less spectacular fashion, into the twentieth century, given increased emphasis by the contemporaneous development of Freudian psychoanalysis (including that of literary character) and Stanislavskyan acting. Such departures lead to an increased subtlety of understanding of concepts of mimesis, a blurring of the tripartite distinction between professional continuity, societal and performative tradition and the genealogy of a role. It is this that will form the focus of Chapter 3.

The discourse of actors over the past two centuries represents a continual engagement with and participation in the mimetic act. This can be seen within the relationship of one acting tradition to another, one generation of canonical performance to another, and in the broad relationship of the profession and art of acting to the society with which it has a reciprocally imitative relationship. It is a discourse that is continually reappropriated by its principal agents in order to privilege one ideology or another or to find a voice in the face of repression. As with the techniques of acting themselves, actors locate themselves in a tradition of coherence and consistency, a continual mimetic genealogy, which belies the fractured and cyclical nature of the processes of performance themselves.

Notes

1 E. Booth, 'A Few Words about Edmund Kean', in B. Matthews and L. Hutton (eds), *Actors and Actresses of Great Britain and The United States: From the Days of David Garrick to the Present Time*, New York: Cassell & Co., 1886, vol. 3, pp. 8–9.

2 Plato, in D. Lee (ed. and trans.), *The Republic*, 395–6, Harmondsworth: Penguin, 1955, p. 156.

3 Quoted by B. Cox in *Lear Diaries*, London: Methuen, 1992, p. 8.

4 He claimed because the friendship undermined the honour – Gladstone had his own box at the Lyceum, close to the stage to overcome his deafness. Irving, journal, quoted by M. Bingham in *Henry Irving and Victorian Theatre*, New York and London: Stein & Day, 1978, p. 265.

5 L. Olivier, *On Acting*, London: Wheelshare, 1986, p. 96.

6 Irving, journal, quoted by Bingham, p. 263.

7 See Lee's edition, p. 421, and also G. Else, *Plato and Aristotle on Poetry*, Chapel Hill, N.C.: 1986, for a discussion of the possibility that book ten takes the position of an appendix, added later in response to or anticipation of criticism of book three.

8 Plato, *The Republic*, 397e, p. 156.

9 See especially his introduction to the edition of his correspondence with Ellen Terry, cited below.

10 McKellen eventually played not Coriolanus, a part he had in any case played before, but Richard III, in a famous production that eventually became the model for Richard Loncraine's 1996 film.

11 R. Girard, 'Mimesis and Violence', in J.G. Williams (ed.), *The Girard Reader*, London: Crossroads, 1996.

12 In J. Richards (ed.) *Sir Henry Irving: Theatre, Culture and Society – Essays, Addresses and Lectures*, Keele: Keele University Press, 1994, p. 276.

13 When reading Irving's written material it is as well to recall the influence of his acting manager, Bram Stoker, who regularly edited, amended or took sole authorial responsibility for Irving's publications. There has been little research done on this matter, and it is currently impossible to state with any certainty in all but a handful of cases who is responsible, and to what degree, for the material bearing Irving's name. See the various works on Irving in the bibliography for further discussion.

14 For a discussion of the operations by which this pseudo-deification occurred see, among others, G. Holderness, *The Shakespeare Myth*, Manchester: Manchester University Press, 1991; J. Joughin (ed.), *Shakespeare and National Culture*, Manchester: Manchester University Press, 1997; I. Kamps (ed.), *Materialist Shakespeare: A History*, London: Verso, 1995; A. Sinfield, *Faultlines: Cultural Materialism and the Politics of Dissident Reading*, Oxford: Clarendon, 1992 etc.

15 Irving, in Richards, *Sir Henry Irving*, p. 276.

16 In the face of escalating debt the Lyceum was taken over by a limited liability corporation, what today would be called receivership, in 1899. See A. Hughes, *Henry Irving, Shakespearean*, Cambridge: Cambridge University Press, 1981.

17 See Derrida, 'The First Session', 1972, reprinted in Attridge (ed.), *Acts of Literature*, London: Routledge, 1992, pp. 127–180.

18 Irving, Introduction to *The Henry Irving Shakespeare*, London: Blackie, 1895, 2 vols, vol. 1, p. 14.

19 Shaw, Preface to Terry and Shaw, *A Correspondence*, ed. C. St John, London: Constable, 1931, p. xxxiv.

20 Ibid., p. xxxiii.

21 Ibid., p. xxxviii.

22 Quoted in N. Auerbach, *Ellen Terry: Player in her Time*, New York and London: Norton, 1987, p. 215.

23 In 1864, aged sixteen, Terry married the painter G.F. Watts, thirty years her senior. During the twelve months before they separated she modelled for him and other Pre-Raphaelites extensively.

24 Quoted in K. Powell, *Women and Victorian Theatre*, Cambridge: Cambridge University Press, 1997, p. 69.

25 Ibid., p. 58.

26 Letter dated 10.7.96, in *Correspondence*.

27 Shaw, Preface, p. xxiv.

28 Auerbach, *Ellen Terry*, p. 212.

29 Ibid., p. 214.

30 Ibid., p. 238.

31 See below, p. 127.

32 E. Terry, *The Story of My Life*, London: Hopkinson, 1927, p. 154.

33 See D. Callaghan, *Shakespeare without Women*, London: Routledge, 2000, esp. p. 91.

34 Powell, *Women and Victorian Theatre*, p. 47.

35 H. Walter, 'The Heroine, the Harpy and the Human Being', *New Theatre Quarterly*, spring 1993, p. 110.

36 T. Campbell, *The Life of Mrs Siddons*, London, 1834 (2 vols), vol. II, p. 9.

37 Ibid., p. 19.

38 Ibid., p. 14.

39 Ibid., p. 14.
40 J.P. Kemble, *Macbeth and King Richard III: An Essay in Answer to Remarks on Some of the Characters of Shakespeare*, first published in 1786 by T&J Egerton, reprinted 1817.
41 R. Manvell, *Sarah Siddons, Portrait of an Actress*, London: Heinemann, 1970, p. 122.
42 Terry, *Four Lectures on Shakespeare*, London: Hopkinson, 1932, p. 162.
43 Also, if her niece Fanny Kemble's account of her failing years is to be believed, Siddons suffered in her last years from senility. If, as is entirely possible, the *Remarks* was written immediately before or during this period, the inconsistency becomes a result of nothing more than the unreliability of advanced age. See E. Ransome (ed.), *The Terrific Kemble*, London: Hamilton, 1978, p. 32.
44 In Auerbach, *Ellen Terry*, p. 259. Emphases as in the original.
45 Walter, *Macbeth*, in Nicholson (ed.), *Actors on Shakespeare* series, 2002, p. 1.
46 Terry, in Auerbach, *Ellen Terry*, p. 259.
47 Terry, *The Story of my Life*, p. 306.
48 F. Kemble, *Notes Upon Some of Shakespeare's Plays*, London, 1882, p. 54.
49 In Auerbach, *Ellen Terry*, p. 237.
50 Letter to Charles Coleman, quoted in ibid., p. 222.
51 Shaw, Preface, p. xix.
52 Terry, *Four Lectures*, p. 80.
53 Ibid., p. 116.
54 S. Case, *Feminism and Theatre*, London: Macmillan, 1988, p. 120.
55 Girard, 'Mimesis and Violence', p. 13.
56 Quoted in Powell, *Women and Victorian Theatre*, p. 52.
57 Ibid., p. 29.
58 Ibid.
59 See J. Gielgud, 'The *Hamlet* Tradition: some notes on costume, scenery and stage business', in R. Gilder (ed.), *John Gielgud's Hamlet, A Record of Performance*, London: Methuen, 1937, p. 84
60 Interview in *Daily Telegraph*, 17.06.1899.
61 Worcester, 1775; Liverpool, 1777; Bath, 1778; Bristol, 1781; Dublin, 1802.
62 See G. Taranow, *The Bernhardt Hamlet – Culture and Context*, London: Peter Lang, 1996, p. 91 for further details.
63 Quoted by R. Hapgood (ed.), *Hamlet, Shakespeare in Production*, Cambridge: Cambridge University Press University Press, 1999, introduction, p. 33.
64 A theory that directly informed the 1920 German film of the play, *Hamlet, the Drama of Vengeance*, directed by Svende Gade and Heinz Schall with Asta Nielsen in the title role. See J.L. Guntner, 'Hamlet, Macbeth and King Lear on Film', in Russell Jackson (ed.), *The Cambridge Companion to Shakespeare on Film*, Cambridge: Cambridge University Press, 2000, pp. 117–34.
65 S. Berkoff, *I am Hamlet*, New York and London: Faber & Faber, 1989, p. 55.
66 See S. West, *The Image of the Actor: Verbal and Visual Representation in the Age of Garrick and Kemble*, London and New York: St Martin's Press, 1991.
67 Taranow, *The Bernhardt Hamlet*, p. 100.
68 See H. Granville-Barker, *Preface to Hamlet*, 1937, reprinted London: Nick Hern, 1993, p. 43.
69 Cited in Taranow, *The Bernhardt Hamlet*, p. 102.
70 Ibid.

71 S. Bernhardt, *The Art of the Theatre*, trans H.J. Sherring, London: G. Bles, 1924, p. 96.

72 C. Wilkes, *A General View of the Stage*, London, 1759.

73 *An Authentic Narrative of Mr Kemble's Retirement from the Stage*, London: John Miller, 1817, pp. xxiii–xxiv.

74 W. Hazlitt, 'Mr. Kean's Othello', in *A View of the English Stage* (1818), in Duncan Wu (ed.), *The Selected Writings of William Hazlitt*, London: Pickering & Chatto, 1998, 9 vols, vol. 3, p. 103.

75 Prepared specifically for this production by Marcel Schwob and Eugene Morand. It was remarkable for, among other things, cutting only 885 lines, fewer than any previous French translation and most English acting versions of the text – Irving habitually cut around 1200 lines, and Tree anything up to 1,700. See Stokes's piece on Bernhardt in J. Stokes, M.R. Booth and Bassnet, *Bernhardt, Terry, Duse: The Actress in Her Time*, Cambridge: Cambridge University Press, p. 1988.

76 G.H. Lewes, 'Foreign Actors on Our Stage', in *On Actors and the Art of Acting*, Leipzig: Bernhard Tauchnitz, 1875, p. 139.

77 Ibid., p. 171.

78 Ibid., pp. 56–7.

79 Ibid., p. 60.

80 Hazlitt, *The Characters of Shakespeare's Plays*, 1817, in Wu, (ed.), *Selected Writings*, vol. 1, p. 143.

81 P. Brook in Ralph Berry (ed.), *On Directing Shakespeare: Interviews with Contemporary Directors*, London: Hamilton, 1989, pp. 132–3.

82 Hazlitt, *The Characters of Shakespeare's Plays*, p. 148.

83 Hazlitt, *A View of the English Stage*, vol. 3, p. 144.

84 See West, *The Image of the Actor*, p. 113. Other accounts of this moment are also described by West. See also R. Asleson (ed.), *A Passion for Performance: Sarah Siddons and Her Portraitists*, Los Angeles, Calif.: J. Paul Getty Museum, 1999.

85 West, *The Image of the Actor*, p. 122.

86 Anatomical attribution of character can be seen as reaching its height in the burgeoning discipline of eugenics, and in the identification of 'criminal' physiognomies through photography by Cesare Lombroso in 1876.

87 In relation to the timing of Old Hamlet's duel, taking place while his wife was in labour, Samuel West commented: 'Couldn't he have put it off for a day or two until his son was born? Perhaps sent a note?' West, interview with Russell Jackson, Swan Theatre, 17.05.01.

88 A.R. Jones and P. Stallybrass, *Renaissance Clothing and the Materials of Memory*, Cambridge: Cambridge University Press, 2000, p. 206.

89 V. Tilley, *Recollections of Vesta Tilley*, London, 1934, p. 233.

90 M. Garber, *Vested Interests: Cross Dressing and Cultural Anxiety*, London: Routledge, 1992, p. 180.

91 R. Von Krafft-Ebing, *Psychopathia Sexualis*, trans. Franklin S. Klaf, London: Bell, 1865, p. 263.

92 Powell, *Women and Victorian Theatre*, p. 35.

93 J. Connolly, quoted in E. Showalter, *The Female Malady: Women, Madness and English Culture, 1830–1980*, New York: Pantheon, 1985.

94 E.G. Craig, 'A Plea for an inquiry after the missing laws of the Art', in *The Theatre Advancing*, London: Bloom, 1947, p. 167.

95 Craig, 'New Departures', in *The Theatre Advancing*, p. 275.
96 P. Lacou-Labarthe, *Typography*, trans. Christopher Fynsk, Stanford, Calif.: University of Stanford Press, 1998, originally published in French in 1979, p. 129.
97 Ibid., p. 133.
98 Ibid.
99 Auerbach, *Ellen Terry*, p. 220.
100 Terry, *The Story of my Life*, p. 304.
101 Auerbach, *Ellen Terry*, p. 222.
102 Letter from Shaw to Terry, 16.9.96.
103 Ibid.
104 O. Wilde, *The Picture of Dorian Gray*, 1891, in *The Complete Plays, Poems, Novels and Stories of Oscar Wilde*, London: Magpie, 1993, p. 74.
105 F. Kemble, *On the Stage*, London, 1863, p. 309.
106 Terry, *Four Lectures*, p. 97.
107 Ibid., p. 110.
108 F. Kemble, journal entry, 29 May 1831, in E. Ransome (ed.), *The Terrific Kemble*, London: Hamilton, 1978, p. 51.
109 Established in 1891. The Actors' Union was formed in 1905, and Equity in 1929.
110 Quoted by A. Booth Clarke, *The Elder and Younger Booths*, New York, 1982, p. 54. Booth was slight and dark, with piercing eyes and a mane of black hair.
111 *The New York Evening Post*, 16.03.1870, quoted in Shattuck, *The Hamlet of Edwin Booth*, Urbana, Ill.: University of Illinois, 1969, p. xv.
112 See Shattuck, *The Hamlet of Edwin Booth*, for a lengthy examination and reconstruction of Booth's performances of Hamlet.
113 Famously, in response to a plea to curtail his record run in deference to Booth, John Barrymore in 1923 deliberately played the part for 101 nights – a suitably Oedipal response for a highly Freudian interpretation.
114 A. Thompson and N. Taylor, '"Father and Mother is One Flesh": Hamlet and the Problems of Paternity' in L. Spaas (ed.), *Paternity and Fatherhood: Myths and Realities*, New York and London: St Martin's Press, 1998, p. 247.

Chapter 3

Noble memories
Playing Hamlet

Hamlet is the greatest play of tradition in our language.

J. Gielgud[1]

The weight of the past of the play is unbearable: globally famous, one of the great cultural icons, 'a hoop', according to Max Beerbohm, 'through which every actor must sooner or later jump'.

P. Franks[2]

Hegel remarks somewhere that all facts and personages of great importance in world history occur, as it were, twice ... Caussidiere for Danton, Louis Blanc for Robespierre, the Nephew for the Uncle ... The tradition of all the dead generations weighs like a nightmare on the brain of the living.

K. Marx[3]

I

Philip Franks's thoughtful account of playing Hamlet, unsuccessfully in his view, encapsulates usefully the problems and trials of playing the role. These can be summarised as a confrontation with the past, epitomised in the presence in his remarks on Beerbohm, and a subsequent identification with the part, leading to a realisation that 'my difficulties are also Hamlet's: he is talking to a group of strangers about a situation he does not fully understand'.[4] This observation results from a conviction that the part requires an 'unusually high level of personal input'; indeed it is his duty to 'pour as much of [my] experience of loss, doubt, fear and lack of faith into the operation as possible'.[5] It is perhaps unsurprising that Franks's final assessment of his attempt at the role is one of 'general inadequacy', given his conceptualisation of the role in almost entirely negative terms. It is also a recognition that he may try to make his own history within the role, but he cannot make it as he pleases.

The echoes, or ghosting, of Marx within Franks's account are almost certainly deliberate, given his education and erudition, as, one would like to think, are the intriguing echoes of *Hamlet* within Marx. Valéry, playfully casting himself in the role of Gravedigger, was not the first to notice this:

> He is bowed under the weight of all the discoveries and varieties of knowledge; incapable of resuming this endless activity, he broods on the tedium of rehearsing the past and the folly of always trying to innovate. Every skull he picks up is an illustrious skull. 'Whose was it? This one was Leonardo ... and this one was Kant ... and Kant begat Hegel, and Hegel begat Marx, and Marx begat ...' Hamlet does not know what to do with all these skulls. But if he forgets them! Will he still be himself?[6]

Nor was he the last, as Derrida's *Specters of Marx* testifies. Indeed Valéry is quoted in Derrida's Hamlettian reading of *The Communist Manifesto*, in which Derrida characteristically casts himself as the hero, a figure with 'a fictive interiority consisting in self-absence'.[7]

Ending with a quotation, an invocation, from earlier in the play than the citations with which it began, Derrida's text promotes a circularity that echoes that of Franks's remark: citing Marx who cited Shakespeare, while Valéry's quasi-biblical genealogy is also revealed through anachronism to be in fact a series of interlinking cycles, the modern 'European' Hamlet beset by the weight of succeeding generations of philosophical thought. This model can be found as well in the rhetoric of actors approaching the role, which simultaneously places the writer in the position of heir to previous players and instrument of Shakespearean incarnation, a slightly displaced inheritance befitting, as Marx hints, not so much a son as a nephew.

Raphael Falco's study of literary genealogy forms an interesting parallel to that of acting. He comments that 'the careful selection (and identification) of a poetic genealogy gave an imprimatur not merely to the individual poet, but to the fledgling [sixteenth-century] literary culture as well'.[8] The emphasis on genealogy amongst actors carries the same weight. The sword of Garrick's Richard III, the battered copy of *Hamlet* passed down from the greatest Hamlet of his generation to his successor, the tenuous and often retrospectively constructed inheritance of technique – all these exist to give a history and a tradition to a notoriously itinerant and nebulous profession.

This chapter will focus on the processes of influence and inheritance as perceived by actors who have played the role, in particular Michael Pennington and Steven Berkoff, both of whom have written at length of their experiences. It will begin by looking at the linear, direct transmission of the role before engaging, via the writing of those connected to a particular production – the Gielgud/Burton 1964 Hamlet – with a more subtle rhetoric that perceives these operations in terms of a radical reinterpretation of mimesis, and is evident most in the comments of Ben Kingsley and Samuel West.

In 1986 T.J. King published 'A Great Chain of Acting', a diagram forming 'an unbroken chain linking actors of successive generations . . . - from William Shakespeare to Laurence Olivier',[9] constituting a family tree with fifteen links, its name echoing an eternalist great chain of being. This in itself is a merely an updated version of a strategy under way as early as the seventeenth century, as recorded by John Downes in *Roscius Anglicanus*:

> The Tragedy of *Hamlet*; *Hamlet* being Perform'd by Mr *Betterton*: Sir *William* [Davenant] (having seen Mr *Taylor* of the *Black-fryars* Company Act it, who being instructed by the Author Mr. *Shakspear*) taught Mr *Betterton* in every Particle of it; which by his exact Performance of it, gain'd him Esteem and Reputation, Superlative to all other Plays.[10]

As the editors of this edition note, this is an impossible genealogy as Joseph Taylor joined the company after the deaths of both Shakespeare and Burbage. The discrepancy is remedied, however, by the substitution of John Lowin in a later entry for *Henry VIII*:

> The part of the king was so right and justly done by Mr *Betterton*, he being Instructed in it by Sir *William*, who had it from Old Mr. *Lowin*, that had his Instructions from Mr. *Shakespear* himself, that I dare and will aver, none can, or will come near him in this Age, in the performance of that part.[11]

A different form of consistency is here being striven for – not the familiar psychological through-line so beloved of twentieth-century actors, nor the mimetic coherence of socio-political positioning as sought by Irving, but a consistency of inheritance and imitation of previous generations of acting. Hamlet is to be true not to himself, nor to his country, but to his father. It is in this purity of genealogy, a kind of divine right, that authenticity of performance is located.

Within the history of the role there can be seen a repeated emphasis on a kind of adoptive primogeniture, with junior Hamlets proclaiming their debt to elder role models, or with prior players nominating successors. If Olivier was keen to abolish memories of Irving, he was equally keen to identify a less traditional figure as his own inspiration: John Barrymore.

Four years before John Gielgud first attempted the part, Barrymore played his version of the 'mother-loving pervert'[12] in a touring production, with the fencing match choreographed by Douglas Fairbanks. He remains the only American actor to have scored significant success in the role in

England. In the audience was Olivier, and his athletic, Oedipal Hamlet of thirteen years later clearly has its origins here. Talking of the issue, Olivier invokes the authority of Shakespeare to sanction his interpretation:

> The Oedipus Complex may, indeed, be responsible for a formidable share of all that is wrong with Hamlet. I myself am only too happy to allow to be added, to Shakespeare's other acknowledged gifts, an intuitive understanding of psychology. Why not? He was the world's greatest man.[13]

Olivier here gives characteristic emphasis to the masculinity of Shakespeare, as he does to his interpretation of the role itself, which perhaps owed as much to Fairbanks as to Barrymore. In an interesting anecdote of his and Peggy Ashcroft's visit to Ernest Jones, Olivier writes:

> At one moment Jones said that there was a particular painting that was of psychopathic interest. It was *The Conception of the Blessed Virgin Mary*, which shows an angel blowing the pollen from a lily into her ear. He said 'Of course, the earhole is also the sign of vicious tendencies, possibly of a homosexual nature'. In amazement I asked 'The earhole?' 'Yes' he said, waited a minute and then – very quietly (not for Peggy's ears) – 'any orifice but the right one.'[14]

One wonders what Ashcroft, sidelined in a remarkably Irvingesque manner, would have made of this – and particularly Olivier's revealing choice of metaphor for her misogynistic exclusion. The bizarre introduction of latent homosexuality into Claudius's fascination with ears endows Olivier's characterisation of Jones with a decided homophobic slant. This Hamlet will most definitely not be either feminine or homoerotic, but will instead be a bold, manly and realistic Prince.

Olivier's Hamlet of action, not reflection, initiated a series of vigorous, virile heroes, particularly on screen. The performances of Burton, Nicol Williamson, Jacobi, Mel Gibson and Branagh all owe something to him. The most visible symbol of this debt is of course Olivier's bleached blond hair. Prior to him, Hamlets had traditionally had brown or black hair, responding to the Romantic, Byronic, Hamlettian archetype. Fechter was the only blond nineteenth-century Hamlet of note, prompting G.H. Lewes to wax lyrical about his 'flaxen curls'.[15] Given these statistics, Olivier's reasoning for bleaching his hair becomes particularly significant. As Rosenberg reports:

> Olivier, black-haired on stage, made himself blond for the film – in order, one observer said, to present a more reflective, ruminative prince, inwardly disturbed. Not so, said Olivier, it was purely

technical: among all the dark men in his cast he wanted that one blond head to stand out.[16]

The casting of one notable stage Hamlet, John Laurie, as Bernardo gives an indication of the subtext of Olivier's explanation – he desired to stand out amongst all those other 'dark men', the legion of past Hamlets. What is interpreted by observers as a tool to illuminate Shakespeare is in fact a vehicle for the display of Olivier himself.

It is within *Hamlet*, therefore, a play that obsesses with inheritance, genealogy and filiality, that we find what Derek Jacobi has called, while directing the play, 'the greatest of all acting traditions'.[17] The documentary recording rehearsals for this *Hamlet*, starring Kenneth Branagh for the Renaissance Theatre Company, pushes this further, with narrator Patrick Stewart intoning: 'It is the role the greatest actors of each generation have always sought to play; an unbroken tradition handed down from one age to the next.'[18] As if to exemplify this remark, Jacobi himself continues with an anecdote. In an anecdote that recalls Olivier watching Barrymore, it was Richard Burton's performance of *Hamlet* at the Old Vic that made up young Derek's mind to become an actor, and he was therefore thrilled when Burton came backstage during Jacobi's performance of the part at the same theatre. During the same production 'there was another visitor who came backstage and told me that seeing the performance had made up his mind to go into acting. His name was Kenneth Branagh.'[19] Branagh's own account of that moment is less portentous, reflecting the affable, blokeish persona he strives to project:

> The damage was done. I began to read the play, to read more of Shakespeare. I resolved to become an actor. Tempting though it is to rewrite one's personal history with the benefit of hindsight, I believe that much of what has followed in my life was affected by that experience.[20]

The genealogy constructed by these two actors, both heavily conscious of tradition, is intriguingly reflected in Branagh's film of *Hamlet* in which Jacobi plays Claudius, putting a knowingly agonistic spin on their relationship, further nuanced by first-time director Jacobi having directed Branagh in his first incarnation in the role on stage. Teleologically, Claudius here directs Hamlet, before the younger man later reverses the relationship. Both actors are also bleached blond in the film in an echo of Olivier's Dane in his 1948 film. Russell Jackson's film diary captures the essence of this relationship in a description of one particular moment:

> The ceremony: Derek completes his work on the film and there's the usual applause, especially strong in his case. Then he springs a

surprise. He holds up a small red-bound copy of the play, that successive actors have passed on to each other with the condition that the
recipient should give it in turn to the finest Hamlet of the next generation. It has come from Forbes Robertson, a great Hamlet at the
turn of the century, to Derek, via Henry Ainley, Michael Redgrave,
Peter O'Toole and others – now he gives it to Ken.[21]

The book becomes a talisman of the tradition itself, an heirloom for an
increasingly dense genealogy. It is the rhetorical structure of this inheritance that is the subject of this discussion. In the previous chapter, the
discourse of a tradition of acting as a whole was analysed according to
Girard's model of mimetic rivalry. The aim of this chapter is to develop
and problematise that model using the text of *Hamlet* itself as a critical tool.

II

In 1980 two radically different *Hamlets* played in London. The first was
directed by John Barton for the RSC and featured Michael Pennington in
the title role, the second was directed by and starred Steven Berkoff. The
Barton/Pennington version was a critical and commercial success. The
Berkoff *Hamlet* received, in the director's own words, 'the most awful bat-
tering from the press', and went on to tour throughout Europe, where it
was received more favourably. In 1989, aged fifty-two, Berkoff published a
revised version of his performance diaries as *I Am Hamlet*.[22] Seven years
later, also aged fifty-two, Pennington published his account of performing
the play as *Hamlet: A User's Guide*.[23]

The books have striking similarities. They work through the play in a
strictly linear fashion using as their starting point a close reading of the
text, so that both books give the impression of a slightly unorthodox and
abridged edition of the play. They are simultaneously accounts of playing
the title role, discussions of acting technique, readings of the play and
moments of autobiography. Both integrate the identity of the writer
strongly with that of Hamlet himself.

Hamlet: A User's Guide differs significantly in that it reflects Pennington's
remarkable diversity of performance experience of the play – he has
played, over thirty years, Fortinbras, Laertes, Hamlet, Claudius and the
Ghost – rather than focusing exclusively on the hero.[24] Berkoff's book
includes a directorial and, intriguingly, a playwright's perspective absent
from the later account, reflecting his multi-faceted theatrical persona.
Both, however, are united in being fascinating and highly sophisticated
works, involving a subtle reading of Shakespeare and a complex understanding of authorial personae. They deal with the weight of previous
generations with skill, recognising with Valéry the anachronistic construction of Hamlet by his successors as they do their own construction by their

varied antecedents. In the history of *Hamlet*, the time is often out of joint and it is insufficient to see the progress of the red-bound book as moving always in one direction only.

Pennington in particular is well aware of the influence of past generations. He begins with an account of hearing of Olivier's death while working with Gielgud on the appropriately titled *Summer's Lease*, by John Mortimer. Olivier was also Pennington's own first encounter with the role which, as with Jacobi and Branagh, propelled him into his choice of career. His text thus begins with the death of the most famous twentieth-century Hamlet and with an account of first seeing him – 'he was my first' – that sounds not unlike a loss of virginity. Olivier becomes both father figure and lover, initiator and begetter, allowing Pennington's text to begin. Additionally, the permanence of the Olivier film of *Hamlet* allows the actor to be both antecedent and contemporary in a manner strikingly close to Bloom's famous model of the anxiety of literary influence.[25] Gielgud, present at the beginning, is there also at the end of the book, when Pennington exhorts us to treasure this 'national resource', who represents 'a great continuum in himself' due to his standing and extraordinary longevity. He becomes the personification of a tradition, born in Ibsen's lifetime and living to see the Branagh/Luhrmann cinematic renaissance in Shakespeare. Consequently, 'for those aware of history, every choice thumps with significance: intimate voices within whisper Garrick and Gielgud, Rylance and Charleson'.[26]

Within this interesting collocation – one (at the time) living past master, one dead contemporary – Pennington is careful to situate himself amongst his successors as well as those who have gone before, implying that the Hamlettian reputation is also a matter of measuring up to those who are yet to come. In this he is almost unique amongst actor/authors, the significant exception being Olivier, who is more than happy that his film roles continue to haunt successive players, remarking that 'it may be the young actor today has to suffer because my shadow has been left on certain roles; not that I'm objecting now, you understand'.[27] With Olivier, this urge is, as we have seen earlier, an urge to supplant, to usurp. With Pennington, in contrast, such rivalry, while not entirely absent, ceases to be the principal motivation. The ideologies present in his writing are more complex.

Talking of Hamlet, Pennington elsewhere remarks:

> He has a yearning for the past that seems to go beyond his personal crisis to be a cultural need. His world is based not only on a contemporary sense of reason but also on an older, deeper morality ... A deep concern for the past and its values runs through him and he perhaps never speaks of the future.[28]

Pennington's nostalgic moralist is reflected in the language used in the text itself, which contains thirty-four instances of words pertaining to memory, twice as many as its nearest Shakespearean rival, *The Tempest*. No other play in the canon has more than a dozen such instances. The play used most often as a vehicle for constructions of acting traditions and genealogies is thus, unsurprisingly, the play most preoccupied to the point of obsession with notions of memory.[29]

Though Hamlet himself may not speak of the future, preferring that the rest be silence, those around him are very much concerned with it. Even the Ghost, the past made present, seems, Olivier-like, to speak only to influence the future – 'Remember me' is an exhortation to future action through past recognition. The protagonist is therefore placed looking backward in a play that denies the past, hysterically remembering in a society that is skilled at forgetting. Similarly, the actor playing the role is always looking back at the Ghosts of previous kings, which are often the very figures that have metaphorically brought them into the world they now inhabit. This impression is reinforced by the occasions on which the Ghost has been played by an actor who had himself been a notable Hamlet years previously. Examples of this include Henry Ainley to F.R. Benson at Stratford in 1914, Paul Scofield to Mel Gibson in Zeffirelli's 1990 film, Gielgud's voice to Burton in 1964, and Berkoff's voice to Richard Dreyfuss in his 1990 Birmingham Old Rep production. Surprisingly, in a film full of Hamlets, Branagh's Ghost, Brian Blessed, never played the role.[30] As Pennington remarks:

> [The Ghost] is not a character in relationship to others or to present events, but rather creating the play's future: and since his world is outside everybody's experience, the actor is imaginatively on the wing, free-associating to show something he has no clearer idea of than any live person.[31]

For once an actor is not bound by any ideas of consistency of characterisation, because the character is unreal – in a sense, there is no character. The actor is in a position similar to that identified by Barthes in his *Textual Analysis of Poe's Valdemar*, in which the dead man says 'I am dead', and so 'the signifier expresses a signified (death) which is contradictory with its enunciation'.[32] Though the Ghost stops short of such an enunciation, its physical presence on stage in the form of the actor endows the speech with the same force, the force, as Barthes comments, of 'a taboo exploded'.

Hamlet, intriguingly, does not so limit his speech with such taboos, famously stating the impossible not once but twice to Horatio at the end of the play – 'I am dead, Horatio', 'Horatio, I am dead' (5.2, 285 & 290). Barthes continues:

> It seems clear that what is taboo in death, what is essentially taboo, is the passage, the threshold, the dying ... the transition between the two states [of life and death], or more exactly, their mutual encroach-

ment, outplays meaning and engenders horror: there is the transgression of an antithesis, of a classification.[33]

Hamlet famously occupies many such 'threshold' spaces throughout the play, often literally, as in the graveyard or on the ramparts, or metaphorically, as when contemplating suicide. It is when these spaces 'encroach', at the Ghost's entrances and at the moment of Hamlet's own poisoning, that madness is most present, as the metaphorical becomes literal; Hamlet's 'mind's eye' becomes a general scene. Barthes writes:

> If the symbolic is the field of neurosis, the return of the literal, which implies the foreclosure of this symbol, opens up the space of psychosis: at this point of the story, all symbolism ends, and with it all neurosis, and it is psychosis which enters the text, through the spectacular foreclosure of the signifier: What is extraordinary ... is indeed madness.[34]

In a psycholinguistic formulation, Hamlet's utterance 'I am dead' marks him out as insane; it is a final, ironic transition into psychosis at the moment of death. He becomes another *memento mori* to be, perhaps, forgotten, his memory erased by Fortinbras's own 'rights of memory'.

Hamlet expresses what his ghostly father, being the spirit of Old Hamlet but not the man himself, cannot – as Hamlet says in a different context, 'the body is with the King, but the King is not with the body. The King is a thing ... of nothing' (4.3, 26–7). This is a speech that equally applies to the office of monarch itself, the constitutive identity both of Hamlet's father and his uncle, as well as the simultaneous division and assimilation of identity that occurs with death. James Calderwood comments that 'In his royal universality Claudius is replete with meaning but devoid of identity – a 'thing' or 'no-thing' – as though the price of office has been paid in the coin of self'.[35] Claudius and King Hamlet become simply 'King' and 'Ghost', a reduction that Hamlet refuses, rejecting the label of 'Revenger' and searching out a more self-fashioned selfhood. The end of this search is, then, Barthes's impossible utterance, the final refusal of signification. Calderwood continues:

> [Hamlet] asserts, not what he is, but what he is not – disjoining himself by word or deed from Old Hamlet, Polonius, Ophelia, Laertes, Gertrude, and, most of all, Claudius. His identity grows complex, not by multiplying relationships but by multiplying disrelationships.[36]

Hamlet's own identity is inevitably 'nothing', refusing as he does all other signifiers except the inescapable final assertion of a total lack of being. In this sense 'I am dead' can be seen as the last answer to 'to be or not to be', a conclusive and definite acceptance of lack, of 'not to be', existing only in the memory of those who will report his 'cause'.

The Ghost, contrastingly, is a literalised memory, the past made present. Pennington deals with this by dissecting the speech almost line by line, reducing (or elevating) it to the status of a musical score to be played solely with regard to effect, not intention. And as with music, he places his greatest emphasis on the final chord:

> *Hamlet, remember me.* This is how the performance will be remembered. The words can be an appeal, or furiously mandatory, or they can be spoken very simply. All the Ghost's qualities jostle behind the four final syllables. If pain isn't in it, you may get a laugh; if firmness isn't, it will be sentimental. If it isn't simple, the audience will soon forget it.[37]

Rightly, the aim of the actor at this moment is to make the audience, not Hamlet, remember the Ghost (the Prince, unless he forgets his lines, will not forget the spirit of his father). As Hillman remarks, 'in Hamlet, to remember is to have one's text again, to re-collect oneself'.[38] The Ghost's extreme verbosity is both a mnemonic aid to the plot, and to future events, and also a feature of memory itself. The text fittingly begins with the recollection of the Ghost's visitation, the memory of a haunting, just as Pennington's text begins with the recalled presence of the deceased Olivier. This necessity to begin with a haunting, an absent present, is, unsurprisingly, Derrida's starting point in his analysis of Marxism – 'A spectre is haunting Europe ...' through the lens of *Hamlet*. Talking simultaneously of communism and Shakespeare, Derrida writes:

> Nor does one see in flesh and blood this Thing that is not a thing, this thing that is invisible between its apparitions, when it reappears. This Thing meanwhile looks at us and sees us not see it even when it is there ... We will call this the visor effect: we do not see who looks at us. Even though in his ghost the king looks like himself, that does not prevent him from looking without being seen: his apparition makes him appear still invisible beneath his armour.[39]

Derrida is of course conveniently overlooking certain textual details within the play: the Ghost wears his 'beaver up', and later, in a part of the play that does not concern Derrida, appears 'in his habit as he lived' – in all probability without armour, or in his 'nightgown', as the First Quarto stage direction indicates. Purgatory does not preclude a change of clothes. Yet the quotation raises interesting points. Perhaps the Ghost is able to watch the action of the play from an unseen position, one reminiscent of a hidden version of Don Andrea in *The Spanish Tragedy*. The Ghost then joins us in the audience as a spectator, the unobserved of all observers.

Derrida also indicates that when the Ghost is first seen on his nocturnal wanderings Shakespeare makes it at once massively present – clunking around in armour – and yet incorporeal – we are unaware of what lies beneath the ironmongery, and, indeed, from the auditorium are unlikely to get more than a glimpse of the actor's face, beaver or no beaver. The Ghost becomes the epitome of all stage characterisation, a presence composed of absence, a physicality without psychology, except that endowed by an audience member's reading of the juxtaposition of their memory of verbal text and the text of the actor's movement. In other words, the Ghost is a literalisation of the process of constructing character, described by Bert States as

> A development that is taking place in the reader or auditor (in interest, understanding, suspense etc.) is assumed to be the consequence of a development taking place in the character, as if the character were unfolding in sections, like a screen.[40]

This has led to several imaginative renderings of the Ghost, from Gielgud, Olivier and Berkoff recording the lines as echoed voiceover, to Peter Hall's giant wheeled edifice in 1964, which became one of three such puppets on the transfer to London. In Stratford the top half of this was played and spoken by Patrick Magee and the silent bottom half, responsible for propelling the thing across the stage, was Michael Pennington, doubling later as a consequently exhausted Fortinbras. In London, Magee's voice was recorded as the actor had been cast in Brook's RSC production of *Marat/Sade*, leaving Pennington to struggle silently while the Ghost's voice echoed in two neighbouring theatres simultaneously.

Pennington's portrayal of the Ghost increased in sophistication thirty years later for the same director, when he doubled the character with his brother. This is an idea as old as Gielgud's suggestion of it in his 1937 essay, and yet, as he remarks there, so loaded with signification that it is surprising it is not more often employed.[41] The audience's visual memory is used here brilliantly, and Hamlet himself cannot escape the memory of his father, embodied as it is at every turn by the figure he must kill.

Curiously, this is one double not employed by Berkoff in his production, which was performed by a cast of nine actors and which employed multiple doubles (including Ophelia as a court stenographer). Speaking of this, Berkoff comments:

> Since we are all players, it must follow that we can enact any role. Therefore it would seem the most natural thing in the world that the King and Queen and Ghost act out their own roles [in *The Murder of Gonzago*]. Normally, a group of players would come on and do this, but this way showed the act as it really happened – as if in the mind's

eye. In a sense the King and Queen are enacting the players who are enacting them. They become the caricatures of themselves. They play their inner lives and not the ones they present to the court.[42]

Such a sophisticated view of the process of characterisation is evident throughout Berkoff's writing in this book, which tends to see characters as extensions of each other, actions that a man or woman may temporarily play. Thus all the cast are continually on stage, watching, 'as if they were witnesses at a trial',[43] while individual scenes are worked out. In this way, 'to confront character properly we must keep one eye on the group and one eye on the individual, who is in a sense always a synecdochic extension of the group itself'.[44] Bert States is here speaking about the construction of character through relationships with others, a construction clearly evident in Berkoff's choral style of performance. Mark Rylance, an actor much admired by Berkoff, came to a similar conclusion when he played the Prince in 1989: 'You have different aspects of a single psyche, so that when you play the conscious one, it is you who are the spokesperson to the audience.'[45] States continues:

> The illusion of discrete individual character is, in some degree, a perceptual compromise. Moreover, we may even speak of a super-character shared by all members of the play's society, in somewhat the way that genetic resemblances are shared by members of the same family.[46]

This 'super-character' comes close to a notion of authorial or intentional unity, in which the component is subordinate to the artistic whole. This is a view shared by Berkoff, and nowhere more clearly than in the title of his book, in which it is initially ambiguous whether he is identifying with character or text. This ambiguity is maintained in his opening descriptions of rehearsing, with just himself and a chair, adding other performers only when he felt it was necessary, and in describing his motives in producing the play, which are that 'since *Hamlet* touches the complete alphabet of human experience every actor feels he is born to play it'.[47] Or, as States prefers, 'the play is as promiscuous as the alphabet'. In an intriguing prefiguration of these comments the eighteenth-century actor Charles Macklin asked 'what is character? The alphabet will tell you. It is that which is distinguished by its own marks from every other thing of its kind.'[48] Character here is defined positively, as having a linguistically endowed identity as distinct as DNA, but, importantly, not connected to the actor himself – Macklin stipulates that the actor must 'take especial care not to mould the character to his [own] looks, tones, gestures and manners'.[49] The definition of character retains an echo of its original palaeographic meaning of a written or printed letter. Character is a typographical construct as well as a construct of type.

When standing on stage awaiting his punning first line, Berkoff remarks of the audience: 'They want to hear how the "title" of the play sounds.' He then begins the blurring of Berkoff/*Hamlet*/Hamlet that continues throughout the text:

> I am alone. I could scream. How dare he?
> **married with mine uncle**
> There he is in the chair, i.e. in my mind's eye. I walk around and survey them and her:
> **Might not beteem the winds of heaven**
> **Visit her face too roughly**
> **... Frailty, thy name is woman.**
> This to Ophelia. All there conveniently sitting in the frame of my mind's eye. So it becomes almost a lecture to the audience; like an examination of police photographs.[50]

Character, actor and director all speak here together, a jumble of voices within the cacophony of the superordinate play, of which each character is just a metonymic example. Typeface plays an appropriately central part in Berkoff's account, with bold type used for quotations from the play only, making Berkoff's own discourse a kind of subtext, except where he uses block capitals to give his stream-of-consciousness rants particular emphasis. This unification of discourse, of player and character, allows Berkoff to formulate at times a close connection with the figure of the author himself:

> I am getting closer to the heart of Shakespeare and this analysis is making him reveal himself to me under the guise of Hamlet ... just as England is under the guise of Denmark, just as I am revealed to myself under the guise of Hamlet.[51]

Here, Hamlet becomes a tool not only for revealing the actor, but for revealing the author as well. Through the presentation of the play, the authority of the author figure is adopted by Berkoff, and his interpretation becomes sanctioned by Shakespeare himself. This is reinforced once again by the appearance of the Ghost, this time in the closet scene: 'I am totally spent and in that moment I feel as if I have stepped out of Berkoff and become Hamlet. I want to avenge myself on society and then dress myself in his clothes. "Society" is Claudius.'[52] Hamlet somehow exists at a deeper level than Berkoff's own identity. Once the detritus of one actor–writer–director is removed, the pristine form of another is revealed. At the same time, Berkoff/Hamlet feels the need to step back into another persona, that of Claudius. Here, Hamlet's resentful envy of Claudius (in this production) and Berkoff's envious resentment of society are twinned, and Hamlet's motives become those of Berkoff, and vice versa. Even the audience is drawn in by virtue of the metatheatrical frame of the ever-present, observing cast. The play is 'part of their consciousness', and so this performance becomes also part of it.

Berkoff's grandiloquent rhetoric even extends to the incorporation of another tradition – that of Christianity.[53] After observing that Polonius's advice to Laertes takes the form of ten precepts or commandments, he goes on to expound the gospel according to Hamlet:

> Laertes was a Judas, Claudius a Pilate and Polonius the fisherman. The Ghost was a spirit of God instructing me and sending me down to do his will. Gertrude was the Virgin Mary and Ophelia, Mary Magdelene. The players were the children that Jesus loved, and Hamlet's soliloquies were sermons to the people. Hamlet was certainly a Jesus figure.[54]

The identification with Hamlet/Christ becomes somewhat eccentric here, as Berkoff becomes a messianic figure spreading the Shakespearean word among the heathen, with 'the greatest demands and trials' experienced, significantly, during tour dates in Israel.

If an abiding preoccupation of Berkoff's work as playwright has been the difficult or impossible integration of the individual with the collective, his two explicitly Christianised plays, *Hamlet* and *Messiah*, reverse that relationship, viewing the collective as part of the individual. His explanation of Hamlet's violent response to the remarriage of his mother is filtered through the metaphor of the trinity and couched in Hamlet's own punning language: 'Father and Mother are one flesh and the son is part of that trinity of flesh. Now Claudius has invaded that sanctuary and this invades Hamlet's own body.'[55] In Berkoff's rhetoric, then, the presence of the author–god is continually affirmed, one playwright–actor performing the role of an actor–playwright–prince created by another playwright–actor. Berkoff is of course continually forming connections between himself, Shakespeare and Hamlet, embodying both in the performance of himself. Ultimately, it is the relationship between these components that is foregrounded, the act of acting as a locus of identity. This emphasis on relationship, on the mimetic act itself, blurs Weimann's distinction between locus and platea, as Hamlet never ceases to be a performance of Berkoff.

This 'figuring forth' of the act of imitation itself, the performance of mimesis, problematises the model established by Girard, discussed earlier. While Berkoff employs a strikingly similar Christianised vocabulary of the triad of mimetic relationships, it is to undermine any notion of rivalry in favour of a spiral of reflexive similitude. This can better be understood by reference to Foucault's analysis of resemblance in *The Order of Things*. He begins by locating the zenith of this trope in the late Renaissance:

Up to the end of the sixteenth century, resemblance played a constructive role in the knowledge of Western culture. It was resemblance that largely guided exegesis and the interpretation of texts; it was resemblance that organised the play of symbols, made possible knowledge of things visible and invisible, and controlled the art of representing them.[56]

In these terms, the play of mimesis within *Hamlet* can be complicated by introducing a vocabulary of similitude which then problematises the straightforward relationship between elements presupposed by Girard. In Foucauldian terms, the identification of Berkoff with Shakespeare/Hamlet is one of sympathy, which he defines as 'an instance of the same so strong and so insistent that it will not rest content to be merely one of the forms of likeness; it has the dangerous power of assimilating, of rendering things identical'.[57] This is mimesis at the extent of its power, when model and imitation become indistinguishable, and Berkoff manages to 'force his soul so to his whole conceit'. This is distinct from the form of rivalry evident in the highly Girardian model of Olivier's agonistic relationship to the tradition he wants to dominate, which Foucault would label emulation:

> The relation of emulation enables things to imitate one another from one end of the universe to the other without connection or proximity, by duplicating itself in a mirror the world abolishes the distance proper to it; in this way it overcomes the place allotted to each thing.[58]

Girard's model of mimesis requires precisely this factor of distance, which is then destroyed by the imitator. Mimesis becomes dependent on an increase in proximity, a closing of the gap. In Berkoff's writing this gap is never present to begin with; he has the actor's grasp, mentioned earlier, of simultaneous contemporaneity with the original, and distance from other imitative objects. For him, Shakespeare is always present and proximal, while the distance exists within the acting tradition, thus giving a circular structure in which all tradition begins and ends with the moment of performance. Pennington illustrates this anecdotally at the end of his book:

> Occasionally, a circle seems truly closed. One evening at the Gielgud Theatre in 1994, I happened on an account by Alexander Hertzen of a performance of Hamlet by Vasily Karatygin ... in 1839:
> *I see a dark night and a pale Hamlet displaying a skull on the tip of his sword and saying 'Here hung those lips and now ha-ha-ha!'*
> I went downstairs to the stage to do the Graveyard Scene. For the first time, either in rehearsal or performance, Stephen Dillane picked up

Yorick's skull on the tip of his dagger and displayed it, with a particularly sardonic laugh ... Believing they have invented them, actors
are led to the same actions, the same improvisations, and the play is a
refrain in all our lives.[59]

For the actor, ever aware of the density of heritage of which he or she is a
part, the starting point remains always the same, and the text is invoked as
present and of the moment to sanction an equally present performance.
The playwright comes to occupy a particular temporality that is almost
that of time itself – as Michael Toolan says, that of 'perceived repetition
within perceived irreversible change'.[60] Shakespeare manages to be both
monumental and cyclical within a linearity of tradition and inheritance,
just as Hamlets recur in the genealogy of Denmark's fathers, but the name
was always until the moment of the play synonymous with kingship.

Both this perceived repetition and this irreversible change depend on
forms of memory for their effectiveness. The position of Shakespeare in
collective socio-cultural memory ('we shall not look upon his like again') is
mirrored by the tradition of successive players of his most iconic and
canonical role. This in turn is echoed within the play by the vocabulary
of inheritance and genealogy, sons and fathers, brothers and murderers. In
this way States is able to collate a series of types and echoes into which
each major character can fit, almost all of which are familial or quasi-
familial categories. States then posits that 'through implicit role repetitions
we are invited to build perceptual bridges between and among characters
... thus character drifts and is known by the company it keeps'.[61]

These bridges are the stuff of character, which is constructed mimetically
and memorially ('Remember me'). Such links are of course strengthened by
doubles such as Claudius/Ghost and the more popular choice of Polonius
and the Gravedigger. Physical mnemonics such as these may have been
further elaborated at the first Globe Theatre if, as seems likely, the actors
playing Hamlet and Polonius had previously played Brutus and Caesar in
Julius Caesar. This would give added resonance both to the brief inter-
change before to the staging of *The Murder of Gonzago* in 3.2, and to the
killing of Polonius two scenes later. The audience would follow the 'line' of
an actor, allowing it to inform their reading of the play in a manner that
perhaps survives today in cinema in the form of the Hollywood star system
and in the European habit of director/actor collaboration.

In short, as Weimann comments, 'memory became a mixed resource of
cultural energy, a not uncontaminated item in the political economy of
circulating pleasure, knowledge, and the very stuff of telling stories'.[62]
Berkoff's sophisticated awareness of the connections between mimesis,
memory and character – character is constructed mimetically, mimesis is
an act of memory and recognition – allows him to develop notions of
similitude and resemblance that exceed conventional understanding. He

is Hamlet because he is an imitation of himself, employing the text to explore Berkoff rather than the other way round. Consequently he 'effects an appropriation, or reappropriation, of language by its speaker, [which] establishes a present relative to a time and place; and it posits a contract with the other in a network of places and relations'.[63] Mimesis in Berkoff can neither be thought of as a representation of a previously existing object or concept, nor can it be defined as a Girardian act of desire desiring desire. It becomes a self-reflexive act, conscious of the other in the meta-phor of the contract, but finally appropriating the authority of the Shakespearean *logos* in a dramatisation of the mimetic act itself, an act with which *Hamlet* and Hamlet obsess.

III

A different kind of resonance was added to Berkoff's production by the context of its performance in the shadow of the Falklands War. The play becomes a mirror for external events, even though the ideas behind this particular production were not ostensibly political:

> We were touring Europe with *Hamlet* when the Falklands War was in full swing, and to an actor, the whole company felt the most extreme revulsion for this horrible waste of human life ... We found continual reinforcement in Shakespeare's words for the petty and unimaginative acts of man – or, rather, of politicians. In consequence certain scenes seemed underlined for us.[64]

Contrastingly, Pennington's production, nearing the end of its run at this stage, avoided such influences, as he writes, 'John Barton's production concerned itself more with the breakdown of family relationships than with the political zeitgeist'.[65]

In a curious echo of this situation, Pennington found himself involved in a highly politicised production of *Coriolanus* in 1990 for his own English Shakespeare Company, which in the context of the fall of communism strove to 'show the age and body of the time its form and pressure'.[66] At the same time, the RSC and John Barton staged an entirely depoliticised production of the same play, which 'lacked what it would not be unfair to call the courage of its own lack of convictions'.[67] The same year also saw Berkoff's first production of the play, which contained no extra-political references, despite the shift of the production to Germany in 1991.[68]

In typical Berkoffian style, the times become an echo of the play *Hamlet*, rather than the other way round, an example once again of Shakespeare's supposed preternatural ability to illuminate context with text. Pennington is doubtless correct when he remarks:

There is a tension in this play between poetic tragedy and political dialectic. A coherent political image should frame the Leidenschaft of the Prince – but what brings us to our feet at the end is the sheer appeal of the man and it doesn't need undermining at the eleventh hour.[69]

Yet he surprisingly fails to pick up on the extent to which the 'sheer appeal of the man' constitutes a major political threat in the play. Hamlet himself may not be primarily a political figure – though a project that involves killing a king and incidentally his chief courtier can hardly fail to be political – but his relationship to the other characters is unavoidably so. The son is also a prince and the father a king, and these status relationships inform the action at least as much as their familial counterparts. Claudius, famously, is never referred to by name in the text (excluding speech prefixes), always as some variant of his political or personal status. Hamlet may well be an attractive, charismatic, personable character, particularly when played by a 'star' actor who also possesses these qualities, but this does not preclude politicisation. As Falco writes, 'charisma is a shared experience. This is perhaps the most important and most misunderstood fact of charismatic group formation.'[70] This particular form of politicised charisma is acknowledged several times in *Hamlet* by Claudius, and is his rationale for proceeding so carefully with his nephew. It is also evident in the processes of performance of the play, as Pennington remarks: 'In the English theatre at least, a director who decided to do the play and then started looking around for a Hamlet would be an oddity.'[71] The play is usually programmed into a repertoire after the selection of a leading actor. In Pennington's case, this came a whole decade after being approached by Barton to play the part. In Berkoff's, it was a decision emerging from the realisation that he would probably never be cast in the role by a third party, and had therefore to do it himself before he became too old. A similar motivation was in evidence in the decision of Simon Russell Beale to play the role:

> I had to do it now, because I'm 39. I'm not Alan Rickman, so I can't do it when I'm 45, still looking lithe and lovely. Next year I can really let myself go! Falstaff here we come! ... You've got to try to analyse why you want to do it, and 80 percent of the reason is that it is a sort of badge of honour.[72]

Once again, the role is configured as a rite of passage, but one which has recently become about maturing as an actor, entering a kind of performative adulthood and moving into the next phase as a performer. The performances of Berkoff, Beale and even Pennington (36 when he played the part), all owe something to the pressures of age – a peculiarly twentieth-century concern with the role. In the previous century Thomas Holcroft could write:

The only fit representative of Hamlet is the man of middle age; whose form, at a distance, may appear youthful; whose mind is penetrating, and stored with ideas; whose feelings are at his command; who is in no danger of being betrayed by his memory; and whose powers of exciting the passions are of the highest order.[73]

In more recent times, such a perspective appears outdated. Johnston Forbes-Robertson, playing his final performance of Hamlet aged sixty in 1913, was the last 'old' Hamlet, and it is generally mooted today that an actor is almost past it at thirty-five[74] – Beale was recently criticised heavily for being too old, as well as being too heavy, and even a thirty-six-year-old Branagh received a certain amount of negative press regarding his age on the release of his film, though this was exacerbated by his casting of twenty-two-year-old Kate Winslet as Ophelia.

Mimetic accuracy is currently obsessed with age in performances of the play, even if Beale and also Richard McCabe can now play the part without paying homage to the Olivier/Barrymore tradition of slim athleticism. The preoccupation with age can be seen as yet another byproduct of the dominance of theatrical naturalism, a misguided concern with who the character is, rather than what he does – *ethos*, rather than *praxis*. The character should be played young, but in theory there is no reason why it should not be played by a fifty-four-year-old Frenchwoman. The imposition of naturalism has led paradoxically to a more ritualistic understanding of the progress of an actor, with key Shakespearean roles checked off along the way and allowing passage to the next. Increasingly, an actor's career path is seen as being mapped out by the roles he chooses: a Richard II or a Hal may indicate a Hamlet is in the offing, a Richard III may point to an Iago, and so on.

Hamlet, as Berkoff understood, is more often than not subordinated to its protagonist, as 'a scene is played almost as a demonstration for Hamlet to analyse for us. As if he sets it up.'[75] There is something of the preacher in the role, and it is often the charisma suggested by the text and displayed by the actor that gives the impression of unity to a discontinuous characterisation. To quote Falco again:

In reviling essentialism and liberal humanism, critics posit both an evolutionary model of the unified subject and an either/or pattern characterising a protagonist as either a continuous interiority or a discontinuous collocation of exterior impressions. But the either/or pattern fails to account for the ambiguous status of group identity and intrasubjective dependence which we find in all charismatic groups.[76]

Hamlet depends upon the other voices in his play as much as does Coriolanus on the voices for which he barters in the marketplace. Equally, the actor playing Hamlet needs the best of casts with which to interrelate. Both Pennington and Berkoff note the uneasy relationship that exists on a dramatic level between the individual and the group:

> Some characters are developed less organically since they are 'straight men' for Hamlet's wit, and this reduces the character's integrity. [Berkoff][77]
>
> His 'madness' almost makes the play unplayable, since it makes fools of the rest of the cast, many of whom are not supposed to be fools. [Pennington][78]

In both instances, but particularly in Berkoff, this indicates a view of the play defined in relation to the protagonist, which is not really supported by the text. Neither Claudius nor Gertrude ever really believes him to be insane, unlike Ophelia, who has good reason to think so. Only Polonius and, perhaps, Rosencrantz and Guildenstern are entirely fooled by Hamlet's feigned madness when they shouldn't be. In addition, the tradition of seeing Hamlet as unquestionably sane is itself a modern one. As Louis Calvert wrote in the early years of the twentieth century:

> I venture to submit that the play is a treatise on mental aberration, Shakespeare contrasting the partial derangement of Hamlet with the total derangement of Ophelia ... we find in the character of Hamlet a marvellous analysis of a brain disordered.[79]

Not only are the rest of the cast fools; so are a significant number of prior Hamlets. Madness is, as Foucault has repeatedly shown, a concept in flux and dependent on the repressive structures of the society and age in which it is located. Following from this, consistency of motivation as a precondition of sanity or full mental health is a feature neither of modern psychology nor Renaissance acting, but exists merely in the conventions of twentieth-century performance characterisation. For one character to appear foolish with Hamlet and shrewd with a third character is only problematic if such spurious consistency is adhered to, and if it is assumed that a person behaves always the same, whoever he or she is interacting with. Pennington in particular, having played Claudius and three other principal characters, is oddly unaware of the extent to which Hamlet depends on the other characters in his choice of (in)action. It is the situation in which he finds himself, the experience of being, as it were, profoundly miscast in the wrong play, which provokes his melancholy. As Granville-Barker commented, 'if Hamlet understood himself the spiritual tragedy would disappear again in the tragedy of action'.[80]

As Pennington rightly asserts from the point of view of Hamlet, his is a tragedy of a man living in the past in a society that seems to have forgotten it. Invoking a different kind of memory again, the world of Elsinore expects its protagonist to belong to Kyd's play rather than Shakespeare's, and this disorientation 'involves him in a rupture of the entire spiritual treaty between himself and the world in which he must live'.[81] This leads him to destroy his history in the name of maintaining it, erasing memory in the attempt to reinscribe it.

The lost *Ur-Hamlet*, whether written by Kyd, as seems most likely, or anyone else, occupies an intriguing position in the rhetoric of Hamlettian tradition. Calderwood comments:

> This play . . . is thus related to Shakespeare's Hamlet both genetically and generically – precisely as Old Hamlet is related to Young Hamlet. As the name 'Hamlet' both is and is not Hamlet's, so the title *Hamlet* is and is not Shakespeare's.[82]

The identity of the character and of the play is split, 'ghostwritten', as Marjorie Garber, Emma Smith and others have described it.[83] Kyd's play, as Barker implies, is responsible for all the flaws in Shakespeare's, becoming a scapegoat for the later playwright's perceived inadequacies while the 1600 *Hamlet* attempts to wrest itself free from the ponderous weight of its previous incarnation. In this sense, every actor to attempt the role is battling an *Ur-Hamlet*, a lost point of origin simultaneously attracting and repelling its progeny.

It is in this temptingly quasi-Oedipal position that the actor playing the role repeatedly finds him- or herself. As Gielgud writes at the conclusion of his significantly titled essay 'The Hamlet Tradition', published the same year as his mentor Granville-Barker's Preface, 'you will see that my mind has been torn in studying the part between a desire to walk in the traditions of the great ones and to carve out some interpretation that I might justly call my own'.[84] Gielgud himself limits his scope in this essay to a description of costume, design and stage business, wisely allowing his performance to stand as his interpretation of the role itself. In his lifelong near-obsession with costume we can, however, detect an emphasis on the external construction of a role that was in large measure a feature of his generation of actors.[85] Interpretation, for Gielgud, was left to a considerable extent to his guide and idol, Granville-Barker, a figure not entirely absent from Pennington's writing.

IV

In the conclusion to his book, Pennington pays homage to a holy trinity of English theatrical tradition, Gordon Craig, Granville-Barker and Gielgud

– a trinity revived by Richard Eyre for his 2000 TV series on the theatre *Changing Stages*, with the substitution of Bernard Shaw for Craig. Granville-Barker and Gielgud in particular haunt the entirety of his text; Gielgud, as has been mentioned, in his honoured, ghostly presence at the beginning and the end, but Granville-Barker less overtly and more profoundly. In a quotation on the jacket of the book, Ronald Harwood enthuses: '[It is] a wonderful book, which takes up for our time where Granville-Barker left off ... Pennington's voice in the reader's ear is clear and precise.'

Aside from an interesting use, given the context, of the metaphor of the ear, the remark is an astute evaluation of the intention of the book. The structure – introduction, methodical trawl through the play, section on characters, conclusion – exactly mimics the structure of Granville-Barker's *Prefaces*, which Pennington, following Gielgud, celebrates as the scholarship most useful to practitioners. The title, self-consciously parodying user's manuals for cars, computers and other complex and expensive pieces of equipment, also implies that the text can guide a novice through the play in very much the way the *Prefaces* were intended to do. We are allowed to follow Pennington's Progress through the play, and if there are no Bunyanesque marginalia to aid exegesis, we have instead a proliferation of footnotes to impart further information and clarification. Nor is he alone in this model – both Marvin Rosenberg's *The Masks of Hamlet* and Bert States's *Hamlet and the Concept of Character* have exactly the same structure, and their informal tone implies that these authors too see themselves as following in the Granville-Barker tradition.

The literary-critical aspirations of Pennington perhaps reflect his change in direction after co-forming the ESC with Michael Bogdanov and taking on a more dramaturgical and administrative role, epitomised in his adaptation of the History plays as *The Wars of the Roses* and his one-man show *Chekhov*. They may also reflect a degree of ambition, a desire to achieve the recognition as a major Shakespearean authority that has been so strangely absent from his acting career.

Both books can therefore be seen as serving a need to establish literary credentials as well as performance ones, the lasting position of Shakespeare in the centre of the literary canon meaning that it is insufficient to be acclaimed as a great stage interpreter unless you reach the dizzying heights of Olivier or Gielgud. Things have not progressed enormously since Irving's edition of Shakespeare.

Irving features strongly at the beginning of Gielgud's essay, just as Sir John cameos in Pennington (and Olivier in Berkoff). He serves to locate Gielgud in the double theatrical tradition of performance and familial heritage that made him seem so much to the manner born, a member of theatrical royalty, in his days at the Old Vic when performances by Irving and Terry still existed in living memory. Gielgud's position in theatrical history is, as Pennington remarks, fascinating. His earliest performances belong to the nineteenth-century tradition, as his essay makes clear, influenced by Fechter and Booth, Tree and, of course, Irving. His last major Shakespearean role was in Greenaway's *Prospero's Books* aged eighty-seven, having seen theatre, screen and acting in general change beyond all recognition in the intervening seven decades.

In between playing Hamlet aged twenty-five in 1929, and appearing as Priam (in Hamlet's mind's eye) in Branagh's film in 1996, Gielgud directed a famous and hugely successful version of the play in 1964 with Richard Burton in the lead role.[86] The production also featured him among the cast as, appropriately, the Ghost. This was no ordinary performance, however. Gielgud never appeared in person; the ghost was signified by a huge shadow projected on to the back wall, and the director's disembodied voice echoed through the auditorium, like so many ghosts of Hamlets past come to haunt Burton. Also at stake, due to the unusual situation in which Burton approached Gielgud to direct him, rather than Gielgud casting Burton, was the relationship between director and principal actor, the competitive desire for surrogate authorship introduced largely by Gielgud's Uncle Edward and which has since dominated the power structures of twentieth-century performance in Europe and North America. Several layers of competitive mimesis were therefore established in the conception of this production.

This manifestation of the play is notable also for the volume of written material available from the cast themselves. In addition to interviews and Gielgud's own recollections, two books were written by members of the cast. Published in 1966, they are *Letters From An Actor*, by William Redfield, who played Guildenstern, and the less than pithily titled *John Gielgud directs Richard Burton in Hamlet: A Journal of Rehearsals*, by Richard Sterne, who played First Gentleman.[87] They could not be more different in tone. Redfield was an experienced and intelligent actor whose knowledge, candour and wit make his book entertaining and anecdotal. Working from transcribed tape-recordings often made by eavesdropping on rehearsals for which he had not been called, and on one occasion hiding under a prop table (though sadly never behind an arras), Sterne's is a careful and descriptive account by a novice performer in his first major show. His desire to write comes from an unconcealed adulation of Gielgud; before rehearsals began Sterne had 'decided that I would take down every word Gielgud said about the play, since I believe he knows more about the part of Hamlet than any living actor'.[88] Redfield seems more amused by the potential fireworks, though a more covert admiration of Burton seeps through his text at times.

The production therefore lies at the heart of a series of layers of discourse, the most prominent of which are constructed at the hands of actors forming a peripheral role in the eventual performance. Whereas the play sidelines Redfield and Sterne, the principal accounts we have of it inevitably sideline the voices of Gielgud and Burton, the very centre of the performance. The two major accounts therefore contain a series of ghostly begetters, whom the authors attempt to reconcile.

Within Redfield's account there is also another spectre at the feast, his friend and co-worker at the Actors' Studio, Marlon Brando. He 'intrudes' him into his account as an overt point of comparison for Burton. And indeed they were comparable. Born in the same year (1924) to working-class families from marginalised but integrated communities within their native countries (Italian and Welsh), both went on to symbolise a radical challenge to previous performance tradition, a revolution in the theatre, even if the extent to which either man actually occupied this role is doubtful. Both are semi-mythical figures. Redfield's contention is that while Brando's challenge was the greater, Burton's was, by 1964 at least, the more real. The reason for this is Shakespeare. As he says:

> The actor is stretched by the verse roles, his muscles grow strong from heroic assignments. They cannot be fudged as naturalistic parts or film assignments can be fudged. More important, the borders of the individual talent are finally defined.[89]

Tradition defines the individual talent. Burton takes the challenge, Brando does not.[90] The film version of the play is called *Richard Burton's Hamlet*. The trailer for this gimmicky two-nights-only theatrical screening of the play simultaneously across the US features Burton giving an uneasy sales pitch while the over-excited voiceover declares:

> Shakespeare's Hamlet – A play for the ages!
> Burton's Hamlet – A performance for the ages![91]

A highly self-conscious attempt is under way to acquire canonicity in the annals of Shakespearean performance, and authority over this particular manifestation of the play. Burton is being inscribed in the history of the play by a marketing machine reliant on his cinematic star profile. Ironically, the implicit attempt to unseat Gielgud from his theatrical throne is undertaken using the machinery and ideologies of television and cinema.

Burton is established by Redfield in a system of mimetic rivalry that operates on three explicit levels: with Gielgud as representative of theatrical canonicity; with Gielgud as director; and with Brando as representative of American theatrical aspiration, and to a lesser degree cinematic stardom. The acknowledgement of the last issues by Burton comes in the form of the choice of an American theatre and a predominantly American cast.

Gielgud's own feelings of rivalry emerge in both texts in the form taken by his direction. Rather than suggest or even instruct his actors, Gielgud generally demonstrated to them. Drawing on his own vast experience of the play, he used a method essentially to chasten the actors into line. When he did not do this, his instructions nevertheless constantly emphasised his own prior expertise:

> It seems to me, Richard, *and I found in playing the part*, that in the concern with details in each scene one forgets the main motivation which must progress through the part as a whole. (Italics added)[92]

Gielgud continually adopts the role not only of director but also of guru, a surrogate Shakespeare and repository of all knowledge. Burton dealt with this tactfully, by asking for advice when necessary but more often than not by deliberately not noting blocking and

> feeling his way through the scenes, making changes each time ... Burton would not try to imitate Gielgud's demonstrations and would sometimes go out of his way to be different. The Hamlet he played was his own.[93]

As before, rivalry relies on appropriation, possession. Burton's aim is to own the part as Gielgud had done, and more and more the production becomes an extremely politic tug of war between Burton and Gielgud, Hamlet and the Ghost, over the corpus of Shakespeare's text.

This positioning of the text as a no-man's-land over which two parties fought was reflected in the design of the production. Both men had agreed upon the idea of staging the play as a kind of rehearsal, an idea of Gielgud's prompted by Granville-Barker's observation that the play itself is a rehearsal. In a note to the programme, Gielgud explained:

> This is *Hamlet* acted in rehearsal clothes, stripped of all extraneous trappings, so the beauty of the language and imagery may shine through unencumbered by an elaborate reconstruction of any particular period.[94]

Thus a virtue was made of lack of interpretation by creating the impression that, like Godot, one would eventually arrive if the spectator would just hang around long enough. William Redfield hung around longer than most, and his initial misgivings as to what, exactly, constituted rehearsal clothes (period? Modern? How do they cohere with each other and with character status?) were confirmed, as was his concern over the need for lighting – absent from a real rehearsal – and set. Redfield became increasingly infuriated with Gielgud's evasions on these points:

> When I think that a roomful of English professors would bend my ear for hours discussing the meaning and interpretation of *Hamlet* while

Gielgud will not even declare openly what period we are choosing, I could turn myself inside out ... Gielgud wants the play to just happen.[95]

The real meaning, the desired signified, would have to come to lie with either Burton or Gielgud, and 'the rest is silence'.[96] Describing an argument over a reading of the line 'Is it the King?' in the closet scene, Redfield comments:

It would make perfect sense for Gielgud to cry out, 'Have I killed the hated one? How wonderful!' but Burton's cry would have to be, 'Oh, God, have I done what I always feared I'd do? How awful!' It is bewitching to watch both men struggle for Shakespeare's meaning while they squirm as individuals beneath the weight of their own psychologies.[97]

Redfield here interestingly implies that the meaning of the character is dictated entirely by the performer – there is no inherent, fixed signified. 'Shakespeare's' meaning then becomes a problematic area for debate between external 'psychologies', either and any decision reverting to the author's ownership the moment it is produced. In the same way that Hamlet's line 'Is it the King?' is a kind of refrain throughout the play, from the doubtful status of the Ghost to Claudius's culpability, so Shakespeare's authority is equally eagerly sought after and appropriated by his interpreters, whose signification lies within their own actions.

That Burton wins this battle but not the war by getting the performance he wants but failing to eclipse Gielgud's reputation is a credit as much to Gielgud's failure as a director as to Burton's success as an actor. Burton wrested his ambition from the ineffectual hands of a redundant Gielgud, and claims his prize. But this prize was far from being a definite decision as to interpretation. Burton's performance remained in itself a kind of final run-through, a near-arrival, lacking that final step. Redfield comments with characteristic epigrammatic flair: 'The actor may be stuck with the character, but the character is also stuck with the actor.'[98] The individual squirming on this occasion is unable to identify authority, kingship, with sufficient certainty. Redfield goes on to remark that though Burton's ability to play Shakespeare is unquestionable, he is nevertheless miscast as Hamlet. The lack of a definite interpretation does not help this initial playing against the grain, and leads Burton to rely on what Redfield characterises as typically English techniques of vocal mannerism, techniques ironically mastered above all by Gielgud.

This leads to the foregrounding and perhaps re-emphasis of acting techniques. Although both trained in broadly the same tradition of English theatre, Gielgud and Burton had vastly different styles. The former was at this stage perhaps seen as overly old-fashioned, whereas Burton was in many ways closer to the Method approach of Brando, though his technical prowess was clearly British. When Redfield's own extreme 'Methodism' is included, his book becomes the site of a collision between, effectively, different views of mimesis. As quoted above, Gielgud wants a smooth external consistency for the play. Nearly thirty years later he wrote:

> I kept on saying to Burton, 'The important thing is to tell the story of the play and to make every scene a progression.' That is what Granville-Barker had once said to me about playing Lear: 'You must start the next scene where you left off in the last one, even if there is another scene between the two'. Every Hamlet must link the strands of the play by an individual, original attitude, and tell the story anew for an audience.[99]

This consistency, however, is far from being the kind of psychological, emotional through-line required by Redfield's Method approach. Gielgud also commented at the time, 'don't worry too much about making sense, though. Words should make sense. But not feelings.'[100] Gielgud is concerned that the story and its imagery are clear for the audience, not that things make sense for the actor. This approach is anathema to Redfield, who passionately exclaims that 'logic is the root of every scene, of every play. The circumstances are of prime importance. Pace, shape, colour, arbitrary differences in attitude – all such things are considered results – externals.'[101] Burton supplies a third, more interesting perspective. Talking of the character, he remarks:

> Sometimes he seems incoherently joined up. He seems to have a lot of anachronisms in him – within himself, I mean. It's very difficult, for instance, for an actor to realise the change between 'The play's the thing wherein I'll catch the conscience of the king', and then within three minutes he's back on stage contemplating suicide . . . That kind of inconsistency is enormously difficult for the actor to smooth over.[102]

Redfield himself comes close to accepting this view, admitting that in this instance his Actors' Studio training may be inadequate:

> Hamlet is a revenge play written during the Elizabethan era when the sort of dovetailed, natural logic we demand of plays today simply was not considered. Over and over, Shakespeare's plays will prove to those who act them that neither Will nor his players cared much for the details of logic. Burton has said to me, 'The play is a series of theatrical effects. If you try to figure them out pedantically, you're lost'. Gielgud has said, 'It is a poem'. The two statements are conjunctive.[103]

This absence of overall consistency became the keynote of Burton's performance, a fact noted and bemoaned by Gielgud for thirty years afterwards. It was, as Redfield comments, a brave decision. It was also one entirely in keeping with the unwittingly deconstructive design. In many ways, the production came ironically and unconsciously close to the absurdist Shakespeare of Brook in its refusal of a final signified, either interpretatively within performance or visually within the design. It also echoed, albeit distantly, the non-conjunctive, externalised style of characterisation used on the Renaissance stage.

V

In the case of this production, however, final meanings were eventually supplied by reference to the overpowering signification of the names attached to it – Burton and Gielgud, and in the wings Elizabeth Taylor and even Brando. But above all, the dominant signified of Western art, Shakespeare, a principle of coherence absent, ironically, from the 1600 performance. Instead of making a Brookian statement about its own lack of meaning, the play becomes a battleground for mimetic competition, the thing wherein Burton will catch the reputation of the king.

The timing of the Burton/Gielgud *Hamlet* is also of relevance here. The early 1960s was a boom period for Shakespeare, a moment of dramatic revisionism the repercussions of which are still being felt today. Though the twentieth-century theatrical deities were still very much in evidence – indeed, it was arguably the apogee of Olivier's career, epitomised in his celebrated RNT *Othello*, which ran contemporaneously with the Gielgud/Burton *Hamlet* – it was also the period of the newly formed RSC, ruled by the *enfant terrible*, Peter Hall, whose *Hamlet* with David Warner (and Michael Pennington as a hoarse Fortinbras) was about to open as Burton finished his New York run. The *Theatre of Cruelty* season, including *Marat/Sade*, presided over by Peter Brook, was in full swing, and his production of *King Lear* with Paul Scofield was still running on Broadway as the Burton *Hamlet* opened.

The clash between Gielgud and Burton can therefore be seen as a microcosm of a larger collision that was soundly shaking British theatre as a whole, symbolised also in the choice of theatre in New York. Alfred Lunt and Lynn Fontanne, the epitome of old-school Shakespeare – the latter was trained by Ellen Terry – had opened their new theatre with a production of Dürrenmatt's caustic *The Visit*, directed by Brook, so making a step into the later twentieth century Gielgud himself was resisting. And as with these individuals, the battleground for theatrical dominance and, increasingly, relevance was Shakespeare, and the prize was ownership of signification, both immediate in terms of the plays, and culturally in the form of the position of the Arts in society.

From this perspective, the Paul Scofield/Peter Brook *King Lear* is a closer correlative than it might at first appear, constituting a unified example of mimetic antagonism towards systems of received Shakespearean performance with which Redfield – a self-confessed Scofield fan – openly sympathises in his text. In his *Lear Log*, Charles Marowitz (assistant director on the Brook *Lear*) recounts a discussion he had with Brook over the character of Edgar. The subheading preceding this account is *Walk through Kensington Gardens in search of Edgar.* In it, he recalls Brook asking him what he considered to be the play's greatest problem:

> I told him that for me it was the character of Edgar, who after three short scenes as a sober, not very bright or demonstrative young man, transforms into the madly capering Bedlam-beggar, Poor Tom. In all the productions I had seen of the play the change had never really worked and I concluded that this was an awkward inconsistency attributable to Shakespeare for which one had to compensate with directorial ingenuity.[104]

Marowitz, like Redfield, starts from a Method perspective. In both plays, there must be Method within the madness. Like Siddons and Terry before them, they find that the portrayal of Shakespearean madness is almost impossible if linear logic is the dominant object of the search. Although far from being a Method director, Brook too looks for consistency. As Marowitz recalls, 'He believed the play had such a hard inner consistency that everything must be there for a purpose and it was necessary to discover Edgar's place in the scheme of things.'[105]

Yet here is a different kind of consistency. Brook is searching for creative, artistic logic as opposed to psychological logic. 'You can't apply psychoanalysis to a character like Lear', he remarks at one point, and goes on to accept Marowitz's amendment of 'mythic, epic or poetic motivation'.[106] For Brook, it is not that the search for consistency is wrong, but that the wrong kind of consistency is being sought out. Marowitz's response to this again recalls Redfield: 'Although all this is true, I cannot help feeling it is only part of the truth and that a subtextual reason has got to be found.'[107]

It is precisely this that Burton denies, commenting at one point that he doubts if *Hamlet* 'has a meaning at all'. He goes on to explain, echoing Redfield, that what he means is that 'practically everything you can think of is in Hamlet',[108] and it is precisely because you think of it that it is there to be found. Both plays are ultimately mimetic of the reader, displaying what she or he hopes to discover, just as Hamlet finds the answers he wants to find. By refusing a final signified, each play embraces a never-ending play of signification in which, as Burton realised, any or no meaning can happily be 'found'. Finally, Burton failed to discover a satisfactory method of playing this discovery, resorting typically to the unification of intention through the imposition of his own personality. Vocal mannerisms and a sardonic chuckle, combined with intense physical presence, give a superficial impression of characterisation in the performance. These tricks disguised what much of the time was not so much a false homogenising of conflicting decisions, but a simple covering up of a lack of decision-making for which Gielgud must bear much of the responsibility.

In contrast, Marowitz felt the Brook *Lear* suffered from too many over-calculated decisions, removing spontaneity from the production. He could also never quite come to terms with Scofield's idiosyncratic working methods:

> Scofield's Lear has slowly begun to emerge. His method is to start from the text and work backwards. He is constantly testing the verse to see if the sound corresponds with the emotional intention. It is a peculiar method which consciously prods technique so that instinct will be called into play. The Method actor starts with feeling and then adds the externals of voice and movement. Scofield uses externals as a gauge with which to measure the truth of any given speech.[109]

This approach is neither the playing of externals so criticised by Redfield nor the Method approach so valued by Marowitz, but rather an intellectual approach which values the verse as an indicator of everything the actor needs to know. Initially, Marowitz found this approach disappointing and dry, but upon revisiting the production some time after it had opened was amazed at the result:

> The shape of his reading was in almost every particular the same, but now it existed as the topmost round of a series of concentric circles which wound down through the actor's nature into Lear's données and then looped firmly around the base which is the mind of William Shakespeare. It was the kind of integration which sometimes takes place in affairs that have gone on for eight and ten years.[110]

The dense signification of Marowitz's writing here bears close inspection. In a single rhetorical operation he identifies Scofield with Lear with Shakespeare, the last forming the centre of a single entity whose other facets include the character of Lear and the actor Scofield. The psychology of Shakespeare here manifests itself in true Borgesian fashion in the performance of Scofield as Lear. Shakespeare is speaking Scofield through the medium of the old king in an occult assimilation of identity. Scofield essentially unifies himself with the model – Shakespeare – in a way that Burton does not. As Marowitz says, 'he had become one with the role'. Despite Burton's appropriative gestures, it is Scofield's understanding of the processes of Shakespearean characterisation that allow him to 'own' Lear, and to establish the kind of popular reputation as the greatest post-war Lear of which Marowitz rightly disapproves.

Scofield recognises that the operations necessary to perform Shakespeare are necessarily mimetic, rather than logical or psychological. The simile used by Marowitz to characterise this process – a romantic affair – is extremely apt, as all forms of desire are necessarily mimetic. Moreover, Marowitz intriguingly does not think of this process as a 'relationship', or a 'marriage', but an 'affair' – in other words, an illicit, secretive, dangerous liaison in which both parties have been involved for some time. Scofield therefore has a covert, unconventional relationship with Shakespeare unseen by the observers, reliant on intuition, passion and a lack of reasoned analysis. Marowitz's impression tallies with Scofield's own account of playing Hamlet:

> There is something inviolate in his character which is proof against analysis and labels. The actor playing him often feels held at arm's length; it is like trying to inhabit a live person rather than the creation of a writer, and it feels like trespassing. We cannot pluck out the heart of his mystery: like ourselves, what is true for him today may not be true tomorrow.[111]

Scofield approaches characterisation like a courtship, the object of his quest taking on features of the unobtainable addressee of Petrarchan convention. He becomes the distant poet, admiring from afar, the moment of consummation imminent yet indefinitely postponed. As Joel Fineman argued brilliantly in regard to Shakespeare's Sonnets,[112] subjectivity is constructed in the gap between the vision of the addressee and the voice of the addresser. The psychology of Scofield and the semiotics of Shakespeare continually renegotiate and reconstruct a sensuous, suitably homoerotic, relationship, one that is always incomplete and unfinished.

In this Scofield is unsurprisingly closer in approach to the poeticism of Brook than the psychology of Marowitz, deliberately retaining the inarticulacy and exploration of an 'affair', and famously rarely discussing his craft in public. Recognising that Shakespearean character constructs and is constructed mimetically – that is to say, socially and politically – Scofield builds his performance in the manner in which his and our everyday identities are also assembled. What he aims for is not 'inner truth', as Redfield does, but 'inner verisimilitude': likeness, mimetic identity.

Interestingly, Burton's performance demonstrates the beginnings of this awareness. In an interview with Sterne, he is asked if there is any part of the role he particularly dislikes. Burton replies that he 'never liked the advice to the players, largely because I disagree with the advice'.[113] He doesn't expand upon this, principally because Sterne is too inexperienced an interviewer to ask him to, but a possible elucidation is provided else-where by Redfield. He comments that Burton clearly is unhappy with this passage and gives his own opinion as to why, based on the fact that he too dislikes it: 'The speech is famous because academicians, critics, and various other non-actors can understand it, thereby electing themselves experts on the oh-so-simple art of acting.'[114]

The speech is essentially an observer's catalogue of features repugnant to a spectator, rather like a review of a performance or, as other commentators have noted, a sequence of good advice to a dramatist about writing char-acter, rather than to an actor about playing it. It offers no real insight as to methodologies of performance in themselves, with the central tenet con-cerning 'the purpose of playing',[115] essentially repeating points made expli-citly in most known theatrical and poetic theory since Horace, most recently and famously by Sidney in his *Apology for Poetry*. In essence it resembles the advice given by Montaigne on the deportment of the ideal courtier: 'The speech that I like is simple and natural speech, the same on paper as on the lips: a succulent, nervous, short and concise manner of speaking, not dainty and nicely combed so much as vehement and brisk.'[116] Hamlet is expounding on the manner of behaviour of his own class, the model Ophelia had previously lamented as being overthrown, rather than professing expertise in the profession of acting.

The desire for consistency and originality characteristic of many twen-tieth-century English approaches to Shakespearean performance can be seen as a product of a mimetic antagonism to a previous theatrical hege-mony. This antagonism can be seen in the theatre of Peter Brook, as its associated system of mimetic rivalry can be seen in microcosm within the 1964 *Hamlet*. In its manifestation in the work of Brook, Scofield and others, it attempts to return to the Shakespearean origin, a theatrical *tabula rasa* in which Brook can find 'what can take the place of blank-verse in the theatre'.[117]

Brook is competing, not *for* Shakespeare, but *with* him, and the desired object here is the act of making theatre itself. In contrast, the American Method returns to a modern, psychological origin in an attempt to find there the processes that create character. However, in ignoring the social and the political this system attempts to erase all that constitutes a public theatrical event, a fact brought into relief when it is used to perform Shakespeare.

VI

Though the 1964 Hamlet presents Gielgud at a juncture when his rhetoric is particularly weakened by the emergence of new and challenging dis-courses of Shakespearean appropriation, this should not blind us to the subtlety of his perception of the operations of Shakespearean authority in other contexts. The bookends to Gielgud's career, represented by Terry and Greenaway, indicate a startling and unusual form of consistency in his understanding of his profession, and his conception of tradition. In outlining his debt to his predecessors, in his 1937 essay 'The Hamlet Tradition' he focuses entirely on costume, as his brief indicates. Yet in other writings it becomes clear that this is not merely an indication of a focus on one aspect of the job – almost all his analysis of roles follow this pattern, and Redfield and Sterne in their accounts write of his preoccupation with costume in a production which, after all, was set in rehearsal clothes.

It is tempting to dismiss this as one of the idiosyncrasies of an eccentric personality, but this would be unfair. What persuaded Gielgud to finally realise his dream of a cinematic *Tempest* after turning down Derek Jarman and the director Peter Sellars, was Peter Greenaway's artistic background:

> The scenario is, I think, extraordinarily original and daring … Greenaway is a painter himself, influenced by Tintoretto and Titian and all the great Renaissance painters, and he organises and choreographs all his scenes with remarkable taste and feeling for depth and colour.[118]

Gielgud himself had directed and acted in a *Much Ado About Nothing* inspired by Piero della Francesca, and remarked 'I do not like Shakespeare being acted in any period later than Jacobean'.[119] When he talks about the tradition of great Hamlets, it is costume and gesture that are important, perhaps unsurprisingly given his background in design and architecture.[120]

More importantly, his viewpoint leads back to a nineteenth-century preoccupation with what West calls 'the image of the actor', as discussed in the previous chapter. The Romantic emphasis on essence evident in Reynolds' painting *The Tragic Muse* is mirrored in Hazlitt's description of Siddons as 'tragedy personified'. It is evident again at the end of the century, as we have seen with Sarah Bernhardt, interested only in the essence of the role, regardless of physical appearance. Painting immortalised not only these essences but ironically their external signifiers; the Prince in black, with skull, cloak and plumed hat, each added by an actor or introduced from the artist's own imagination. So ingrained was the interpretation of the inner truth by means, literally, of the suits of woe that when Terry asked if she could wear black as Ophelia she was famously rebuked by a shocked Walter Lacy (Irving's adviser): 'There is only one character in this play who wears black, Madam!'[121]

Significantly, Gielgud agrees that Ophelia and Laertes should both wear black after the death of Polonius, at which point Hamlet should change to a different colour. A century later, problems of costuming had

not evolved much, as Clare Higgins found when playing Regan in
Deborah Warner's 1990 RNT *King Lear*: 'In most productions of Lear I
have seen, one daughter comes in with long blonde hair and a blue dress
and two daughters have dark hair and black dresses; and you think "I
already know what's going to happen".'[122] Higgins's natural instinct was
to undermine this process, which she rightly saw as contributing to a
'deadening' of the play. When asked what she intended to wear in the
role she informed them she had chosen a white dress: 'I was told I could
not play Regan in a white dress. That brought home the incredible expectations people have.'[123] That this should happen in such an experimental
environment as Warner's Lear is particularly remarkable. Higgins is not
the only modern female actor to encounter problems of this nature, as
Frances Barber's account of playing Ophelia in Ron Daniels's 1984 RSC
production testifies.

Barber was told in no uncertain terms by Daniels, 'Frankie, you can't
play her as a feminist, it's not in the text.'[124] Despite Barber's not uncon-
vincing arguments to the contrary, Daniels refused to be moved. So did
Barber:

> Stubbornly refusing to be blown about by argument or threat, I
> entered those initial days of rehearsal with the notion that the play
> we were embarking upon was really called 'Ophelia and her Downfall'.
> I was intent upon discovering a way of playing her that revealed the
> masculine as well as the feminine qualities Hamlet lacked.[125]

There are echoes of Walter and other actors in her obsessive focus on the
character, but the interesting part is Barber's conviction of the aptness of
her reading, and of the implicit consideration of her relationship with
Hamlet. Barber is content to see Ophelia as an adjunct to Hamlet, supplying that which he lacks, but is aware that this reading does not have to
make her weak, only powerless. The distinction between the two is something Barber understands but Daniels does not – a difference that Barber
very strongly locates in gendered terms. Barber's conception of Ophelia is
that she is 'strong', 'spirited' 'forthright', but 'powerless', 'only an observer'.

This superficial paradox alarmed a director looking for a coherent and
categorised Ophelia, instantly recognisable from a long tradition of
tropes for the role. Barber's own insecurity of expression interestingly
reflects that of Ophelia, resulting in a paradox of articulation in her
own work that in itself mimicked her reading of the character. The
reason for this insecurity is not just a difficult relationship with the
director; it can also be traced to Barber's other chief preoccupations –
verse speaking, and in particular the history of the role.

The weight of dead generations is conveyed more literally than either
Marx or Philip Franks intended in Barber's essay, as she recounts

chatting to the stagehands who were to catch her when she is dropped into her grave by Hamlet after his tussle with Laertes.

> As we chatted away in this hole underneath the stage, the stagehand, who had been at the Memorial theatre since its opening, said, 'I've caught them all down here you know, all the Ophelias'. 'Oh, really', I replied, implying, I hoped, that this was not a good time to remind me of all the illustrious actresses who had played the role before. 'Oh, yes', he said, 'Glenda Jackson, Helen Mirren, Carole Royle, yes I've caught them all, you know. And they've all gone on to big things you know.' 'Yes', I replied weakly, I did know. 'Mind you', he answered, 'none of them was wearing as many clothes as you are'. Well, if only in the grave scene, I thought, at least I've made the character my own.[126]

Facetious though Barber is clearly being, the anecdote reveals the frustration of trying to do something different with a role that is held down by the detritus of a moribund tradition. Barber is not trying to be novel for its own sake, but to carry out an intelligent reappraisal of a difficult part. Ultimately it is only at the point of the character's erasure, when all that is present is Barber's own body, that she is permitted to be different – a difference which even then resides in the imposed externals of costume.[127]

Caught between the extreme externalism of costume and the extreme abstraction of post-Romantic conceptions of mimetic performance, the actor could be both an extremely liberated figure, as in the case of Bernhardt, or repressed, as with Terry or Barber, depending on the particular juxtaposition of traditions with which they found themselves. Situated thus, it becomes difficult to formulate a useful mimetic relationship to the craft. Garrick, Siddons, Terry, Irving, Gielgud and Olivier would all form connections with highly reputable writers and artists, moving between being mimetic model and agent of mimesis themselves, though almost always in relation to an omnipresent ghostly father. A supposedly profound erasure of identity would endow them with immortality – as in the play itself, attempts to suppress memory, to forget, are themselves agents of the further multiplication of mnemonic symbols.

Gielgud's debt to this lasting pictorial tradition – expressed at its simplest in the darkened auditorium and proscenium frame – is, as he confesses, immense. What can be seen in his writing is an understanding of the interrelationship of the symbolic world of art and the semiotic world of performance. Throughout his account, Gielgud proposes variations on the traditional signifiers, a plurality of methods of expression, hardly ever discussing performance at the level of the signified. Despite his emphasis on the benefits of being the right age for the part, his conception is still largely based on the dialectic of essential and external without the intermediary discourse of the psychological.[128]

Writing of his relationship with Gielgud, Olivier comments: 'I was the outsider and John was the jewel ... He was giving the familiar tradition fresh life, whereas I was completely disregarding the old in favour of something new.'[129] Olivier's bold Hamlet placed an emphasis on physicality absent since Kean, and once again a tradition of doing, of gesture, was established. Garrick in his production cut many passages suggesting irresolution. In his film of the play, Olivier also made drastic cuts to emphasise action. Most effectively, however, he played soliloquies as voiceovers, giving the impression of instant thought rather than delayed meditation – a technique used again recently in Julie Taymor's *Titus* to give the impression that time stands still as Marcus first sees the mutilated Lavinia. In this way, Olivier helped pave the way for an increased visualisation of psychological intention through physical action. This can be seen as introducing a rhetoric of the verb, of doing, into blocking and stage configuration. As Toolan says, 'the finite verb is the unmarked, preferred and unexceptional vehicle for expression of plot events'.[130] And so an emphasis on action and, moreover, consistency of action was put in place, helped of course by the parallel adoption and celebration of post-Stanislavskyan acting techniques, most famously the American Method.

VII

This movement rendered even more problematic another major Shakespearean tradition, or sub-tradition, that of the soliloquy, which often has no direct plot or action value at all. *Hamlet*, of course, contains the most famous soliloquy in Shakespeare, indeed arguably the most famous speech in the whole of literature in English. The place of this speech in a performance adds further layers of paradox to its meaning. The ultimate expression of paralysis must be moved, that is, spoken by a moving body in time. Pennington remarks that the speech 'hovers over the play like a great wing'.[131] Samuel West comments that 'we are not in the play now'.[132] Berkoff describes the audience

> politely looking on as if secretly engaging in some rite in which they had been privileged to partake: the world's most famous speech and done in English. They knew that this was the one, and they would politely and attentively become very quiet and still, most keen to follow each word and each change of thought. There is a curse on famous speeches that makes what was simple and direct suddenly complex and mysterious – too riddled with hidden depths to be easily mined, and having secret codes to get to the bottom of it and that will result in revelation. So one has to be all the more simple and clear: direct and honest – that will create the grandest possible effect. (But this is not what I always did ...).[133]

Indeed, Berkoff became so obsessed with the speech that he performed it differently almost every time, believing 'you have to show the audience who you are',[134] that is, show them that you are Berkoff, as well as Hamlet. He tried it with a cutthroat razor held just above his wrist, pacing up and down, galloping through it, even writing it on a blackboard, but never managing to make it seem fresh or new. Rather than talk us through it, Pennington adopts his Granville-Barker hat and discusses its dramatic function in the play:

> According to Albert Camus, suicide is the only philosophical question of any interest; and Hamlet's eye-to-eye encounter with it, expressed with all his intellectual lucidity, is perhaps the nearest drama can come to pure philosophy. Like many great insights, it is essentially banal, a trite (or profound) phrasing of a profound (or trite) question.[135]

A literary tradition here fills in for a purely dramatic one.

Playing the role only a year or two before Pennington, Derek Jacobi came up with the idea of speaking the speech directly to Ophelia, placing it in the context of an unresponsive dialogue. This had the additional benefit of motivating his anger at Ophelia, who now is in the position of failing to reciprocate, even dismissing, such emotional candour. Even though this gives the actor playing Ophelia an even more difficult job, it has been copied on several occasions since, including in the version directed by Jacobi and starring Branagh in Birmingham in 1988, and most recently in the Bill Alexander/Richard McCabe production again at the Birmingham Rep in 1998.

Jacobi himself explained:

> He's saying it to her, but he's also saying it at her, through her, around her. He doesn't need her response. And I think that it's legitimate to say that she's about to say something and so the lines at the end, the 'soft you now, the fair Ophelia' is how he quiets her.[136]

In the *Discovering Hamlet* video he reiterates that the speech is 'not a soliloquy but a dramatic speech to Ophelia'. For Ophelia, her lack of lines does not solve the problem of how she should physically react to this situation, rather exacerbating it. Jacobi may have found a way of putting his signature on the part and making the ensuing scene easier into the bargain, but Ophelia now has the problem of how to respond silently to the world's most famous speech, which now becomes, theatrically speaking, very much about action. In conclusion, Jacobi comments:

> It was an approach. I will take it to my grave that it was not a gimmick and we never said, 'well, how are we going to do To Be

Or Not To Be a new way?' It truly wasn't that. It was an attack. But for me, the situation and the emotion really bear that out.[137]

In sharp contrast, the intelligent approach taken by Ben Kingsley in Buzz Goodbody's landmark production of 1975 makes the impossibility of making a decision about the speech part of the motivation for the speech:

> You are going to continue with a play (the players' play) and the play (the one you're in). The strongest sensation before I went on was – is it worth continuing – are we doing anything by carrying on with this play? Is it worth it? Is it justifiable, this agony, drenched in sweat and shaky, all the emotions we were exploiting and playing with, in the best sense of the word – and particularly, I must say, after the death of our director – sitting back there I used to hit terrible despair and help-lessness and questioned everything. I could have chosen to opt out. I could have chosen suicide. But I did not. I chose to cross over into adulthood, to go on like a man and an adult, to complete the journey. Which is everything that that soliloquy is about and that the play is all about: joining the adult world, having to make adult decisions.[138]

For Kingsley the playing of this particular role became more than just 'a hoop to jump through' in his career. The death of Goodbody while the production was still in preview endowed it with a personal immediacy and poignancy that influenced every aspect of his interpretation. It became an analysis of himself and an attempt to find meaning in Goodbody's death – a tragedy born from the ruins of real tragedy:

> You see, this is what happened to Buzz. She got us all through 'To be or not to be' and said 'I'm not joining you on the other side'. Knowing a bit about suicide, knowing a bit about that terrifying leap from childhood to adulthood, and knowing that she had a very difficult childhood, I understood that she found letting go of that and moving into adulthood very painful.[139]

The extent to which Kingsley is here using his reading of the play to help him understand the death of his director, or using his explanation of Goodbody's death to help him understand the play, is unclear. In fact, it is both, the two tragedies informing each other and interacting in Kingsley's mind as he plays the role. He takes Franks's realisation about the connectedness of Hamlet's experience and that of the actor and pushes it further, identifies with the role not just as Berkoff does, playing the performativity, but in a more profound sense. With Kingsley the play becomes a way of reading the world outside it, and he consciously ham-mered home the metatheatrical resonances within his performance. This went as far as leaving the building midway through the 'Rogue and Peasant Slave' soliloquy:

> I said to the director, 'why don't I leave the play here? Why don't I just say, with my actions, 'fuck it'?' It even sounded like 'fuck it', FOH! As if to declare, 'Goodbye, ladies and gentlemen, I can't do it, I don't think I can do it, you probably don't think I'm a very good Hamlet anyway. So fuck it!'[140]

The personal pronoun here is entirely ambiguous, devoid of the distinctions evident in Berkoff between actor and role. For Kingsley, they become the same. There is no foregrounding of the otherness of performance, no playing of metatheatricality as with Berkoff. Kingsley returned to the theatre because:

> The play had to go on: the play's the thing. The only way to solve the problem is to do this play and also to do this play within this play. If the evening doesn't continue, neither I as an actor nor Hamlet as protagonist will ever resolve themselves.[141]

As Berkoff also does, Kingsley foregrounds the playing of mimesis itself. This is a choice evident also in the rhetoric of Samuel West. The crucial point in his performance comes with the arrival of the players who, he says in a particularly Stoppardian moment, have already 'read the play'. The Player–King then becomes 'the director of Hamlet's performance throughout the rest of the play'[142] through his performance of Pyrrhus. The fact that the actor playing the Player–King also doubled as Fortinbras in this production meant that, for West, 'Pyrrhus also played Fortinbras'. Hamlet thus understood that the winner in this play would be modelled on this fourth avenging son, the victory suitably pyrrhic.

Unlike Berkoff, neither West nor Kingsley retains the boundaries between the levels of mimesis on display. As Weimann says about the character of Hamlet, 'the multiplicity in the forms of mimesis used in his "characterisation" is stronger than any consistency in the social and psychological attributes of the "character" himself'.[143] This is precisely the approach of both West and Kingsley. The result is not so much a mimetic metadrama, as a *mise en abyme*, a model in which the boundaries are removed and the slippage of levels of signification is theoretically endless. This, as Weimann and others have observed, is the pattern of theatrical representation within the text itself, a truly Shakespearean construction in which character, as States remarks, resides in the gaps, the slips between acts. In *Hamlet* these gaps become *abymes*, and are large enough to contain an enormous plurality of readings. As Barthes writes, 'undecidability is not a weakness, but a structural condition … there is no unequivocal determination of the enunciation: in an utterance, several codes and several voices are there, without priority'.[144] Consistency is a principle intrinsic neither to character nor to the language that constitutes it. Weimann continues:

> The most stringent link with Hamlet's mimetic theory and practice is provided by the fact that Hamlet is both a product and, as it were, a producer of mimesis, a character performed in a role and one who himself performs and commissions a performance.[145]

Kingsley exploits this 'double coincidence', as he calls it, and makes it not only the defining feature of his performance, but crucially also of his experience of playing the role. A series of shadow-Hamlets is set up, with Goodbody established in Kingsley's discourse as herself a Hamlet figure. Kingsley, in attempting to deal with Goodbody's death and seeing her ghostly authorship of his performance every night becomes in his personal life another Hamlet. This is in turn fed into the actor who must play the role, into the role itself, and then into the roles that Hamlet himself plays within the play. A chain of Hamlets exists, each defining the next and deferring the last and inducing what Pennington calls in Hamlet 'a feeling of vertigo'. So complex is this chain of reference in Kingsley that it overflows all boundaries of the theatrical event, playing with the memory of Goodbody, a previous Hamlet succeeded and avenged by Kingsley. Such a waste of potential becomes Kingsley's key into Hamlet because 'that's what they say about Hamlet. That's what Fortinbras says about Hamlet at the end of the play.'[146]

Kingsley is also playing Goodbody-as-Hamlet as well as responding to her parenting role. Nor is the history of the Hamlet tradition forgotten, but is also brought in, integrated in another vertiginous moment that takes place, appropriately enough, after the play scene in a brief exchange with Bob Peck's Player–King:

> I ask Peck for the sword. I hold out my hand, and he gives me the prop. It's a real sword, the one I kill Polonius with. As I am the royal patron, the prince, and he is there at my behest, he has no choice but to give me that sword, but he gave it to me in a very special way – as if to say, 'Manhood, here you are'. Giving a sword is also part of the great acting tradition. The sword that Edmund Kean used in Richard III was given to Olivier. It was handed down through a whole line of great actors, including Irving and Gielgud. So, this gesture is a magic talisman for actors.[147]

The phallic sword becomes another rite, not only of adulthood this time, but also of the profession shared by both actors and both characters, in which, as we have seen, the role becomes an index of the authority of the actor within his profession. A *mise en abyme* of tradition is played out, with the sword embodying several layers of mimesis within Kingsley's description. It becomes an agent for the production of mimesis, memory and vengeance, a complex and appropriate emblem for the play itself. As with West, the Player–King becomes the instigator of a multiplication of all the mimetic systems within Hamlet and within *Hamlet*, the Ghost replaced by the Player as begetter of meaning. A similar heightening of the symbolism of a prop can be found in the 2000–2001 RSC productions of the history cycle, from *Richard II* to *Richard III*. In this sequence, the crown worn by Sam West as Richard II, wrested from him by David Troughton's Bolingbroke, passed down the lineage of kings, through all eight plays, until it came to rest on the head of Richmond, played by Troughton's real-life son, also called Sam. As Weimann remarks:

> What the product-as-process quality of these multiple functions of mimesis achieve is a simultaneity in the awareness of life in the theatre, and the theatre as a supreme form of life: the indivisibility, that is, of the appropriation of the world through and on the stage and the appropriation of the stage through and in the world.[148]

Kingsley appropriates the processes of Shakespearean mimesis itself, constructing an identity that cannot be limited to a performance self but which spills out into the very real world of suicide, memory and indecision as well as to the play-world. Shakespearean authority is no longer invoked in the sense of sanctioning a reading or an interpretation, but in the processes of a construction of selfhood itself. This endlessly cyclical process challenges the conventional, linear structures of neoclassical mimesis as verisimilar and imitative, in accordance with which, as Weimann says, 'Hamlet would serve purely as a character and never as an actor, always the product of characterisation, never as a process of bringing it out'.[149] Kingsley allows us to posit mimesis in a new, performative sense that no longer relies on boundaries but exists on shifting sands of sympathy and analogy, identification and emulation that can move forward as well as back in a vertiginous structure of *mise en abyme*.

Notes

1   J. Gielgud, 'The *Hamlet* Tradition: some notes on costume, scenery and stage business', in R. Gilder (ed.), *John Gielgud's Hamlet, A Record of Performance*, London: Methuen, 1937.
2   P. Franks on Hamlet, in Jackson and Smallwood (eds), *Players of Shakespeare 3*, Cambridge: Cambridge University Press, 1993, p. 189.
3   K. Marx, *The Eighteenth Brumaire of Louis Bonaparte*, in D. McLellan (ed.), *The Selected Writings of Karl Marx*, Oxford: Oxford University Press, 1977, p. 300.
4   Franks, *Players 3*, p. 195.

5 Ibid., p. 190.
6 P. Valéry, 'The Crisis of the Spirit' (1919) in J.R. Lawler (trans. and ed.), *Paul Valéry: An Anthology*, London: Routledge, 1977, pp. 94–107, p.100.
7 R. Hillman, *Self-Speaking in Medieval and Early Modern English Drama – Subjectivity, Discourse and the Stage*, London: Macmillan, 1997, p.107.
8 R. Falco, *Conceived Presences, Literary Genealogy in Renaissance England*, Cambridge, Mass.: Harvard, 1994, p. 11.
9 T.J. King, 'Shakespeare to Olivier: A Great Chain of Acting, 1598–1935', *Notes and Queries*, September 1986, pp. 397–8. The links are: Shakespeare, Christopher Beeston, Michael Moone, Thomas Betterton, Colley Cibber, Hannah Pritchard, David Garrick, Sarah Siddons, Charles Kemble, Edmund Kean, Charles Kean, Ellen Terry, Henry Irving, Johnston Forbes-Robertson, Mrs Patrick Campbell, John Gielgud and Laurence Olivier.
10 J. Downes (1708) in Judith Milhous and Robert D. Hume (eds), *Roscius Anglicanus: or an Historical Review of the Stage*, London: London Society for Theatre Research, 1987, [21], p. 51.
11 Ibid. [24], p. 55.
12 Barrymore, quoted by R. Hapgood (ed.), *Hamlet, Shakespeare in Production*, Cambridge: Cambridge University Press, 1999, p. 59. The word 'loving' is probably a euphemism.
13 Olivier, *On Acting*, p. 48.
14 Ibid., p. 49.
15 Lewes, in Hapgood, *Hamlet*, p. 30. According to the *Hamlet on the Ramparts* website, http://shea.mit.edu/ramparts2000, only E.H. Sothern, Tree and Gielgud had hair that was not obviously black before Olivier.
16 M. Rosenberg, *The Masks of Hamlet*, Newark: University of Delaware Press; London: Associated University Presses, 1992, p. 134.
17 Jacobi in *Discovering Hamlet*, written and directed by Mark Olshaker, narrated by Patrick Stewart, Unicorn/PBS Home Video, 1990.
18 Narration to *Discovering Hamlet*.
19 Jacobi in *Discovering Hamlet*.
20 K. Branagh, *Hamlet, by William Shakespeare: Screenplay, Introduction & Film Diary*, London: Chatto & Windus, 1996, Introduction, p. v.
21 R. Jackson, 'Film Diary', in Branagh, *Hamlet*, p. 211.
22 S. Berkoff, *I am Hamlet*, London: Faber & Faber, 1989.
23 M. Pennington, *Hamlet: A User's Guide*, London: Nick Hern, 1996.
24 Pennington's various acting experience of *Hamlet* is unique. His only rival is Eric Maxon, who never played the Prince, but who played Claudius in 1910, Horatio in 1927, 1929, 1930 and 1933, Laertes in 1910 and 1924, Polonius in 1936, and was costume designer to the play in 1929, all at Stratford.
25 See in particular, *The Anxiety of Influence*, Oxford: Oxford University Press, 1973, but also relevant to this argument is his *The Western Canon*, London: Macmillan, 1996.
26 Pennington, *User's Guide*, p. 187.
27 Olivier, *On Acting*, London: Wheelshare, 1986, p. 51.
28 Pennington, on Hamlet, in Brockbank (ed.), *Players of Shakespeare 1*, Cambridge: Cambridge University Press, 1984.
29 *Hamlet* contains twelve uses of the word 'remember', ten of 'memory', four of 'remembrance' five of 'forgot', and three other variations. *The Tempest* has eleven of 'remember' and six of 'remembrance' *1 Henry IV* has nine uses of

'forget', as does *Othello* and *King Lear*, which also has nine uses of 'memory'. *Twelfth Night* and *As You Like It* both contain nine uses of the word 'remember'.

30 Branagh's film contains no less than four Hamlets apart from himself – Jacobi (Claudius), Michael Maloney (Laertes), Gielgud (Priam), and Simon Russell Beale (2nd Gravedigger), though Beale's performance came of course some time after the film was released. In comparison, Zeffirelli's version has, aside from Gibson, three Hamlets: Scofield, Stephen Dillane (Horatio), and Maloney again (Rosencrantz). Olivier makes do with just one, John Laurie (Bernardo).

31 Pennington, *User's Guide*, p. 155.

32 R. Barthes, *Textual Analysis of Poe's Valdemar*, 1973, trans. G. Bennington, in D. Lodge (ed.), *Modern Criticism and Theory*, Harlow: Longman, 1988, pp. 172–95, p. 190.

33 Barthes, *Valdemar*, p. 182.

34 Ibid., p. 190.

35 J.L. Calderwood, '*Hamlet*: The Name of Action', *Modern Language Quarterly*, vol. 39 no. 4, December 1978, pp. 332–62, p. 335.

36 Ibid., p. 345.

37 Pennington, *User's Guide*, pp. 158–9.

38 Hillman, *Self-Speaking in Medieval and Early Modern English Drama*, p. 144.

39 J. Derrida, *Specters of Marx – The State of the Debt, The Work of Mourning and The New International*, trans. P. Kamuf, London: Routledge, 1994, p. 34.

40 B.O. States, *Hamlet and the Concept of Character*, Baltimore, Md.: Johns Hopkins Press, 1992, p. 8.

41 Peter Hall is rather fond of it, using it also in his 1984 production at the NT, with Denis Quilley playing the brothers.

42 Berkoff, *I am Hamlet*, p. 123.

43 Ibid., p. viii.

44 States, *Hamlet and the Concept of Character*, p. xx.

45 M. Cox (ed.), *Shakespeare Comes to Broadmoor*, London: Jessica Kingsley, 1992, pp. 30–31.

46 States, *Hamlet and the Concept of Character*, p. xx.

47 Berkoff, *I am Hamlet*, p. vii.

48 C. Macklin, 'The Art and Duty of an Actor', in J.T. Kirkman, *Memoirs of the Life of Charles Macklin, Esq, principally compiled from his own papers and memorandums*, London: Lockington, Allen and Company, 1799, vol. 1, pp. 362–6, p. 66.

49 Ibid., p. 122.

50 Berkoff, *I am Hamlet*, p. 12.

51 Ibid., p. 44.

52 Ibid., p. 147.

53 Berkoff is not alone in making this connection. See for example Harold Fisch's *Hamlet and the Word: The Covenant Pattern in Shakespeare*, London: Ungar, 1971.

54 Berkoff, *I am Hamlet*, p. 153.

55 Ibid., p. 13.

56 M. Foucault, *The Order of Things*, London: Tavistock, 1970, p. 17.

57 Ibid., p. 23.

58 Ibid., p. 19.

59 Pennington, *User's Guide*, p. 212.

60 M. Toolan, *Narrative: A Critical Linguistic Introduction*, London: Routledge, 1988, p. 48.
61 States, *Hamlet and the Concept of Character*, p. 104.
62 R. Weimann, *Author's Pen and Actor's Voice: Playing and Writing in Shakespeare's Theatre*, Cambridge: Cambridge University Press, 2000, p. 236.
63 Quoted by Weimann, *Author's Pen*, p. 17.
64 Berkoff, *I am Hamlet*, p. 28.
65 Pennington, *User's Guide*, p. 13.
66 For Pennington's most politicised response to the Falklands, in the form of the ESC History Cycle, see Pennington and Bogdanov, *The English Shakespeare Company: The Wars of the Roses*, London: Nick Hern, 1990.
67 P. Holland, *English Shakespeares*, Cambridge: Cambridge University Press, 1997, p. 31.
68 See S. Berkoff, *Coriolanus in Deutschland*, London: Amber Lane, 1992.
69 Pennington, *User's Guide*, p. 10.
70 R. Falco, *Charismatic Authority in Early Modern English Tragedy*, Baltimore, Md.: Johns Hopkins University Press, 2000, p. 2.
71 Pennington, *User's Guide*, p. 32.
72 Beale, interviewed by J. Coldstream, *Daily Telegraph*, 19.8.2000.
73 T. Holcroft, 'The Art of Acting', *The Theatrical Recorder*, vol. II, no. VII, 1805, p. 46.
74 Even Samuel West, playing the role at the RSC in 2001 aged thirty-four and looking much younger, has commented that he felt time was running out as far as opportunities to play the part were concerned.
75 Berkoff, *I am Hamlet*, p. 25.
76 Falco, *Charismatic Authority*, p. 10.
77 Berkoff, *I am Hamlet*, p. 121.
78 Pennington, *User's Guide*, p. 19.
79 L. Calvert, *An Actor's Hamlet*, London: Mills & Boon, 1912, p. xiii.
80 H. Granville-Barker, *Preface to Hamlet*, 1937, reprinted London: Nick Hern, 1993, p. 289.
81 Ibid., p. 263.
82 Calderwood, '*Hamlet*: The Name of Action', p. 348.
83 See M. Garber, *Shakespeare's Ghost Writers: Literature as Uncanny Causality*, London: Methuen, 1987, and also E. Smith, 'Ghost Writing: Hamlet and the Ur-Hamlet', in Andrew Murphy (ed.), *The Renaissance Text*, Manchester: Manchester University Press, 2000, pp. 177–91.
84 Gielgud, in Gilder, *John Gielgud's Hamlet*, p. 169.
85 Gielgud's costume for his 1937 production of the play is called by Marvin Rosenberg a 'Fauntleroy suit', *The Masks of Hamlet*, New York and London: Associated University Presses, 1997, p. 119. It was predictably all in black with the exception of a broad white collar which would have caught the light and reflected it onto his face, at least partly explaining the ethereal, poetic impression received by most observers, and making him look not unlike a perambulating pint of Guinness.
86 *Hamlet*, directed by John Gielgud, opened at the Lunt–Fontanne Theatre, New York, on 9 April 1964, and ran for a record 185 performances.
87 W. Redfield, *Letters from An Actor*, New York: Cassell & Co., 1966; R. Sterne, *John Gielgud directs Richard Burton in Hamlet: A Journal of Rehearsals*, New York: Random House, 1966.

88 Sterne, *John Gielgud directs*, p. 4.
89 Redfield, *Letters*, p. 9.
90 Brando, of course, did play Mark Antony in Joseph L. Mankiewicz's 1953 film of *Julius Caesar*, also, coincidentally, with John Gielgud. But Redfield's point is as much stage v. film as verse v. prose.
91 *The Richard Burton Hamlet*, produced by William Sargent and Alfred Crown, Atlantic Programmes Lt. Broadcast 1964.
92 Sterne, *John Gielgud directs*, p. 66.
93 Ibid., p. 23.
94 Programme to *Hamlet*, Lunt–Fontanne Theatre, New York, 1964.
95 Redfield, *Letters*, p. 73.
96 Ibid.
97 Ibid., p. 75.
98 Ibid., p. 76.
99 Gielgud with J. Miller, *Shakespeare: Hit or Miss*, London: Sidgwick and Jackson, 1991, p. 42.
100 Redfield, *Letters*, p. 86.
101 Ibid.
102 Interviewed by Sterne in *John Gielgud directs*, p. 331.
103 Redfield, *Letters*, p. 78.
104 Marowitz, *Lear Log*, in D. Williams (ed.), *Peter Brook: A Theatrical Casebook*, London: Methuen, 1992, pp. 6–23, p. 7.
105 Ibid., p. 7.
106 Ibid., p. 9.
107 Ibid., p. 71.
108 Burton, in Sterne, *John Gielgud directs*, p. 331.
109 Marowitz, *Lear Log*, p. 16.
110 Ibid., p. 21.
111 Quoted in J. Cook, *Shakespeare's Players*, London: Harrap, 1983, p. 110.
112 See J. Fineman, *Shakespeare's Perjur'd Eye*, Berkeley: Calif., 1986, and also *The Subjectivity Effect in Western Literary Tradition*, Cambridge, Mass.: MIT Press, 1997.
113 Burton, in Sterne, *John Gielgud directs*, p. 326.
114 Redfield, *Letters*, p. 62.
115 *Hamlet*, 3:2, 20–23, in Wells and Taylor (eds), *The Complete Works*, Oxford: Oxford University Press, 1987.
116 Montaigne, 'Of the Education of Boys', in Screech (trans. and ed.), *The Complete Essays*, p. 171.
117 Brook, in S. Trussler, 'Private Experiment – In Public', *Plays and Players*, November 1964.
118 Gielgud with J. Miller, *Acting Shakespeare*, London: Pan, 1997, p. 99.
119 Ibid., p. 85.
120 One of his most significant achievements at the Old Vic was the establishment of the Motleys in charge of costume and set design, heralding something of a revolution in these areas over the next two decades. Motley: Sophia Audrey Harris, 1900–66, Margaret F. Harris, 1904–, Elizabeth Montgomery, 1902–93. For more information on their work, see Michael Mullin, *Design by Motley*, Newark, Del.: University of Delaware Press, 1996.
121 Anecdote related by Gielgud in Gilder, *John Gielgud's Hamlet*. Other versions have Irving himself offering the rebuke.

122 C. Higgins on Regan in *Shakespeare Comes to Broadmoor*, p. 73.
123 Ibid.
124 F. Barber on Ophelia in Jackson and Smallwood (eds), *Players of Shakespeare 2*, p. 139.
125 Ibid., p. 140.
126 Ibid., p. 149.
127 For a reading of Ophelia in the grave, which incidentally advocates many of the interpretative choices proffered by Barber and quashed by Daniels, see C. Rutter, *Enter the Body – Women and Representation on Shakespeare's Stage*, London: Routledge, 2001.
128 Interestingly, in his 1937 New York production he cast an Ophelia a decade older than himself, and who at the time was a bigger screen than he was a stage star: Lillian Gish.
129 Rosenberg, *The Masks of Hamlet*, p. 44.
130 Toolan, *Narrative*, p. 35.
131 Pennington, *User's Guide*, p. 21.
132 Samuel West in conversation with Russell Jackson, Swan Theatre, 17.05.01.
133 Berkoff, *I am Hamlet*, p. 97.
134 Ibid., p. 99.
135 Pennington, *User's Guide*, p. 80.
136 D. Jacobi, in M.Z. Maher, *Modern Hamlets and their Soliloquies*, Ames, Ia.: Iowa State University Press, 1992, p. 107.
137 Maher, *Modern Hamlets*, p. 109.
138 Kingsley, in ibid., pp. 81–2.
139 Ibid., p. 82.
140 Ibid., p. 80.
141 Ibid., p. 81.
142 West in conversation with Jackson, Swan Theatre, 17.05.01.
143 R. Weimann, 'Mimesis in Hamlet', in P. Parker and G. Hartman (eds), *Shakespeare and the Question of Theory*, London: Methuen, 1985, pp. 275–91, p. 282.
144 Barthes, *Valdemar*, p. 194.
145 Ibid., p. 288.
146 Kingsley, in Maher, *Modern Hamlets*, p. 68.
147 Ibid., p. 85.
148 Weimann, 'Mimesis in Hamlet', p. 288.
149 Ibid., p. 283.

Chapter 4

Acting the woman
Feminist appropriations in *Clamorous Voices*

These actresses are political, in the widest sense of the word. By redefining Shakespeare's heroines they have opened up new perspectives on how 'his' women are portrayed on stage.

C. Rutter[1]

All theatre's political, because whatever you do, if it's only coming on with a tennis racket and saying 'Anyone for tennis?' you're either confirming the status quo and celebrating it or you are on some level challenging it and asking questions about it. There can be ways of attempting those plays which can be genuinely subversive.

J. Stevenson[2]

I

The voices clamouring throughout this text belong to five actors and an academic.[3] Paola Dionisotti, Sinead Cusack and Fiona Shaw talk about playing Katherina in *The Taming of the Shrew*. Paola Dionisotti and Juliet Stevenson discuss *Measure for Measure*'s Isabella, and Sinead Cusack shares her thoughts on *Lady Macbeth*. Harriet Walter remembers playing Helena in *All's Well That Ends Well* and Imogen in *Cymbeline*, and Juliet Stevenson and Fiona Shaw discuss their Rosalind and Celia, played in the same production of *As You Like It*. The introduction to the volume and the interviews themselves were the responsibility of Carol Rutter. Each actor recounts the experience of playing two major Shakespearean roles, 'redefining', according to Rutter, the presentation of ' "his" women' on stage. The placing of the pronoun 'his' between questioning inverted commas informs the reader as much as could any overt statement of the purpose of the book. This is to reclaim these, and by implication other, Shakespearean roles for the actors playing them. It is also to 'interrogate their playwright', to question the author's exclusive ownership of the text from within the glare of performance.

The parenthetical 'his' also underlines the explicitly gendered nature of this relocation of meaning. *Clamorous Voices* endeavours not to reclaim the Shakespearean text for performance in general, though this is an inevitable byproduct of the work, but for female performance in particular. The patriarchal prescription of interpretation hinted at by the possessive 'his' is rejected in favour of a feminist reclamation of these roles for the women who have occupied them.[4] The purpose of this chapter is to investigate the extent to which this project has been achieved, and to analyse the often sophisticated rhetoric used by these women to characterise their relationship with this most authoritative of male writers.

Clamorous Voices is clearly a political text. Not only is its self-proclaimed agenda political, but so also are the approaches of the actors who speak so insightfully within it. All come to the roles they discuss with an intention to probe the text and fight their corners in rehearsal in order to 'rediscover' the part, to 'reclaim' it for themselves. This attempted reappropriation of Shakespeare is fraught with difficulties and contradictions, evident not least within the subtitle of the book – 'Shakespeare's Women Today' – which ambiguously conflates actor and role as possessions of the patriarchal bard the contributors seek to dispossess. This tension of political ownership runs throughout the book as women try to negotiate their contemporary relationship with historical and historicised texts.

Paola Dionisotti remarks that: 'I am loath to take on Shakespeare's writing. I usually feel that if there's a problem in the play, it's me, not him.'[5] Shakespeare's received textual authority is something to which all five actors to some extent defer. Juliet Stevenson explains that 'if you make a decision to impose a stage image on Shakespeare's language ... or if production choices set a different rhythm to the one the language is setting, you may be creating trouble for yourselves'.[6]

The final point of reference for all performance is assumed to be the text, to which the decisions of the actors in this volume are subservient. Yet, despite Dionisotti's reverence, this does not simply represent a celebration of the Shakespearean or textual status quo. Although all contributors have a profound admiration for Shakespeare generally, when it comes to examining roles individually, the case is significantly different. Stevenson remarks:

> If you are playing one of Shakespeare's women, you are by definition in a supporting role. You appear in relationship to the man – as wife, daughter, mother, lover. The man is the motor, the initiator of the action; he sets the pace of the play and the woman is usually in a reactive, not an active, position.[7]

This is of course not always the case, particularly in comedies, but superficially at least it is an observation borne out by the roles described –

daughter, sister/virgin, wife, lovers – beginning with the most troublesome of daughters, Katherina.

II

The discussion of Katherina is dominated by Fiona Shaw, who at the time of being interviewed had just finished playing the part in Jonathan Miller's 1987 RSC production. Her experience of the role, echoing several of the female contributors to the *Players of Shakespeare* series, was one of frustration with a director with whose fixed ideas she did not agree. Her view was that Miller was 'translating the taming of the shrew into the realignment of the delinquent',[8] a view ostensibly shared by one reviewer at least – Michael Billington remarked that the play he had seen was 'less *The Taming of the Shrew* than *The Rehabilitation of the Maladjusted*'.[9]

Petruccio was portrayed by Brian Cox as a quasi-medical figure, coaxing Kate back to some state of normal health represented by the climactic speech. This psychoanalytic approach represents Kate's development as both positive and necessary, and, more importantly, impossible without the intervention of this man. Miller himself claimed to have detected within the text the 'behaviour patterns of unloved children',[10] leading to his conclusion that the play is about 'The beautifying of a girl who thought herself ugly and unloved'.[11] This comment pinpoints the difference between the apparently echoing comments of Billington and Shaw. Billington, responding to Cox's weary, grizzled and calm Petruccio, diagnosed the doctor/patient relationship but assumed both parties to be adult. From inside the production, however, Shaw was repeatedly placed in the juvenile confines of delinquency. In this way, the status games played along gender and class lines in the text were unbalanced in performance by the introduction of the further mediating factor of age.

In this production Katherina was very much a daughter, defined in relation to Baptista. Shaw found this problematic, seeing in Katherina a mature woman repressed by her environment rather than an unloved child unable to express herself. She says:

> Every now and again there's a character who really isn't Shakespeare's most interesting heroine but who nevertheless says something of primary importance, which is that part of the problem of our whole society is that women have been told they may not speak.[12]

This lack of speech, this silence, became for Shaw the crux of the performance. As she says, in a comment that is taken for the title of this chapter of *Clamorous Voices*, 'We must interpret this silence'.[13] This interpretation of silence becomes significant for this actor's negotiation with Shakespeare –

Shaw is no longer reading into the text, but into the absence of text; she is not engaging with Shakespeare's words but with his gaps. Such a focus was not lost on reviewers, one of whom commented that the part was 'acted with relish, vigour and understanding – especially in her silences – by Fiona Shaw'.[14]

The location of the debate within what the text does not say has political repercussions for the kind of rhetoric used by Shaw when talking about Shakespeare. She remarks:

> Clearly there has been a system at work which modern feminist theory has brought brilliantly to light: a double-think, where men have described the reality and women have conformed to that description of it.[15]

This act of conforming – a silent act – where the patriarchy has controlled the means of expression is, for Shaw, subverted by Katherina's eloquent linguistic game in act five, where the status quo is ostensibly upheld while being simultaneously and interconnectedly undermined. She becomes free, 'Even to the uttermost, as I please, in words.'[16] Shaw's description of a masculine 'double-think' must, however, surely also apply to Shakespeare, as male author and centre of the patriarchal canon. In this light, not only Katherina but also Shaw is, in her interpretation of the part, conforming to a male description of reality. This was certainly the belief of the protesting female activists who interrupted one performance of the play to assert Shaw's complicity with the misogynist discourse of which the play is considered implicitly a part.

The notion of a sexist Shakespeare is avoided by all three actors discussing the part of Katherina. For Shaw, the final speech does not escape from its phallocentric constraints, it acknowledges them and follows them to their logical and devastating conclusion: 'She is saying "I acknowledge the system. I don't think we can change this" – which is a terrible indictment of a system of patriarchy that is so strong it is unchangeable even for its own good.'[17]

Patriarchy, at the individual level, dominates men as much as it does women, Petruccio as much as Katherina, but in significantly different ways. The self-referentiality of Katherina's speech allows it to comment upon her situation without explicitly dissecting it. Shaw rehabilitates Shakespeare from the charge of misogyny by focusing meaning within the gaps and silences of his text, the parts free from patriarchal ideology both in the writing and in the imposition of a 'complicatedly conservative' director's beliefs. It is within these gaps that her performance is most strongly located. Denis Salter, in a discussion of postcolonial performance of Shakespeare, asks: 'How can the postcolonial margins write, speak, and act back to the imperial centre when trying to articulate themselves through the very language that itself partially constitutes the problem of estrangement?'[18] Shaw answers this for 'marginalised women' and for Katherina by centring interpretation on non-linguistic performance – the gaps – and allowing this to act as a commentary on the text.

A performance is thus freed from the implications of a patriarchal text, and this process can be ascribed to Shakespeare's deliberately constructed gaps in Katherina's language. Commenting that participating in an almost all-male rehearsal room gave her an unexpected insight into Katherina's predicament in a male-dominated society, Shaw learned to be 'watchful', to use her silences constructively and defensively, a technique that persisted into performance and into her characterisation of Kate:

> The Kate I played in *The Shrew* was a direct product of the rehearsal process. I was conscious of wanting to radiate the sense of terribly clouded confusion that overwhelms you when you are the only woman around. That was Kate's position, and it was mine: she in that mad marriage, me in rehearsal.[19]

The performance is explicitly as much a product of the environment in which Shaw constructs it as the part is of that of the Renaissance, or as Katherina's actions are of her situation within the play. This moves her approach from one of psychologised convention to one of politicised subversion that is familiar to many female actors within the context of a Shakespeare production. As Penny Gay remarks:

> Fiona Shaw's reading ... is distinctly different from Miller's. It is political, rather than psychological; as a modern feminist actress, she consciously opposes her politics to his (though his are disguised as an ideologically neutral, 'scientific' reading of history).[20]

The collision of the actor's feminist ideologies with a respected Shakespearean text necessitated the development of an alternative approach to preparing the part. Shaw's armoury of acting techniques is supplemented by a political method of locating the performance in the gaps, the omissions of the text – the moments of Shaw's greatest presence are constructed in those of the text's absences.

Paola Dionisotti explains that 'the story any production tells is not just the story of the play, it's also the story of those actors as they rehearsed it'.[21] Shaw's Shrew became the epitome of this, a story of gender conflict and textual controversy that uncannily mirrored the play in which the performance was situated. In many ways it lived out the phrase 'Shakespeare's woman today' to the full, as Shaw became a second Kate combating a second Petruccio. The uneasy relationship with the playwright that this occasioned is encapsulated in Shaw's witty summary of the play as 'underwritten and overendowed', her admission that with this play 'Shakespeare sails close to the wind', but finally that it remains 'terribly fundamental, almost transcendental'.[22] Her performance decentres the textual meaning of the play and her Kate deconstructs the socially constructed hierarchies that have hitherto repressed her, but Shaw finally comes to rest at a point of closure that is the transcendental signified of the Shakespearean author-function.

A curious paradox is in evidence here. Shaw rightly critiques the male-dominated environment in which she works, and at the same time acknowledges Katherina's subversion of Paduan patriarchy, and yet she remains entirely obedient to the social processes of the construction of meaning that are masked behind the Shakespearean author-function. It is a paradox that recurs in the comments of this and other actors and is not engaged with directly until the accounts of Stevenson and Walter, as will be seen later.

Fiona Shaw's other contribution to *Clamorous Voices* is her discussion of Celia, a discussion that both in this volume and elsewhere contains striking similarities with her attitude towards Katherina. She exclaims: 'Celia in *As You Like It* is one of the best written roles ever. What's extraordinary is that she can do so much in such a short time. Compared to the amount of speech that Rosalind has, Celia's impact is enormous.'[23] Shaw emphasises the concision, the preciseness of the part. As with Katherina, the appeal lies in an opportunity to read between the lines, to 'create the character more laterally'.[24] This is partly due to the sheer linguistic imbalance of Celia's scenes, in which she is so vocal at court and so reticent in Arden. As Shaw says, 'Celia sets out thinking the play is about Celia. But when she gets to Arden she finds out that she is no Lord Hamlet, but an attendant lord in the land of love.'[25]

Rather than pursue this belief through to the end of the play, Shaw sets about, in Rutter's words, 'recuperating the role': 'Those scenes in Arden were written as trios, and I was determined that the trios be trios. The problem is, Celia never speaks to Orlando in these scenes. Not a word!'[26] Here, Shaw begins to indicate the differences between what are superficially similar cases of reclaiming silence. Celia is deliberately written in as a mute witness to the shenanigans of the lovers, her physical presence as significant as her vocal silence, whereas Katherina is denied the opportunity to speak in society at large.

More than with Katherina, it is within these absences that the crux of Shaw's performance interpretation of Celia is located. This leads to a tension between this agenda and the evidence of Celia's diminishing participation within the play – Shaw readily admits that the move to Arden represents 'the end of Celia's play', yet it also represents in many ways the beginning of Fiona's play, as 'for the actress playing Celia the major challenge ... [is] that of Celia's silence'.[27]

The dominance of the first part, relinquished with grace in this production by Juliet Stevenson's Rosalind, is all well and good, but 'what is Celia's attitude to it all' in the second half? 'Lateral characterisation' becomes a sprint of virtuoso invention as Shaw set out to recuperate her character through a series of comic glances, stances and other stage business that at times threatened to upstage Rosalind entirely. The obvious interpretation of this move as the result of an actor's desire to expand her part was picked up by some reviewers,[28] but it can also be seen as consistent both with the general exuberance of the production and with the egotism of the first-act Celia of both Shaw and Shakespeare. Interestingly, Shaw and Stevenson's suggestion that part of the frisson of watching the play lies in the supposed competitiveness of the actors playing their roles is borne out here. No one worries about Orlando upstaging Rosalind, or indeed Oliver upstaging his brother (though one reviewer felt he did in this production[29]). The gender of the female performer is consistently characterised as other in both auditorium and rehearsal room, and, as these actors demonstrate, becomes an active constituent in the construction of a role in a manner which is rarely the case for a male actor.[30]

Shaw's engagement with Shakespeare is very much with what she calls his silences. It is the textual absences that allow her fully to realise her character and to stamp her mark upon the performance. She describes *As You Like It* as the play that first confirmed her love of Shakespeare, and phrases this infatuation in a fascinating manner: 'it was the play in which I fell through the looking glass in relation to Shakespeare'.[31] Moving from T.S. Eliot to Lewis Carroll in her metaphorical descriptions of this play, Shaw implies the extent to which she forms her character as a projection of herself. Celia becomes an extension of her own personality, and, as, given half a chance, Shaw would definitely be a presence in the latter half of the play, so will Celia. By focusing on the silences and the gaps, moulding her performance around her presence in Shakespeare's absences, Shaw appropriates the text for herself and subordinates the role to the actor.

This strategy is ideologically implicated in Shaw's positioning of herself as part of what she calls the 'women's movement'. Her feminist sensibilities are crucial to an understanding of her technique and central to her approach to this 'lateral characterisation'. This is evinced not only in direct statements of the need to reclaim performance in general and Shakespearean performance in particular for women – statements which she shares with other female actors and directors – but in her continual merging of the world of the character with the world of the actor and the position of women in society. This was clearly apparent in Shaw's complex mirroring of Katherina with her own place in the rehearsal room, and vice versa. It is apparent again in her approach to Celia and her relationship with Stevenson as Rosalind:

> Like Rosalind and Celia, what we encountered was a journey ... we
> were lucky that the production gave us, finally, the space in which to
> draw upon our own experience, our own humour and our own lunacies,
> passions and sensibilities – and, primarily, upon our own friendship.[32]

Rosalind and Celia become extensions of Juliet and Fiona, as the gaps and
absences in the text are occupied by the personalities and ideologies of the
actors, decentring the text and reclaiming the role for the player. Shaw
very much goes through the looking glass of her own image to project the
character on stage, and Shakespeare's woman becomes Shaw's woman, if
only for the duration of that performance. This constitutes an understanding of mimesis that is contingent, dependent on a representation of relations rather than subjects; Shaw refigures gaps, omissions and the
inevitably extra-textual dynamic between character and actor. This is
mimesis without a fixed model, an imitation of absence.

III

The complex mechanisms of Shaw's reclamation of character are suitably
mirrored and further developed by her friend and Rosalind, Juliet
Stevenson. Talking of Rosalind's attitude in the first part of the play,
she remarks:

> She seems to be very private in her utterances. Indeed, except when
> alone with Celia, she hardly speaks at all: and the fact that she doesn't
> speak has to be focused upon, her very silence has to be given space.
> Her distraction, her speechlessness, her lack of centre have to be
> placed, because out of that come all her choices in the second half
> of the play.[33]

Not only do the 'underwritten' roles of Katherina and Celia require an
investigation of silence, one of the lengthiest roles (in terms of number of
words) in the canon also requires this approach. The case of Rosalind,
however, is markedly different. Here is an example of a role that is neither
underwritten nor passive, yet requires Stevenson to feel the necessity of
focusing on her silences and 'her speechlessness'. This is not the contradiction that it at first appears. Stevenson describes the world of the court as

> a world totally dominated by the male principle and its attendant
> values, a world in which we are shortly to see that the prevalent
> idea of a good time is to watch a wrestler bashing hell out of three
> young men and going for his fourth when he's killed them.[34]

Rosalind has no position or immediate family at the court. She is defined as the daughter of the exiled Duke, the offspring of an absence. Unlike Celia, she is not recognised as belonging to this world and has nothing to enable her 'to place herself'. This lack of place, of 'centre', as Stevenson terms it, is manifested in her speechlessness. Once again, mimesis is seen as arising from absence and undefined relation. The silences of Rosalind result from circumstance and location, and her acquisition of eloquence occurs only in Arden, where she adopts the surrogate and split identity of Ganymede. This quasi-Lacanian interpretation was borne out by Adrian Noble's directorial concept, in which Arden was entered through a mirror and became a kind of staged unconscious, and where role-reversal was the norm. The courtiers became forest lords, Duke Frederick became Duke Senior, and Rosalind's voice was found while Celia's was lost.

This psychoanalytic approach was not lost on the reviewers of the play, particularly Michael Billington, the strapline for whose article in the *Guardian* was 'Jung Ones in Arden'. He further revealed his ability to read programme notes by commenting that 'Juliet Stevenson's Rosalind and Hilton MacRae's Orlando embody the Jungian animus and anima, each having something of the other's sexual nature.'[35] This refers directly to Noble's insertion of several Jung quotations in the programme, including the Jungian idea of a dream as being structured like a play, in which the dreamer 'plays many parts', including actor, playwright and spectator.[36] As Stevenson and Shaw comment, 'The play is so clearly not a rural romp, and Shakespeare's description of the forest bears no relation to the familiar or recognisable ... It is both an image from our nightmares and a place of infinite potential. Above all, we felt, it is a metaphor'.[37] The play-world is here understood not to be a mimetic construction, unlike characterisation, but rather a psychological or ideological landscape, a metaphorical echo of the minds of the characters. Shaw and Stevenson quickly found this textual interpretation to be problematic in performance, writing that 'it both occupied too much space and prominence, and seemed to become excessively metaphorical – in the end, we discovered, one cannot act with a metaphor'.[38]

The decision was therefore made to reduce the volume of stage imagery and keep the psychoanalytic symbolism general and vague. Stevenson's broadly psychological conception of the role and of the play as a whole remained, however, and her articulation of the problems of Rosalind's silence is grounded in a vocabulary of psycholinguistics. Rosalind's assumption of a second, masculine identity liberates her voice above all else, though interestingly for Stevenson this was very much connected to the differences of physicality:

Literally and physically the disguise releases her: you have to imagine going into doublet and hose from Elizabethan petticoat and farthingale and a rib-cracking corset. To get out of that corset must be such a release! (In fact I know it is: I loved getting out of that vogue gown into trousers, having tottered around in tight skirts and heels for the first hour). Rosalind can stretch her limbs, she can breath properly, and she's able to embark on increasingly long sweeps of thought and expression that take her ever deeper into new terrain.[39]

Once again, the actor's performance experience informs that of the character. Strikingly, however, it is Stevenson's physicality that feeds her interpretation, rather than her psychology. She locates her gender in its exterior trappings, rather than placing it as an unchanging given of performance identity. Femininity becomes as performative as the masculinity of Ganymede. Judith Butler has theorised that 'there is no gender identity behind the expressions of gender; that identity is performatively constituted by the very "expressions" that are said to be its results'.[40] Paraphrasing Rosalind, Stevenson exclaims:

> Women will get out at keyholes, or casements, or chimneys ... we will change our shape, like some strange Protean beast, and we will get out. If you [men] do repress us, you will have to take the consequences. You are directly responsible ... Your 'power' puts you in jeopardy, for if you create us, you create our waywardness too.[41]

Throughout this passage Stevenson is skirting around the fascinating proposition that gender may be as metaphorical as the forest of Arden, that the reason she cannot 'act with a metaphor' is not so much the impracticality of the design, but the overly naturalistic conception of character with which she is used to working. She falls in the gap between mimetic character and metaphorical interpretation.

Stevenson's often sophisticated analysis of the nature of her performance as Rosalind negotiates several aspects of her relationship to the Shakespearean text. The themes identified by director and cast during the rehearsal period lend a psychoanalytic dimension not just to her approach to the role but to her understanding of the play and of her own performance. Her emphasis on the decentred nature of silence within the characterisation of the part recalls that of Shaw, and has similar connections with the gendered nature of her investigation of the part and attempted reclamation of it from a phallogocentric appropriation. Connected to both these threads is Stevenson's emphasis on the physicality of performance and in particular the use of voice, the vehicle of both her psychologising of performance and her deconstruction of character. Finally, there is her awareness of the political nature of all theatre as expressed in the quotation at the beginning of this chapter, which has clear repercussions in her politicisation of the play and her participation within it.

The combination of all these elements represents a highly complex and dynamic relationship to the Shakespearean text in performance, a relationship that is most easily approached through the unifying element of these themes within performance – her use of voice. Stevenson's voice is always clamorous, even when silent, the agent of her politicised appropriation of the Shakespearean character. Her decentring of the role becomes a reinscription of that character within not just the conventional vehicle of the actor's body, but specifically and significantly within her own individual voice. In her summary of what the play means to her, Stevenson comments:

> It isn't about confirming cosy opinions or settled stereotypes. It isn't about a woman in search of romantic love. The search is for knowledge and for faith, and in that search Rosalind is clamorous – as clamorous as 'a parrot against rain'![42]

Above all, Rosalind wants to discover a second Eve in a new Eden. This is a parallel perhaps also evident within the stage imagery, which included a moment when Orlando and Ganymede gaze into an onstage brook, as she begins her 'magician' speech in 5.2, and he sees her identity change from within her reflection.[43]

These connections extend also to encompass Lacan's description of the mirror stage leading to the construction of juvenile identity: 'The child sees itself as a unity in the world ... before it is objectified in the dialectic of identification with the other, and before language restores to it its function as subject.'[44] Such a moment of reflexive identification is evident also in Harriet Walter's interesting observation concerning the moment of visual assimilation with the character:

> Unavoidably there is also a physical image in my mind of another actress playing her [the character]. She looks like Helen Mirren, Judy Parfitt, Peggy Ashcroft etc. (When does a part begin to look like me? Possibly not until I stand up in rehearsals without book in hand and look into the eyes of a fellow actor who is looking at me as the Duchess).[45]

Character is constructed dialectically with other performers on stage, just as in Noble's production Ganymede changes to Rosalind in the mind's eye of Orlando. He observed Ganymede's metamorphosis as if it were a reflection of himself, a completion of the identity split at the entry into language. The agent of this unification is the speech of Rosalind through the voice of Stevenson – the point of connection between the actor and the text. This moment then represents an onstage unification of the actor with the character and also a merging of the characters of the two lovers, each supplying that which the other lacks. The production achieved this through a merging of the physicality of the actor, particularly her voice, with stage imagery that is a powerful assertion of the dominance of stage presence over textual absence.

Richard Paul Knowles describes the development of voice work within the theatre as 'the trend towards liberating and freeing and a more psychological approach to analysis [combined with] . . . a new found desire for truth'.[46] This is reflected in the titles of many of the voice manuals now on sale: *The Need For Words*, *The Right to Speak*, *Freeing the Voice*, and so on.[47] The valid and essential training of the voice to operate freely and safely, uninhibited by the physiological constraints accrued over a lifetime of vocal abuse, is often combined in these books with an ideology of discovery of truth. Like Stevenson's Rosalind, the actor is taught that 'physical depth – deep breathing – is silently conflated with emotional depth, psychological depth, and the "deep meaning" of language, especially Shakespeare's'.[48]

This depth of exploration of the voice will yield the key not just to speaking Shakespeare, but also to uncovering the hidden truths of his words. By working on your physical centre, your diaphragm, the transcendental centre of the deified text will be revealed. As Kirstin Linklater enthuses, 'the more truly Shakespeare's text is spoken, the more . . . the poison of pain can transform to a life-restoring elixir through the alchemy of speaking Shakespeare's words'.[49] This view of voice sees it as central to truth, the vehicle for uncorking the genius of Shakespeare within the performer; the presence of the spoken word is identified to an immutable degree with the presence of truth – if the word is spoken correctly. This leads to a form of aural logocentrism in which the actor becomes a vehicle for possession by a deified message.[50]

Such ideologies can also be found within the title of the volume under discussion. The radical appropriation of Shakespeare by the actors here interviewed is implied by the use of the trope of their voices. The book continually takes pains to emphasise the verbal, spoken nature of the performers' contributions as opposed to the quasi-literary responses contained in *Players of Shakespeare*, for example. This device also, I would argue, becomes a trope for the gender of the contributors – women speak, clamorously; men write, formally. The voice becomes a site not just for meaning but for the gender identity of the speaker, a fact that becomes quite ironic when the emphases the actors place on silence, and the textual, silent nature of the printed book are concerned – the voices are contained within the text; they are Shakespeare's women.

Juliet Stevenson's employment of voice contains traces of this aural logocentrism, but it is problematised in crucial ways. An indication of this is given in her analysis of the final scenes of *As You Like It*. After Rosalind's line 'Nor ne'er wed woman, if you be not she', 'That's it,' says Stevenson:

Rosalind doesn't speak again. Rosalind, The Mouth, who has talked non-stop for the past three hours, is silent. And Celia stopped talking at the end of Act IV! ... They are silent for the same reason that they fell silent in Act I when the court invaded their attic: that the patriarchy is reasserting itself. A male god dispenses marriage: 'You and you no cross shall part/ You and you are heart in heart'. You can read that as magically cohering; but you might read these slight aphorisms the god comes up with as impossibly trite.[51]

Truth and harmony are not necessarily the reasons for Rosalind's silence; repression is also an option. Equally, truth and closure are not necessarily contained within the words spoken on stage – perhaps what they eventually contain is the status quo, an artificial order rather than a universal truth. Interestingly, Stevenson is not the first Rosalind to notice the abrupt sense of closure in the play. Over six decades previously Lillie Langtry remarked that 'the play after that scene [5.2] is over, and the only thing to whip it up at the end is the much-liked epilogue'.[52]

The play's subversive nature disappears with Ganymede. The end of the play, so often interpreted as magical and transcendent, could in fact be no more than the restoration of the established pattern after a period of licensed carnival, the final dance a 'dynamic ritualising of order'. In response to Noble's pointing out that Shakespeare was a 'monarchist, a reactionary, a bourgeois and a conservative' Stevenson argues in favour of a principle of uncertainty, a denial of closure and a slippage of meaning:

I don't think Shakespeare's plays ever attempt to answer questions. They ask questions, and they leave those question marks hanging over the heads of the actors and the audience at the end of the play ... What directors often like to do is to send the audience home with a package which has done the work for them... usually by celebrating the very status quo which the play has set out to challenge.[53]

The political nature of the Shakespearean text is therefore the responsibility of the interpreters, not of the author. Ideologies contained within the text are evaded in favour of the Shakespearean playtext as a *tabula rasa* on which meaning is imposed. The refusal to acknowledge immanent meaning in the text also becomes an excuse to abdicate textual responsibility – Shakespeare only ever asked questions; he never made statements.

Stevenson's own political agenda prevents her from innocently perpetuating any ideology of inherent, unchanging meaning and allows her to begin to question within her performance the system that advocates such belief systems. She positions herself as an appropriator of the text, a clamorous interrogator of it and of its silences, using the text as a means for temporarily unifying her own performance identity. This foregrounds the text's fragmented nature with the purpose of hinting at its inevitably politicised, ideological construction.

Stevenson's role, like that of Rosalind, is a three hours' questioning and probing of this powerful text, a search for knowledge which is always frustrated but which subordinates the authority of the transcendental playwright to the brief authority in which Stevenson dresses herself. Her tool for this is the manipulation of the union of performer with role, a temporary creation of a questioning subject that decentres the text through the medium of the interrogative voice.

The title of the chapter devoted to this production in *Clamorous Voices* is 'Rosalind: Iconoclast in Arden'. It is concerned to demonstrate the subversive elements of Rosalind's activities in the forest, and also shows Stevenson's approach to the role to be equally iconoclastic. Yet, as her attitude to the ideologies of the Shakespearean text in itself suggests, the icons she is primarily subverting are those of prescriptive, contemporary, patriarchal culture – the male director; unchanging, naturalised conservative meanings; theatrical training and practice. The one icon that largely escapes incrimination is Shakespeare. The author–god may be theoretically reduced to a form of the Foucauldian author-function in terms of the freedom Stevenson allows herself in constructing a performative identity uninhibited by any notions of propriety or tradition, yet the iconic author returns with a vengeance in the paradoxical fashion that Stevenson employs the name of Shakespeare to sanction this subversion.

It is possible that rather than an unconditional acceptance of the authority of the playwright, what this strategy demonstrates is an understanding that the site of interpretation is not so much the text as the layers of critical heritage and performance tradition that lie upon it. The text is indeed a construct, but it is a construct in which Stevenson as an actor must locate herself in order to realise her performance.

IV

This chapter of *Clamorous Voices* looks not just at the individual work of one actor but also focuses on the relationship between the two principal performers, Shaw and Stevenson, and, by extension, the onstage relationship between Celia and Rosalind. The professed resolve of these actors in tackling the play was to 'jettison stereotype', both in terms of their working methods and in the presentation of the two characters on stage:

> We soon discovered a mutual interest in redefining that friendship, sharing as we did a frustration about the portrayal of female friendships on stage. It often seems that the audience's relish of that friendship is based on the actresses' working in spite of each other – the kind

of traditional 'feminine behaviour' which is based on divisiveness rather than bonding.[54]

The iconoclasm of this approach is based upon the formation of intriguing new identities within the rehearsal room and on stage. The character is identified with the performer not just in conventional ways, psychologically or archetypically, but ideologically. These actors look for ways in which the political (rather than domestic or emotional or everyday) experience of the character mirrors their own. A further level of recognition is then introduced as the actors' experience within rehearsal is seen to mirror that of the characters within the text. A multiple reflection of identity is in evidence, with all these images drawn together on stage to create a complex and charged act of mimesis. Macro- and microscopic levels are juxtaposed and then merged to create a form of gendered solidarity between actor and role that is essentially political. Stevenson links herself with Rosalind in many ways, and also establishes connections with Shaw as Celia in rehearsal and Celia as Shaw in performance. The friendship cultivated between the two reads almost as a deliberate attempt to create a platform on which their work can be built rather than a natural case of attracting personalities. Like people in extreme circumstances, they form a fast friendship as if it were necessary for their survival.

The merging of identities between the two women is consistently foregrounded, not least in their discussions of the roles, which they have repeatedly carried out together. A prime example of this is the *Players of Shakespeare* article that is co-authored by them both. Just as in the play, one character is silent when the other is vocal, so in these actors' accounts of the production they speak in turn and together, their print identities depending on the presence of the other. The politics of their feminism not only informs their approach to their work; it defines it. Their relationship with the text is couched in a rhetoric of political awareness and a heavily gendered agenda, reflecting their performance choices and rehearsal-room construction of identities.

They conclude their collaborative article in *Players 2* by commenting: 'If the struggle for women is the struggle to be human in a world which declares them only to be female, then this was the territory of *As You Like It* which most engaged and challenged us.'[55] Interestingly, this carefully phrased concluding remark is itself unwittingly commented upon within Stevenson's *Clamorous Voices* chapter:

> The word 'if' here enters as a protagonist ... 'if' you believe, it will happen. But 'if' is also a challenge: now is the time your deeds must match your words, and so must mine ... As Touchstone will say, 'Much virtue in "if".'[56]

In the case of Stevenson, her deeds very much match her questioning of the words, and also the interrogation of the silences to emphasise an investigation that is highly modern in nature though the vehicle is still the territory of a 400-year-old forest. Her awareness of the political nature of theatre and the sophisticated manner in which she carefully deconstructs and subverts the status quo within her performance led this Rosalind to be, on the surface at least, very much Stevenson's woman today.

This politicisation is once again sanctioned through reference to the authorial subject; Stevenson is propelled along this subversive path by the authority of the Shakespearean name. Whilst this name is used uncompromisingly to attack and establish different political standpoints, the force with which this is done remains Shakespearean. The text itself is never attacked, it is inscribed by Stevenson as precisely the neutral agent of purity that it was believed to be by the New Criticism. The distinction between the two standpoints is simply a political one – for Stevenson, this purity is not conservative, it is radical – a questioning rather than an eternalising of ideology. But still this presupposes the existence of ideology outside the text, to which the plays are an uncontaminated response. In themselves, they are insulated and untarnished. Only if this is supposed to be the case can Stevenson's political operations be successful; only if the neutrality of the text is real can it be this driving force for a political interrogation of the ideologies of the status quo. Much virtue, indeed, in 'if'.

Stevenson's brand of iconoclasm had been evident also in the previous Stratford season when she played Isabella, in a production of *Measure for Measure* again directed by Adrian Noble. In many ways, the iconoclastic approach taken by the actor is more rigorous here than in *As You Like It*. Once again, Stevenson finds herself focusing on the word 'if', in a rhetorical move that pre-empts her later discussion:

> 'If' occurs thousands of times in this play. It's a protagonist in *Measure for Measure*. 'If' takes us into compromise, that muddy territory. But it provides for possibility, for miracle. 'If' is the imaginative means of projecting someone else's experiences onto yourself. It is a doorway, leading to empathy, identification, recognition.[57]

As did the Forest of Arden, Vienna here acquires another resident in the shape of the word 'if'. Language becomes a character in itself, to be interacted with. It also becomes a tangible prop to be used on stage, as Stevenson explains in the context of Isabella's debates with Angelo: 'They're parrying with verbs, fighting this out with scrupulous variations on the infinitive "to be".'[58]

This literalisation of the corpus with which she works hints at Stevenson's view of the Shakespearean word, which is far from unconditional awe. On the contrary, she argues, negotiates and experiments with it exactly as she would a fellow cast member, and so it comes in precisely for the kind of rigorous analysis she devotes to all other aspects of her performance.

More than this, in her obsession with the conjunction 'if', Stevenson begins to outline a sophisticated understanding of mimesis as an approach to characterisation. Her performance of both Rosalind and Isabella is focused around the empathetic 'if' of make-believe. In *As You Like It* this becomes the magical transformative power of myth, close, in fact, to the loose Stanislavskyan concept of 'magic if'; in *Measure for Measure* it is the humane, merciful power of empathy. In this she is, consciously or otherwise, also echoing Peter Brook: 'In everyday life, "if" is a fiction, in the theatre "if" is an experiment. In everyday life, "if" is an evasion, in the theatre "if" is the truth. When we are persuaded to believe in this truth, then the theatre and life are one.'[59]

In theorising imaginative processes by reference to the conjunction 'if', both Brook and Stevenson can be understood as acting according to principles of mimetic fictionality; engagement with a work of art operates as a game of imaginative make-believe in which the work is used as a prop in the creation of a fictional world, in which we then participate. The philosopher Kendall Walton explains:

> Representations are things possessing the social function of serving as props in games of make-believe, although they also prompt imaginings and are sometimes objects of them as well. A prop is something which, by virtue of conditional principles of generation, mandates imaginings ... Propositions whose imaginings are mandated are fictional, and the fact that a given proposition is fictional is a fictional truth.[60]

Stevenson is thus moving from a conception of the playworld as a post-Stanislavskyan surrogate reality to a conception of it as a parallel, fictional world with its own rules. Her employment of a process of fictionality enables her to switch between aspects of character without searching for consistency, as she would from one game to another. But it does not lessen the power of the performance, nor does it indicate complete detachment from her work. As Walton states:

> These worlds are merely fictional, and we are well aware that they are. But from inside they seem actual – what fictionally is the case is, fictionally, really the case – and our presence in them ... gives us a sense of intimacy with characters and their other contents. It is this experience that underlies much of the fascination representations have for us and their power over us.[61]

This leads not to a search for truth, but for fiction, not a commitment to belief, but to imagination. This is a theory of mimesis that has much in common with Sidneyan ideas, familiar to Shakespeare, of a 'figuring-forth' of perception via imaginative representation, and characterises Stevenson's approach as highly unusual and rhetorically dense.

Stevenson's understanding of fictionality extended to her costume, as she refused to wear the conventional nun's habit and be thus categorised throughout by such a strong signifier. As she said, 'the actress, not the dress, should do the acting'. She continues: 'There ought never to be a sense that Isabella is in fancy dress, because I think one of the points the play is making is that the Duke is.'[62] The Duke is operating on a different fictional level, and one of the principal indicators of this is costume, which must neither lose its metatheatrical currency for him nor acquire it for her. The notions of virginity and virtue indicated by nun's apparel are also relevant here, as Stevenson resists the concept, unwillingly undergone by Paola Dionisotti's Isabella, of a habit becoming gradually soiled as the play proceeds.

V

Virtue becomes central to both actors' discussions of the character, as indicated by the title of the chapter: 'Isabella: Virtue Betrayed?' Rutter sets the scene with characteristic brio: "Feminist" had made its way into the vocabulary; chastity was being reclaimed as a sexual option; Isabella was ripe for recuperating; and Juliet was ready to take on the challenge.'[63] Stevenson herself expands on this more calmly:

> Characters in Shakespeare's plays have become mythologised, half-buried under a rubble of literary and theatrical tradition, which generates certain preconceptions, particularly moral ones. The women are judged far more harshly than the men, and those judgements serve to restrict their parameters as characters.[64]

It is not the Shakespearean character that is flawed, but the accumulation of ideological detritus that weighs the role down. Stevenson saw it as her task to remove this 'rubble'. Once again, it is the rubble of subsequent ideological practice rather than any inscription of that ideology within the text itself. Her initial targets were preconceived notions of Isabella and her reasons for entering the novitiate:

> With Isabella, the assumption is that she is fleeing into the convent because she's frightened of her own sexuality. That's a moral judgement ... I had only one instinct about Isabella when I started, which was that she should be looked at not as a frigid hysteric with a big problem about sex, but that we should kick off by exploring the positive reasons for entering a convent.[65]

These reasons are, in a nutshell, that 'she provides a focus for Vienna to see itself'.[66] Isabella, in Stevenson's reading, becomes a moral mirror in which a corrupt or flawed society can see its deficiencies reflected back at itself. Once again, Stevenson is using metaphors of mirrors and reflection to construct a character, this time to position that character within the play. That position is of conscience, a Christian corrective to the amorality of Vienna, and it was with this woman of principle that Stevenson identified. As with Rosalind, there are echoes here of Stevenson's own view of herself, encapsulated in Rutter's repeated descriptions of her as 'iconoclast'. In this case, Stevenson has to destroy the iconic representation of Isabella, defined in relation to the sexually promiscuous male characters as frigid or lacking in humanity. Instead of going along with this comfortable objectification of the character, she chose to rehabilitate her subjectivity, discover her inconsistencies. In this case, the focus is the explicitly gendered concept of virtue that Stevenson sought to problematise – much 'if', indeed, in virtue.

Yet again, the actor picks up on the initial silence of the character: 'What I found interesting is how little Isabella has to say', and these silences become the key to the role. She wanted the audience to 'listen to this person. Listen afresh . . . she shapes, and continually reshapes, where she's going through her language.'[67] The centre of her performance was again linguistic, both in terms of what the character says and does not say, words and silence. It is this logocentrism that also becomes the reflective embodiment of the character's morality, Isabella's words exposing the truth within other characters as Stevenson discovers Isabella's truth within her lines – 'They are as they speak'. In response again to the directorial impositions experienced by Dionisotti four years earlier, Stevenson ensured that few of her lines were cut, believing that 'the energy of the language Isabella uses is a reflection of the enormous bank of strength she has in her. If a director deprives her of that language, he deprives her of her strength.'[68] Understanding clearly the power given to her by the text, Stevenson here effects an appropriation of Shakespeare's words, 'reclaiming' the words themselves. As Marjorie Garber comments:

> 'Man' and 'woman' are already constructed within drama; within what is often recognised as 'great' drama, or 'great' theatre, the imaginative possibilities of a critique of gender in and through representation are already encoded as a system of signification.[69]

In rehabilitating the character from years of stereotypical representation, Stevenson is subjectifying a role whose customary reception is one of objectification, and attempting to project that subjectivity onto the audience by exactly the methods of identification and empathy she mentions earlier. More specifically, however, she is attempting to reach a certain sector of the audience in particular:

[It is] of no interest to women, watching women being victims. What's interesting is to watch how women collude with what is done to them or how they create it, their part in it. Our active participation in it is much more interesting to explore than our blamelessness, our victimisation. I want women's roles to be as complex in performance as men's, to restore them to their flawed and rounded complexity.[70]

Her audience here is female, and Stevenson is inferring an active participation in the performance event by the spectator. Her approach therefore is aiming also to appropriate a response from the women in the audience, a response that endows both the character and themselves with agency.

In doing this she achieves two things. First, she accomplishes her political aim of restoring three-dimensionality to a wrongly stereotyped character – an accomplishment not lost on reviewers, of whom Irving Wardle was representative when he commented that Stevenson portrayed 'a heroine as emotionally direct as Beethoven's Leonora'.[71] Second, and more problematically, she recentres her performance on the character's language. She runs the risk of replacing the errors of previous misinterpretation with an icon of her own making; the new-improved, reflective Isabella who is herself the centre of the play's moral universe. Stevenson

discovered an Isabella who is confronting the collapse of values, of beliefs of justice, of virtue. If the same perilous mouth that is condemning her brother for fornication is soliciting her, and if there is no appeal to justice because the judge himself is corrupt, that's chaos; by saying 'yes' to Angelo, Isabella would be committing herself to chaos. It's not her chastity that's at sake, it's order ... It is more than a personal decision: it has political resonances too.[72]

The personal becomes the political as it must in Stevenson's interpretation – her own gender becomes political upon the stage, as does Isabella's. Actor and role are reciprocally reflective, each centring the other in a reconstruction of iconography that idealises Isabella rather than demonises her, realises her virtue rather than resents her supposed priggishness. Even more than with Rosalind, Stevenson here is re-emphasising the power of the Shakespearean word, commenting that 'as a philosopher Shakespeare may well have been a conservative, but as a playwright he's a radical'.[73] Stevenson is at first glance here asserting the value of Shakespeare as artist, above and beyond his politics, with the interesting grammatical subtext that his conservatism is in the past tense whereas his radicalism is contemporary and continuing. However, her earlier assertion that 'all theatre's political' allows us to read this more subtly. If the politics of theatre reside in its form and structure, and if Shakespeare is formally radical, then consequently there exists a continual tension in Shakespearean texts between overt political conservatism and covert radicalism. *As You Like It* and *Measure for Measure* are both demonstrated in her arguments to reinscribe the status quo at the end, despite the political radicalism of the heroines. Plot becomes the vehicle for order, and character for subversion.

Yet this formulation results in an easy binary that privileges the performer. Nor is it a formulation that Stevenson accepts, and Isabella, advocate of order and stability, becomes the paradoxical agent of deconstruction. This is achieved through the most famous silence in all of the texts discussed in *Clamorous Voices* – that of Isabella's response to the Duke's proposal of marriage at the end of the play.

Rutter observes in the introduction that 'all of them [the contributors] are sceptical of happy endings'.[74] Stevenson takes this further in a comment on Shakespearean endings in general: 'There isn't a fixed end to a play. The script ends. The words run out. But the ending – that's something that has to be renegotiated every performance.'[75] Closure is provided by the actor on stage, not by the words on the page. The negotiation that takes place between actors and audience provides a unique and temporary point of finality every time the play is performed. Stevenson talks of renegotiating the end of *Measure for Measure* in every performance. Walter comments that her production of *All's Well* ended 'on a knife edge' each time due to the contrasting views of the director, Trevor Nunn, Bertram (Mike Gwilym) and Walter herself. Such moments of reproduction are in a constant state of flux. In the case of *Measure for Measure*, Paola Dionisotti was clear as to Isabella's reply to Vincentio:

> The fact that Shakespeare doesn't script Isabella's answer to the Duke's proposal but just leaves it with his line, 'Give me thy hand', tells me she doesn't give him her hand. I think it's quite clear. Shakespeare is leaving an extremely big void there, a figure who goes completely silent and makes no commitment. She doesn't. He asks. But she doesn't.[76]

One of the most interesting aspects of this commentary is its complete contradiction of her actions in performance – Dionisotti's Isabella in fact eagerly accepted the Duke, a fact remarked upon by several contemporary reviewers. Typical of these was Michael Billington, who in a piece describing the production as 'spellbinding', remarked:

> Paola Dionisotti offers us an unconventional Isabella ... She presents us with a girl gradually waking up to her own femininity and delighting in the Duke's serpentine ploys. I wish she could find something a little more momentous than squeals of 'oh' (as if someone had just pinched her bottom) to register her burgeoning humanity. But her coy

flutter when the Duke suddenly kisses her and her delight in being a woman at least prepares the ground psychologically for her acceptance of the final marriage offer.[77]

Billington's rhetoric here conveniently includes many of the features found to be worth unpacking by Stevenson: the correspondence established between 'femininity' and sexuality and then 'humanity', and the equation of this movement with psychological coherence. A stereotyped view of female sexuality – even if this is largely the result of Kyle's directorial impositions – becomes a signifier for psychological realism in this article. Nor is he alone in this. Jane Lapotaire finds herself employing a similar language of sexual innuendo and psychological continuity in discussing her Isabella:

> That's what turns Angelo on so much, not that she is beautiful, but her energy and passion channelled into chastising him. It makes him think what it would be like channelled into a fulfilled female ... To me it is right that at the end she accepts the Duke. She has made a similar journey into self-discovery. They are ideally suited.[78]

The revealing and unconscious sexual imagery used by Lapotaire – 'channelling' into a 'female' – points to the superficiality of her discourse. It is precisely this stereotyping of gender and conventional acceptance of superficial pantomime as 'psychology' that Stevenson attempted to subvert five years later.

Dionisotti's evasion of this performance decision in her later account reflects her strained relationship with her director, Barry Kyle. As with Shaw's characterisation of Katherina, the actor's problematic experience with the male director comes to inform her relationship with a problematic male character, in this case the Duke. In describing rehearsing the scene in which Isabella is persuaded to participate in the 'bed-trick' scheme, Dionisotti remarks:

> No person who thought the way I had told the audience I thought, and the way I believed and behaved, would then have been persuaded by what was going on in that scene. I did handsprings trying to make sense of it. Finally the only way I could play it was to endow the Friar with total paternalism. I constructed a persona who was the experienced man of the church. And since I was quite new to the church he became my unquestioned authority figure. Except that I was constantly disturbed by the things he was suggesting.[79]

The echoes here of an unhappy relationship with a strong-minded director are, I suggest, pronounced, and can even be extended to an unquestioning faith in the authority of Shakespeare to get her through the experience. The character's religious faith becomes an excuse for the actor to find some level of belief in her role.

The third nun/whore in that production, Juliet Stevenson, made sure that the same problems would not arise when she tackled the role, and her account is notable for a clear reaction against Dionisotti's characterisation, despite her assertion that the latter's version was 'wonderful'. Stevenson's interpretation was certainly more her own, and developed from her concept of virtue. Harriet Walter, discussing Helena, remarks:

> I confess to finding ideas like 'virtue', 'honour', 'chastity' – big concepts in Shakespeare – hard to get into. Helena showed me a way through that, which was to do with substituting the word 'integrity' – me being true to me, a sense of self ... Maybe this helps with someone like Isabella in *Measure for Measure*, if you replace 'chastity' with 'integrity'.[80]

This was precisely Stevenson's solution, endowing the character with 'an awesome sense of integrity'.[81] Importantly, this does not lead automatically to the adoption of a strong, Stanislavskyan through-line, but rather to a location of the character's selfhood within morality, rather than psychology. Stevenson is not making a moral judgement on the character, but constructing the character as a series of moral choices. She exemplifies this by quoting Isabella's speech in 2.2:

> There is a vice that most I do abhor,
> And most desire should meet the blow of justice,
> For which I would not plead, but that I must,
> For which I must not plead, but that I am
> At war 'twixt will and will not. (29–33)

It is in the gap between these moral absolutes that the character of Isabella is located:

> She's absolutely split in two ... She's pulled between two moving vehicles in the speech. Her quandary is there in all those verbs that keep replacing one another: 'I would not', 'I must', 'I must not', 'I am'. The way I am hangs suspended at the end of the line leaves her dangling over a precipice.[82]

Stevenson emphasises the active nature of morality as a sequence of decisions, rather than a passive state of acceptance. Character as morality is extant only within the action, the verb, and is as transitive as the grammar that contains it. She explains this further:

Shakespeare's characters live in the moment they speak. They don't premeditate their soliloquies in the wings and bring them on prepared. They are as they speak. An image is chosen, which leads to the next image, each thought to the next, and if you follow the structure of the verse, you will discover the way the character's mind is working towards its conclusion.[83]

A preoccupation with virtue and morality leads to a sense of momentary integrity – character is not a developmental, linear model but an assembly of actions, realised as a whole by the presence of the actor's body. As in Truffaut's film, continuity and coherence are therefore always constructed retrospectively by the spectator, using the binding signifier of the body. This process avoids the logocentrism of conventional interpretation by virtue of the continual reinscription of the subject moment by moment – the text is manifested as utterance, rather than the performance being subordinate to the language.

Walton's work on fictionality again becomes relevant here, as he differentiates between the experience of an actor and that of a spectator in a theatrical performance:

Whether it is fictional that the character portrayed is afraid depends just on what the actor says and does and how he contorts his face, regardless of what he actually thinks or feels. It makes no difference whether his actual emotional state is anything like one of fear.[84]

In contrast, the experience of the spectator, here called Charles, is more internal:

Fictional truths about Charles are generated partly by what he thinks and feels, by his actual mental state. It is partly the fact that he experiences [a form of] quasi-fear, the fact that he feels his heart pounding, his muscles tensed and so on, that make it fictional that he is afraid; it would not be appropriate to describe him as afraid if he were not in some such state.[85]

Importantly, it is not necessary for the actor to participate in this state for the effect to be achieved, and psychological constructions of a performance by an actor can be seen as deriving from that actor's experience as a spectator (including on stage observing) rather than from his or her experience in performance. As a result of Charles's experience, 'his realisation that fictionally he is afraid is based largely on introspection, just as his realisation that he is really afraid would be'.[86]

The meaning of a performance is located and constructed in the mind of the spectator willingly engaging in the fiction created in part by the actor on stage. Stevenson's emphasis on the conditional nature of the language of the characters she plays, and the placing of her performance self in textual gaps and silences, aids this redirection of the performance towards the audience and effects a deconstruction of her own theatrical presence.

This approach can also be seen as a method of deconstructing the traditions in which the actor is located, as another embodiment of the heritage of a role. Again, the ethical nature of performance is invoked in the shape of a peculiarly gendered kind of history – reputation. Katherine Eisaman Maus has convincingly argued for a construction of Early Modern selfhood through a process of narrativisation, in which interiority is conveyed through the establishment of a related history. In relation to the position of women, this can become extremely problematic, as Maus exemplifies by reference to *Othello*:

> [Othello] does not know how to imagine Desdemona apart from her history, but in the play world, for a young woman to have a history can mean only one thing. Insofar as she is a person, Othello imagines, she must have something to narrate; but if she has something to narrate, she is no longer innocent.[87]

Presupposition of subjectivity implies presupposition of guilt. This is precisely the bind that Stevenson finds herself combating in her approach to Isabella, and it is encountered too by Harriet Walter in her experience of playing Helena and Imogen (in *All's Well That Ends Well* and *Cymbeline* respectively).

VI

Walter begins by echoing sentiments expressed by the other actors in the volume:

> The most frustrating thing about playing Shakespeare's women is having to dislodge the audience's preconceptions of who they are. Shakespeare's men don't have 'reputations'. His women do. The men can be compromised or compromising. The women can be neither. The women have to be liked.[88]

Leaving aside the contentious issue of whether Shakespeare's men are construed as having reputations (as we have seen, an actor preparing to play Hamlet may disagree vehemently), this passage is familiar in intent from those of Stevenson and Shaw, and predicates another position from which contemporary assumptions can be attacked, perhaps deconstructed, but the transcendence of the sacred text be ultimately reaffirmed. She swiftly deviates from this path, however, and in startling fashion. When describing her ideological approach, she comments: 'First you have to clear away the heroine's reputation. Then you have to clear away the received idea about the character. Then you have to clear away the idea of character itself.'[89]

This comment is remarkable for several reasons. First, there is the differentiation made between the reputation of the heroine and the received idea about the character. This indicates a particularly gendered understanding of the way in which characters are stereotyped. They are portrayed, as Stevenson implied, in relation to their virtue or chastity – a sexual identity is ascribed to them – before general assumptions of character are even considered. Edward Burns comments:

> Fame, in European humanist tradition, is the process by which history is made, the process by which the individuals of whose stories history is made up join the 'already known'. It is also the process by which they are defined as individuals. They become an epitome of their deeds, a kind of schema of the virtues and vices that those deeds represent.[90]

This process of fame can be crippling for a female character defined largely by several centuries of limited or prejudiced interpretation. If reputation and fame are constituent parts of their scripted identities, they are also extant in the parallel history of the play's production and reception.

Walter's distinction between these aspects of female stereotyping, however, implies an awareness of the value system in which Shakespeare is operating as much as that of modern society. She is putting into operation an awareness of what Rutter has elsewhere called the 'anti-play' contained within every performance of Shakespeare today.[91] This represents the ghostly presence of traces of the original staging from which the text results within every modern reproduction. In her later writing Walter also refuses to divide these ideologies into safe categories of past and present – rather she is aware of their largely indissoluble nature:

> In Shakespeare's day actors wore their own sixteenth-century dress even playing ancient Greeks. It was understood that the play was not about Then but about Now. When we watch the latest production of a classical play, we are necessarily watching Now's take on Then, and it is our own connection to both which gives the exercise its relevance.[92]

Whilst Walter is generalising – the Peacham illustration to *Titus Andronicus* has long indicated the use of some historical costuming on the Renaissance stage[93] – she is doing so to put forward an important point. Ideological debris is not just a result of modern response to the text; it is there in the text itself, to be confronted and dealt with. Walter wryly remarks: 'I find it curious to think that as a modern actress my opportunities in the

Shakespearean repertoire have been determined by the limitations or excellences of two or three generations of Elizabethan boy players.'[94]

This movement towards a critique of the text and the conditions of its original production is followed also by an awareness of the necessity of critiquing the methodology of that text's reproduction today – 'You have to clear away the idea of character itself.' This is a response to the post-Stanislavskyan anachronism of modern actor-training, an emerging awareness of the inadequacy of such an approach for Shakespeare. Walter goes on to argue: 'We tend to think of "character" as something psychologically coherent or consistent, something that has sub-text. Shakespeare doesn't think of "characters" like this.'[95] Juliet Stevenson acknowledges this point when she remarks that 'the language tells you who the character is moment by moment, word by word. You need not, should not, be bound by notions of psychological consistency.'[96]

Though they ultimately retain ideas of superordinate coherence, in the case of both actors this constitutes an important challenge to established ideologies of performance, reminiscent of the comments of McDiarmid and Troughton encountered in Chapter 1. Peggy Ashcroft comments that 'it's the actress's job to make a character whole', while Jane Lapotaire remarks that 'whatever psychological explanation you come up with, it's got to be watertight for you'.[97] The actors in *Clamorous Voices* are running against the grain of their own job description.

Julia Kristeva, in her essay 'Women's Time', comments:

> It can now be seen how women ... might try to understand their sexual and symbolic differences in the framework of social, cultural and professional realisation, in order to try, by seeing their position therein, either to fulfil their own experience to a maximum or – but always starting from this point – to go further and call into question the very apparatus itself.[98]

This questioning, of the apparatus of the Shakespearean text, of that of modern ideological appropriations of it, of that of her own inculcated ideological, professional and political position towards these things, is evident throughout the responses of Stevenson and Walter to playing Shakespeare. The position from which Walter begins this questioning is no less sophisticated:

> Our language is not really our own. It is an established tradition, a club we are forced to join in infancy and whose rules we agree to obey ... If we can make language our own, we can bend it to suit our needs, but when language feels like 'theirs', it becomes a gag on the soul.[99]

In a sense this is a problematic, even contradictory, statement. Walter acknowledges the constructedness of the linguistic order and simultaneously posits the existence of the soul without this order, a classic logocentric formulation ripe for deconstruction. Yet the coherence within this contradiction, the force of the desire for unity with which Derrida identifies such a move, requires investigation.

Perhaps more than any other of the actors talking through *Clamorous Voices*, Walter makes repeated and determined use of a discourse of subjectivity. She talks of reconciling her artistic choices with 'her conscience', she 'knows [her] own values'. In a convenient summary of her own approach that is fast becoming a motto for her various publications, she states that 'Acting is what I do with who I am.'[100] She continually relates her ideological manoeuvres to, if not a fixed, then certainly a repeatedly redefinable notion of self.

As with other actors, this sense of her own identity is transferred into a consideration of that of the character. In discussing Imogen, for example, she remarks:

> There is a great sense of self. And the challenge of finding out what that self consists of: what is the heart of me if you strip everything away? My crown, my power, my position, my ideals, my husband. And from now on, even my sexual identity. What is me? ... That's what it means to be a female achiever in these plays. It's not about getting a man, 'achieving' a husband. It's about finding out what your self consists of.[101]

Walter's feminism, no less real than that of her co-speakers, focuses on the relationship between a personal idea of subjectivity, problematised by that of the inconsistent character, with the various strategies of ideology that constitute both actor and character. Walter's selfhood is central, but not fixed. Her approach involves a constant redefinition of herself and relocation of character under the constraints of an arbitrary linguistic order. She predicates her approach not on a permanent signified but a recognisable if changeable signifier. This once again is close to Kristeva's concept of a 'fluid and free subjectivity' with the intent to

> bring out – along with the singularity of each person and, even more, along with the multiplicity of every person's possible identifications – the relativity of his/her symbolic as well as biological existence, according to the variation in his/her specific symbolic categories.[102]

By interiorising social ideologies and making her own self the ideological focus on the stage, by problematising the relationship of actor with text and with author-function, Walter suggests a reappropriation of the sacred word that is, like Kristeva, at once feminist, psychoanalytic, subjective and radically disruptive. This is a move that, also like Kristeva, is at the expense of any unifying exterior discourse, including those of feminism or psychoanalysis themselves, an evasion of any monolithic presence outside that of the constantly changing body of the actor herself.

Moreover, Walter's awareness of the inseparable juxtaposition of play and anti-play hints at a further reconfiguration of the relationship of performance to text. Stevenson's quasi-Marxian approach focuses on the means of contemporary production, but Walter implies a more subtle and gendered re-emphasis on reproduction. All performance is necessarily reproduction, a re-entry of the text into the performative arena that problematises the linear relationship between author, text and performance presupposed by other commentators. It is a view echoed much later by Deborah Warner, who describes her approach to theatre as wanting 'the possibility of the performance re-birthing and engaging an audience night after night'. Moreover, her directorial role is 'to enable the organic process to happen so that the actors' performances can live'.[103] In other words, she acts as midwife to the performance.

Kristeva talks of the process of maternal reproduction as 'the slow, difficult and delightful apprenticeship in ... forgetting oneself',[104] and goes on to locate art as another arena in which this reproductive erasure can occur: 'It is in the aspiration towards artistic ... creation that woman's desire for affirmation now manifests itself.'[105]

The union of actor with role in the case of Walter is not a submerging or a conflation of identity, but a reproduction of it, a formulation of another self, seen as the goal of both actor and role. The cyclical nature of this reproductive aim incorporates both repeated performance and the continuing reproduction of the text on stage, metamorphosing and reinventing itself every time. It thus offers an account of authorial positioning and ideological interaction with self that is truly radical. It can also be extended further to become a critique of the linear, unique and universalist discourses of Stanislavskyan training, which are not only anachronistic but can also be seen as inherently patriarchal, privileging and reaffirming the ideological apparatus of the political status quo.

Even this position, however, has its flaws. Walter's quasi-Kristevan approach appropriates her gender as agent of deconstruction and, in Rutter's buzzword, recuperation. Yet gender itself can be seen as, far from being a stable signified, a signifier in a constant state of flux. As Butler comments:

> The presumption of a binary gender system implicitly retains the belief in a mimetic relation of gender to sex whereby gender mirrors sex or is otherwise constructed by it. When the constructed status of gender is theorised as radically independent of sex, gender itself

becomes a free-floating artifice, with the consequence that 'man' and 'masculine' might just as easily signify a female body as a male one, and 'woman' and 'feminine' a male body as easily as a female one.[106]

The result of this is that:

> Because there is neither an 'essence' that gender expresses or externalises nor an objective ideal to which gender aspires, and because gender is not a fact, the various acts of gender create the idea of gender and without these acts there would be no gender at all.[107]

In short, if gender, as with other aspects of self, is a 'free-floating signifer', then any ideas of maternal biological determinism are untenable.

VII

Juliet Stevenson begins to approach this stance in her analysis of Rosalind, when she writes: 'Her capacity to play all roles and to manipulate her own disguise successfully is potentially a danger to Rosalind: Rosalind might have so interesting a time as Ganymede that she's unable to commit herself to Rosalind again.'[108] Quite how radical this view is can be seen by comparing it to previously accepted wisdom about the gender of the character. Jane Lapotaire writes: 'The crucial thing for me is that Rosalind never becomes a boy at all, her psychology is totally feminine, her attitudes are feminine – she is a fully rounded and understanding woman.'[109] This is a view closer to conventional, even outdated, notions of femininity than it is to Stevenson's reconceptions: Helen Faucit declared in 1893:

> I need scarcely say how necessary it is for the actress, while carrying it through with a vivacity and dash that shall avert from Orlando's mind every suspicion of her sex, to preserve a refinement of tone and manner suitable to a woman of Rosalind's high station and cultured intellect.[110]

For Stevenson, Rosalind enters into another level of fictionality, the character begins to perform, and so any sense of stable gender identity is lost. Rosalind's identity is explored through 'vigorous role-play', in which the performance of Rosalind as Ganymede is potentially subverted when 'Ganymede starts performing'. This idea of a performative gender identity comes very close here to Butler's own thesis:

> Acts, gestures, and desire produce the effect of and internal core or substance, but produce this on the surface of the body, through the play of signifying absences that suggest, but never reveal, the organising principle of identity as a cause. Such ... enactments, generally

construed, are performative in the sense that the essence or identity that they otherwise purport to express are fabrications manufactured and sustained through corporeal signs and other discursive means.[111]

As Butler herself points out, this has significant repercussions for the Kristevan notion of maternal power and the authority of reproduction. If gender is always performative and there is no pre-discursive point of origin, then the Kristevan binary of the symbolic and the semiotic on which her concept of maternal subversion depends is itself deconstructed, as is its unavoidable emphasis on the normative force of the heterosexual drive.

Unsurprisingly, this leads to problems for the actor, for if the stability of gender, selfhood and the performative subject is questioned, then notions of integrity have to be jettisoned along with those of interiority. Thus the emphasis placed by Walter and Stevenson on moral integrity in their discussions of Isabella and Helena is cast in doubt. Yet it is not a complete and coherent moral standpoint, a kind of Aristotelian understanding of character as *ethos*, that these actors are claiming. Rather it comes closer to a construction of a role as evidenced through *praxis*, through action. As Walter comments:

> You play each scene or each beat, however contradictory, or however incompatible it seems with what has gone before or comes after. You play the moment for its integrity, for what it is. Then, by the end of the play, the character is an accumulation of all those separate moments.[112]

Integrity is momentary and always already past, fleeting and deferred, constituted by exterior rationalisation of repetition. In this can be found an echo of Nietzsche's formulation that 'there is no being behind doing, effecting, becoming; the doer is merely a fiction added to the deed – the deed is everything'.[113]

We have here a return to Walton's idea of fictionality, in which what matters is the game, the fiction itself, in which the artefact is a prop to aid the participant – in the case of theatre, the spectator, not the actor. Stevenson's earlier comment on the participation of the female spectator in the victimisation of women on stage is relevant here – she understands her role in the fiction, understands that she is a player in a world created by the spectator. Only by conceiving of the theatrical event in this fashion, indeed, can the actor hope to have a political impact, to change the way a spectator thinks. Theatrical power is situated in the decentring of a performer's presence – in the gaps and silences so obsessed upon by all the actors in this volume. Located within the fiction, the actor is free to experiment with levels of performativity that paradoxically require inconsistency and disjunction. As Stevenson says:

It's like acting. You go on stage and you're two people: you are yourself, the actress, but you are also a character; you are bound by the dictates of playing somebody else within a piece of make-believe. You may be feeling all manner of things about what a fellow actor is doing, but you don't have the means in the fiction to express that. What you do have is a variety of choices by which you can make those feelings manifest, without destroying the fiction.[114]

Stevenson here articulates a sophisticated concept of performativity that extends to her own role as actor. Juliet is performing an actor playing Rosalind performing Ganymede who then, in her words, 'begins to perform'. Butler asks 'what kind of gender performance will enact and reveal the performativity of gender itself in a way that destabilises the naturalised categories of identity and desire?'.[115] Stevenson here provides the answer. Such a sophisticated performance of Rosalind points to a kind of mimesis that is always already 'figured forth' and displaced, imitating not an original but the fiction of such an original.

Agency, such as it is, is located within the variations of this endless recurrence of mimesis. A realisation of this allows concepts of authority and representation to be subverted from within, permitting the possibility of a form of liberation. In this way, the fictionality of character liberates the performativity of the gender of the actor, undermining and interrogating patriarchal, logocentric notions of psychology, linear construction, reputation, tradition and selfhood. Consequently 'the deconstruction of identity is not the deconstruction of politics; rather, it establishes as political the very terms through which identity is articulated'.[116] In the rhetoric of Stevenson, Shaw and Walter these terms are extremely subtle indeed, perhaps more so than Butler herself envisages in her work on gender performativity.

These actors begin with an engagement with text that is located in absence, in what is left unsaid, and therefore in their own gendered bodies as signifiers of meaning. They move to a negotiation with the Shakespearean author-function that resists a simple denunciation or reaffirmation of authority, instead working to refashion that authority through textual absence and through the dynamic between a fluctuating notion of character and that of embodied performance. In addition, the shifting history of interpretation and performance experience itself textures their approaches: the enforced awareness of their gender identity in rehearsal, in performance, and in the reputations and traditions of roleplaying within their profession. This in turn is further nuanced by the exigencies of playing opposite other gendered performers employing similar operations from within the constructs of characters themselves carrying out gender performances, frequently inside multiple layers of fictionality. Above all, the notion of a fixed self interacting with a stable character is radically jettisoned; both the actors' own identities and that of the characters they embody are continuously redefined within the context of each individual performance moment.

This can be seen as a remarkably sophisticated reworking of mimesis. Instead of Girardian ideas of mimetic competition, or even Lacou-Labarthe's post-Derridian concept of mimesis as an act of depropriation, Stevenson and Walter in particular postulate a notion of mimetic responsibility to the moment and resist any imposed ideas of regular or fixed containment of meaning. In this formulation, performance is understood as existing in the juxtaposition of a repeated and reciprocal series of mimetic acts, drawing on the signification of text, history and the bodies enunciating these discourses, and decipherable to a spectator only through that spectator's active participation in the fiction. A conventional hermeneutics of interpretation is rejected in favour of a destabilised mimesis of performance and performativity. The final achievement of these actors is to begin to discard the previously accepted baggage of performance ideologies in favour of a liberating and continually redefinable performativity of selfhood, one that in turn continually redefines the drama they appropriate as a vehicle for this process of refashioning.

Notes

1 C. Rutter, *Clamorous Voices: Shakespeare's Women Today*, ed. by Faith Evans, London: The Women's Press, 1988, p. xi. All subsequent references to this text will use the abbreviation *CV*.

2 J. Stevenson, in 'Theatre in Thatcher's Britain: Organising the Opposition', *NTQ Symposium*, 1988, p. 121.

3 Throughout the discussion I have preferred the gender-neutral noun 'actor' to 'actress', while of course retaining the latter word when it is used by actors themselves.

4 For feminist discussions of Shakespeare see, among many others, R.P. Barker and I. Kamps, *Shakespeare and Gender*, London: Verso, 1996; S. Case, *Performing Feminisms: Feminist Critical Theory and Theatre*, Baltimore, Md.: Johns Hopkins University Press, 1990, and *Feminism and Theatre*, London: Macmillan, 1988; C. Lenz, G. Greene and C. Neeley (eds), *The Woman's Part: Feminist Criticism of Shakespeare*, Urbana, Ill.: University of Illinois Press, 1980; E. Schafer, *Ms-Directing Shakespeare*, London: The Women's Press, 1998 etc.

5 *CV*, p. xxv.

6 Ibid., p. 100.

7 Ibid., p. xxiv.

8 Ibid., p. 6.

9 M. Billington, *The Guardian*, 10.9.87.

10 J. Miller, interview with T. Grimley, *Birmingham Post*, 29.8.87.

11 Ibid.

12 *CV*, p. 17.

13 Ibid., p. 8.

14 J.C. Trewin, *Birmingham Post*, 9.9.87.

15 *CV*, p. 20.
16 *The Taming of the Shrew*, 4.3, 80, in Wells and Taylor (eds), *Complete Works*, 1987.
17 *CV*, p. 24.
18 D. Salter, 'Acting Shakespeare in Postcolonial Space', in J. Bulman (ed.), *Shakespeare: Theory and Performance*, London: Routledge, 1995, pp. 113–33, p. 115.
19 *CV*, p. xvii.
20 P. Gay, *As She Likes It*, London: Routledge, 1994, p. 118.
21 *CV*, p. xviii.
22 Ibid., p. 25.
23 Shaw in C. Woddis (ed.) *Sheer Bloody Magic: Conversations with Actresses*, London: Virago, 1991, p. 135.
24 *CV*, p. 101.
25 Ibid., p. 114.
26 Ibid., p. 115.
27 Shaw and Stevenson, 'Celia and Rosalind in *As You Like It*', in Jackson and Smallwood (eds), *Players of Shakespeare 2*, Cambridge: Cambridge University Press, 1988, pp. 55–71, p. 67.
28 See, for example, J.C. Trewin's *Birmingham Post* review of 24.4.1985.
29 Billington, *The Guardian*, 25.4.85, characterised Bruce Alexander's Oliver as 'a Machiavellian in an anorak'.
30 An interesting comparison, as described in Chapter 1, is the dominance of Shylock in *The Merchant of Venice*, and the accepted shift of emphasis onto that character from Portia.
31 Woddis, *Sheer Bloody Magic*, p. 135.
32 Shaw and Stevenson, *Players 2*, p. 71.
33 *CV*, p. 101.
34 Shaw and Stevenson, *Players 2*, p. 59.
35 Billington, *The Guardian*, 25.4.85.
36 This was clearly an offshoot of the production's symbolism, and remained firmly that. The archive video reveals that the production no more than hinted at the Jungian themes, and they find no place in the discussions of the play by Stevenson or Shaw, or indeed in interviews given at the time by Noble or in the account in *Players of Shakespeare 2* by the production's Jaques, Alan Rickman. Nevertheless, the suggestion of Arden as a loosely psychological world of the unconscious was deliberate, even if its precise psychoanalytic school of thought was left unclear, with Jung, Freud and Lacan all jostling for position in the production's imagery.
37 Shaw and Stevenson, *Players 2*, p. 63.
38 Ibid., p. 64.
39 *CV*, p. 104.
40 J. Butler, *Gender Trouble*, London: Routledge, 1990, p. 25.
41 *CV*, p. 114.
42 Ibid., p. 121.
43 The connections with Eve's discovery of self in Book Four of *Paradise Lost* are strong: 'As I bent down to look, just opposite,/A shape within the watery gleam appeared/Bending to look on me', J. Milton, *Paradise Lost*, bk 4, 460–62, in S. Orgel and J. Goldberg (eds), *John Milton*, Oxford: Oxford University Press, 1991.

44 J. Lacan, 'The Mirror Stage', in *Ecrits*, London: Routledge, 1977, p. 2.
45 'H. Walter on Playing "The Duchess of Malfi"', in M. White, *Renaissance Drama in Action*, London: Routledge 1998, pp. 88–100, p. 89.
46 R.P. Knowles, 'Shakespeare, Voice and Ideology: Interrogating the Natural Voice', in Bulman, *Shakespeare, Theory and Performance*, 1995, pp. 92–113, p. 95.
47 All by P. Rodenburg and published by London: Methuen in 1993, 1992 and 1994 respectively.
48 Knowles, 'Shakespeare, Voice and Ideology', p. 98.
49 K. Linklater, *Freeing Shakespeare's Voice*, New York and London: Theatre Communications Group, 1992, p. 196.
50 It is important to note that such mystification of vocal technique is largely unshared by Cicely Berry, perhaps the most significant figure in the field, or indeed her associates Lyn Darnley and Andrew Wade. See, for example, C. Berry's *The Actor and His Text*, New York: Charles Scribner's Sons, 1988, and *Voice and the Actor*, London: Harrap, 1973.
51 *CV*, p. 119.
52 L. Langtry, *The Days I Knew*, London, 1925.
53 *CV*, p. 120.
54 Shaw and Stevenson, *Players 2*, p. 57.
55 Ibid., p. 71.
56 *CV*, p. 118.
57 Ibid., p. 47.
58 Ibid.
59 P. Brook, *The Empty Space*, Harmondsworth: Penguin, 1968, p. 157.
60 K.L. Walton, *Mimesis as Make-Believe*, Cambridge, Mass.: Harvard, 1990, p. 69.
61 Ibid., p. 273.
62 Ibid., p. 42.
63 Ibid., p. 40.
64 Ibid., p. 40.
65 Ibid., p. 41.
66 Ibid., p. 50.
67 Ibid., p. 42.
68 Ibid., p. 42.
69 M. Garber, *Vested Interests: Cross Dressing and Cultural Anxiety*, London: Routledge, 1992, p. 15.
70 *CV*, p. xxvii.
71 I. Wardle, *The Times*, 6.10.83.
72 CV, p. 51.
73 Ibid., p. 28.
74 Ibid., p. xxvii.
75 Ibid., p. 51.
76 Ibid., p. 40.
77 Billington, *The Guardian*, 29.6.78.
78 Lapotaire, quoted in J. Cook, *Women In Shakespeare*, London: Harrap, 1980, p. 43.
79 *CV*, p. 39.
80 Ibid., p. 76.
81 Ibid., p. 48.
82 Ibid., p. 45.

83 Ibid., p. 43.
84 Walton, *Mimesis as Make-Believe*, p. 242.
85 Ibid., p. 243.
86 Ibid., p. 240.
87 K.E. Maus, *Inwardness and Theatre in the English Renaissance*, Chicago, Ill.: University of Chicago Press, 1995, p. 124.
88 CV, p. 73.
89 Ibid., p. 76.
90 E. Burns, *Character, Acting and Being on the Pre-Modern Stage*, London: Macmillan, 1990, p. 63.
91 See C. Rutter, 'Kate, Bianca, Ruth and Sarah: Playing the Woman's Part in *The Taming of the Shrew*', in M. Collins (ed.), *Shakespeare's Sweet Thunder: Essays on the Early Comedies*, London: Associated University Presses, 1997, pp. 176–215.
92 H. Walter, *Other People's Shoes*, London: Viking, 1999, p. 239.
93 See Bate's 1995 Arden edition of *Titus*, pp. 39–42 for a discussion of the drawing.
94 *CV*, p. xxiv.
95 Ibid., p. 76.
96 Ibid., p. 43.
97 Cook, *Women in Shakespeare*, pp. 39 and 43.
98 J. Kristeva, 'Women's Time', in T. Moi (ed.), *The Kristeva Reader*, London: Blackwell, 1986, pp. 197–214, p. 198.
99 Walter, *Other People's Shoes*, p. 181.
100 See, for example, the dust-jacket of *Other People's Shoes*; CV, p. 94; Walter, 'The Heroine, the Harpy and the Human Being', *New Theatre Quarterly*, spring 1993; interview in *Daily Telegraph*, 5.8.95 etc.
101 *CV*, p. 96.
102 Kristeva, 'Women's Time', p. 210.
103 D. Warner in G. Giannachi and M. Luckhurst (eds), *On Directing*, New York and London: Faber, 1999, pp. 137 and 138.
104 Kristeva, 'Women's Time', p. 206.
105 Ibid., p. 207.
106 Butler, *Gender Trouble*, p. 6.
107 Ibid., p. 140.
108 *CV*, p. 106.
109 Cook, *Women in Shakespeare*, p. 20.
110 H. Faucit, Lady Martin, *Of Some of Shakespeare's Female Characters*, London, 1893, p. 165.
111 Butler, *Gender Trouble*, p. 139.
112 *CV*, p. 76.
113 Nietzsche, *The Genealogy of Morals*, trans. W. Kaufmann, London: Vintage, 1969, p. 45.
114 *CV*, p. 109.
115 Butler, *Gender Trouble*, p. 139.
116 Ibid., p. 141.

A bad epitaph

The play's the thing, all right, but there is no play at all without the
actor.

W. Redfield[1]

Pardon my folly, writing of folly; if you knew [me], you would say *'nec
mirum'*. If my pardon may be purchased then so [be it], if not you may bid
me keep my fools company.

R. Armin[2]

In the preface to his edition of Robert Armin's *Fool Upon Fool* E.F.
Lippincott speculates that 'for its original audience, the work may
have had added appeal through its association with the London theatre,
much as today the writings of even relatively unimportant theatrical
persons have a kind of fascination'.[3] The concept of an actor writing
about his profession, be it in so circuitous a fashion as Armin, here
requires justification through a connection with the glamour of theatrical
otherness. Much like the autobiographies of twentieth-century film stars,
the work is seen as existing as a public relations byproduct of a parallel
career. Lippincott continues: 'For us, Armin is significant not because he
may have written this and a few other ephemeral works but because he
played Shakespeare's great fool roles – Touchstone, Feste, the unnamed
Fool in King Lear.'[4] Armin is decisively stripped of any literary merit
and located simply as a tool of a greater writer – the roles he plays are
'Shakespeare's', despite the undoubted influence the clown would have
had on their performance. Armin is here the subject of a re-appropriative
move in favour of Shakespeare the canonical author. The actor, even in
the moment of his presence as writer and as player, is elided, made
absent to such an extent that Armin's work is treated almost as part
of the Shakespeare apocrypha, retitled by Lippincott and shoehorned
into what is really a separate genre, as *A Shakespeare Jestbook*.[5] Like
Groucho Marx, perhaps the Elizabethan clown's greatest cinematic

heir, Armin is presented as being unworthy of belonging to any tradition that would have him as a member.

Part of my project in this book has been to contribute to the rehabilitation of actors as commentators on the texts they perform, and on the conditions of their performance, rather than viewing them purely as adjuncts to a broader Shakespearean scholarship. Talking of the importance of theatrical performance as commentary on Shakespeare, W.B. Worthen writes that in order 'to make its insights valuable, we need to locate its claims as criticism [and] to displace the enervating polarization of "text against performance"'.[6] The twin points identified here focus on the need both to identify a new critical discourse, and to amend an existing one. Worthen is undoubtedly correct to note that the latter task needs to be achieved before the former can begin: for performance criticism to be truly productive, it must learn to exist between the two disciplines of textual criticism and theatrical practice. In this sense, this book has sought broadly to initiate a methodological shift towards alternative, but valuable, objects of study.

The accounts of actors fall naturally into this gap, by their very nature bridging the two disciplines. It is disappointing therefore to read Worthen's own, somewhat unguarded, appraisal of these texts as 'an unreliable and possibly irrelevant index of the performances they describe'.[7] Such remarks, recalling Lippincott's reference to 'unimportant theatrical persons', hardly contribute positively to his own loosely deconstructionist project of reconciliation. It is indeed the case that recollections of performance by performers are rarely an accurate reproduction of the circumstances of that production, but in this they are no more 'unreliable' than any other such subjective moments. They are of undoubted archival value, but their real significance lies elsewhere. It has been my intention to demonstrate that these texts are far from 'irrelevant'; in fact they constitute a vital and unexamined field of inquiry that cannot but enhance the subtlety and value of performance theory and practice.

In the particular case of Shakespeare I have argued that their significance resides in an understanding of authorial invocation and appropriation that leads to the construction of a complex and diverse spectrum of performative identities, both within a specific performance of a play and in the form of a more general rhetorical positioning. Such identity can be seen as conservative and reassuring, as in the case of theatrical tradition and history, though as I have demonstrated such history is rarely free from subversive or questioning moments. It can also be explicitly radical and challenging, as in the case of feminist appropriations of performance, though conversely these instances too are often combined with unconsciously traditionalist manoeuvres. In all cases a relationship with the cultural artefact of the Shakespearean name has to be negotiated, as does the issue of the construction of a performance self in relation to such a powerful author-function. The processes by which these operations are carried out have been detailed in the body of my text.

The value of such an analysis lies predominantly in the increased understanding of the workings of the text and of the cultural positioning of Shakespeare afforded by these accounts and essays, both in the larger discourse of society and, crucially, within the institutions of theatre themselves. These actors talk of how Shakespeare means theatrically, not only to a spectator – the usual concern of performance criticism – but also to the performer, who for a time inhabits the Shakespearean signifier more fully than any other reader of the plays. If we are sufficiently attentive, we can gain insights from the writings of actors that may otherwise be hidden to conventional scholarship.

Such writing enables us also to consider and evaluate strategies and techniques of performance more closely and thus to appreciate in more detail the workings of a still under-theorised art form. The staging of Shakespeare and its accompanying influence on the projection of textual meaning, both historically and in our own time, still requires more attention from the academy. The written work of actors is an essential contribution therefore to Performance Studies in general, as well as to those working with Shakespeare in particular. Performance theory operates largely through a reading of Shakespeare via the sign of the actor's performance. My intention has been to problematise that sign by means of the actor's self-reflexive discourse upon her or his own semiotic status.

Additionally, these accounts facilitate the comprehension of the workings of a profession that has produced some of the dominant social, cultural and iconographic sign systems of the twentieth century. In the West, this profession is still influenced by an umbilical connection to Shakespeare above any other single figure. The contours of internal traditions of inheritance and totemic transmission are therefore a necessary object of study within the cultural history of Shakespearean reception. Furthermore, actors' essays on performance can also contribute to the continuing understanding of the politically hegemonic appropriation of the dramatist over the nineteenth and twentieth centuries, and can act as a critical paradigm for his attempted reclamation by contemporary liberal ideologies, in this country and elsewhere.

The accounts of actors continually challenge and undermine received wisdom about performance in general, and acting Shakespeare in particular. At its most nuanced, this writing posits a construction of selfhood that exists very much on discursive boundaries, a liminal positioning produced in a triangular relationship with author-function and spectator. This is a position evident in the figure of Robert Armin; speaker of the Shakespearean text, improvisor of his own material within that role, and commentator and biographer of his own profession. By emphasising a commitment to playing a role as well as constructing a character, and thinking in terms of *praxis* as much as *ethos*, many of the actors here discussed are actively reconfiguring the manner in which Shakespearean characterisation is theorised, and the means by which the Shakespearean text functions on the stage.

Above all, this represents an engagement with processes of mimesis, with the ways in which the various discourses surrounding a Shakespearean text are negotiated and investigated and then projected onto a performance. Increasing numbers of actors are engaging with these operations in sophisticated and complex ways that challenge and recast the perspectives of academic theory. What is happening in the theatre is at least as illuminating and as compelling as what is happening in the study.

In this area, as in many others, I have indicated that there is much that the academy can learn from practitioners about the collision of Early Modern selfhood with more modern conceptions of subjectivity. Both in the particularities of technique and the generalities of politics (especially those of gender), actors continually have to confront notions of ideology, psychology and socialisation alien to their own. In doing this they are forced to engage directly with the mechanisms of a text's construction in a manner more forceful than other readers of the texts, which emphasises the considerable historical gap between the time of this construction and our own. Actors continually have to make these plays work today by somehow bridging that gap, a near-impossible process that often leads to the default employment of a discourse of universality. As Harriet Walter has written:

> Just because the feminist movement has created a language and found a voice, does not mean that late twentieth century women are a completely new breed unlike any known before. I have held on to this idea, as a means of building a bridge between myself and the characters from the past I have had to play.[8]

The ideologies evident in the invocation of the Shakespearean name by practitioners are of course not exclusive to them. It is in their aptly representational and condensed presence in these accounts that we can learn more of the operations by which Shakespeare is refashioned as our contemporary by those who appropriate the plays. In engaging in the process of authorial invocation, these accounts in their diversity provide a complex model of self-fashioning, both of the actor in relation to the text, and of the spectator in relation to the text of the actor's performance. In their inevitable, if sublimated, engagement with the rhetorical processes of mimesis the more sophisticated of these accounts detail the difficult and intricate means by which Shakespearean authority is produced, and its connection to superordinate discourses which also to a large extent construct the reader and the spectator.

Finally, by discussing from within the operations of mimesis the diverse negotiations with authority that constitute rhetorical invocation, particularly in connection with subjectivity, history, politics and ideology, the publications of actors constitute a vital and influential addition to the study of Shakespeare in performance. I have proposed ways in which this corpus can be approached and integrated into more familiar critical methodologies; there are of course other routes for analysis and other texts to examine.

In view of the limited amount of material I could include in this book, and of the sceptical views of most of the actors mentioned towards theatrical closure, it is perhaps fitting that I should end with Carol Rutter's account of trying to draw the interviews that constitute *Clamorous Voices* to a close, only to be met with cries of 'Wait! Wait! There's more to say about this!'[9]

Notes

1 W. Redfield, *Letters from an Actor*, New York: Cassell & Co., 1966, p. 30.
2 R. Armin, 'Conclusio', *A Nest of Ninnies* (1608), in J.P. Feather (ed.), *The Collected Works of Robert Armin*, New York and London: Johnson Reprint Corporation, 1972, 2 vols, vol. 1, G3.
3 H.F. Lippincott, preface to *A Shakespeare Jestbook: Robert Armin's Foole Upon Foole (1600), A Critical Old-spelling Edition*, Salzburg: Salzburg Studies in English Literature, 1973, p. vii.
4 Ibid.
5 By the standards of similar books by contemporary authors Armin's writing is unusually free of debts to his predecessors. See Feather's introduction to *Quips Upon Questions* in *The Collected Works of Robert Armin*, vol. 1.
6 W.B. Worthen, *Shakespeare and the Authority of Performance*, Cambridge: Cambridge University Press, 1997, p. 190.
7 Ibid., p. 42.
8 H. Walter. 'The Heroine, the Harpy and the Human Being', *New Theatre Quarterly*, spring 1993, p. 110
9 C. Rutter, *Clamorous Voices*, London: The Women's Press, 1988, p. xxvii.

Appendix

Details of *Players of Shakespeare* essays, 1985–98

Players of Shakespeare 1, edited by Philip Brockbank, 1985

Actor	Role	Pages
Patrick Stewart	Shylock in *The Merchant of Venice*	11–28
Sinead Cusack	Portia in *The Merchant of Venice*	29–40
Donald Sinden	Malvolio in *Twelfth Night*	41–66
John Bowe	Orlando in *As You Like It*	67–76
Geoffrey Hutchings	Lavatch in *All's Well That Ends Well*	77–90
Brenda Bruce	Nurse in *Romeo and Juliet*	91–102
Tony Church	Polonius in *Hamlet*	103–14
Michael Pennington	Hamlet	115–28
Richard Pasco	Timon of Athens	129–38
Roger Rees	Posthumus in *Cymbeline*	139–52
Gemma Jones	Hermione in *The Winter's Tale*	153–66
David Suchet	Caliban in *The Tempest*	167–79

Players of Shakespeare 2, edited by Russell Jackson and Robert Smallwood, 1988

Actor	Role	Pages
Daniel Massey	The Duke in *Measure for Measure*	13–32
Edward Petherbridge	Armado in *Love's Labour's Lost*	33–44
Ian McDiarmid	Shylock in *The Merchant of Venice*	45–54
Fiona Shaw and Juliet Stevenson	Celia and Rosalind in *As You Like It*	55–72
Alan Rickman	Jaques in *As You Like It*	73–80
Zoë Wanamaker	Viola in *Twelfth Night*	81–92
Kenneth Branagh	Henry V	93–106
Roger Allam	Mercutio in *Romeo and Juliet*	107–20
Niamh Cusack	Juliet in *Romeo and Juliet*	121–36
Frances Barber	Ophelia in *Hamlet*	137–50
Antony Sher	The Fool in *King Lear*	151–66
Ben Kingsley	Othello	167–78
David Suchet	Iago in *Othello*	179–99

Players of Shakespeare 3, edited by Russell Jackson and Robert Smallwood, 1993

Actor	Role	Pages
Roger Allam	The Duke in *Measure for Measure*	21–41
Maggie Steed	Beatrice in *Much Ado About Nothing*	42–51
Deborah Findlay	Portia in *The Merchant of Venice*	52–67
Gregory Doran	Solanio in *The Merchant of Venice*	68–76
Sophie Thompson	Rosalind and Celia in *As You Like It*	77–86
Nicholas Woodeson	King John	87–98
Ralph Fiennes	King Henry VI	99–113
Penny Downie	Queen Margaret in *Henry VI* and *Richard III*	114–39
Anton Lesser	Richard of Gloucester in *Henry VI* and *Richard III*	140–59
Simon Russell Beale	Thersites in *Troilus and Cressida*	160–73
Brian Cox	Titus Andronicus	174–88
Philip Franks	Hamlet	189–200
Harriet Walter	Imogen in *Cymbeline*	201–19

Players of Shakespeare 4, edited by Robert Smallwood, 1998

Actor	Role	Pages
Christopher Luscombe	Launcelot Gobbo in *The Merchant of Venice* and Moth in *Love's Labour's Lost*	18–29
David Tennant	Touchstone in *As You Like It*	30–44
Michael Siberry	Petruccio in *The Taming of the Shrew*	45–59
Richard McCabe	Autolycus in *The Winter's Tale*	60–70
David Troughton	Richard III	71–100
Susan Brown	Queen Elizabeth in *Richard III*	101–13
Paul Jesson	Henry VIII	114–31
Jane Lapotaire	Queen Katherine in *Henry VIII*	132–51
Philip Voss	Menenius in *Coriolanus*	152–64
Julian Glover	Friar Lawrence in *Romeo and Juliet*	165–76
John Nettles	Brutus in *Julius Caesar*	177–92
Derek Jacobi	Macbeth	193–210

Bibliography

Adelman, Janet, 'Iago's Alter Ego: Race as Projection in *Othello*', in Stephen Orgel and Sean Keilen (eds), *Political Shakespeare*, New York and London: Garland 1999, pp. 111–31.

Agate, James (ed.), *These Were Actors: Extracts from a Newspaper Cutting Book, 1811–1833*, London: Hutchinson and Co., 1946.

Alexander, Catherine M.S. and Wells, Stanley (eds), *Shakespeare and Race*, Cambridge: Cambridge University Press, 2000.

Anon., *An Authentic Narrative of Mr Kemble's Retirement from the Stage*, London: John Miller, 1817.

Archer, William, *Masks or Faces?* in Denis Diderot, *The Paradox of Acting* and William Archer, *Masks or Faces?* With an introduction by Lee Strasberg, New York: Hill and Wang, 1957.

Aristotle, *On Rhetoric: A Theory of Civic Discourse*, trans. and ed. George A. Kennedy, Oxford: Oxford University Press, 1991.

——*Poetics*, trans. and commentary Gerald Else, Ann Arbor, Mich.: University of Michigan Press, 1967.

——*Poetics*, trans. and ed. Malcolm Heath, Harmondsworth: Penguin, 1996.

Armin, Robert, *Foole Upon Foole, or Six Sortes of Sottes* and *A Nest of Ninnies* in J.P. Feather (ed.), *The Collected Works of Robert Armin*, 2 vols, New York and London: Johnson Reprint Corporation, 1972, vol. 1.

——*A Shakespeare Jestbook: Robert Armin's Foole Upon Foole, 1600, A Critical Old-spelling Edition*, ed. H. F. Lippincott, Salzburg: Salzburg Studies in English Literature, 1973.

Armstrong, Philip, 'Watching Hamlet Watching: Lacan, Shakespeare and the Mirror/Stage' in Terence Hawkes (ed.), *Alternative Shakespeares 2*, London: Routledge, 1996, pp. 216–36.

Artaud, Antonin, *The Theatre and its Double*, trans. Mary Caroline Richards, New York: Grove, 1958.

Asleson, Robyn (ed.), *A Passion for Performance: Sarah Siddons and Her Portraitists*, Los Angeles, Calif.: J. Paul Getty Museum, 1999.

Aston, Elaine and Savona, George, *Theatre as Sign System: A Semiotics of Text and Performance*, London: Routledge, 1991.

MRI has greater sensitivity for detecting vascular lesions, but so much so that periventricular changes and mild/ moderate white matter lesions are seen in over 50 per cent of non-demented elderly subjects (O'Brien *et al.* 1996). While the classic studies of Tomlinson *et al.* (1970) suggested that between 50 and 100 mls of infarcted tissue was needed to develop dementia, imaging studies do support the current notion that both severity and location of lesions are important (Liu *et al.* 1992), though much work still needs to be undertaken to establish the value of imaging changes. Until then, neuroimaging changes should be interpreted in conjunction with clinical history and cognitive and neurological examination. A common mistake is the overinterpretation of small and insignificant cerebrovascular lesions in patients with otherwise typical features of AD or other dementias.

SPECT scanning may be diagnostically useful in VaD, showing a patchy, asymmetric distribution of cerebral blood flow instead of the bilateral, symmetric changes suggestive of AD or DLB (if temporoparietal) or frontal lobe dementia (if frontal). Confirmation of this SPECT utility is still required. The usefulness of other imaging techniques, such as functional MRI, remains to be established.

Summary

The diagnosis of VaD or mixed dementia requires the synthesis of clinical assessment with correlation of neuroimaging vascular lesions. Which of the currently proposed diagnostic criteria will achieve the most widespread use and have the most accurate clinical pathological correlations is not yet clear. Similarly how to integrate neuropathological findings for final diagnosis is not yet settled. With up to 30 per cent of dementia having mixed pathologies of AD and vascular disease, resolution of some of these issues is mandatory to further our clinical approach and to set the way for appropriate patient selection for emerging VaD pharmacological treatments. Whether there will be a differential response of AD, VaD, and mixed dementias to cholinesterase inhibitors or muscarinic agonists remains to be established.

Dementia with Lewy bodies

It has been increasingly recognized that a primary progressive disorder with the clinical profile of fluctuating cognitive impairment, parkinsonism, and psychotic features, characterized neuropathologically by the presence of Lewy bodies in the cortex, is an important cause of dementia. A variety of diagnostic labels have been attached to this condition, including the Lewy body variant of Alzheimer's disease (Hansen *et al.* 1990), dementia associated with cortical Lewy bodies (Byrne *et al.* 1991), diffuse Lewy body disease (Dickson *et al.* 1991), and senile dementia of Lewy body type (Perry *et al.* 1990). A recent consensus meeting advocated use of the term dementia with Lewy bodies (DLB) (McKeith *et al.* 1996), which will be adopted here.

The prevalence of DLB in the community is unknown, but recent neuropathological autopsy studies have found DLB in 15 to 25 per cent of all cases, suggesting it may be the largest pathological subgroup after pure AD. Accurate antemortem diagnosis of DLB is important as such patients have a characteristic and often rapidly progressive clinical syndrome, respond adversely to neuroleptic (antipsychotic) medication, which may hasten their decline, and may possibly be the best responders to cholinesterase inhibitors (McKeith *et al.* 1996).

Clinical diagnosis

The use of standardized criteria

At present, there are no internationally agreed criteria for diagnosing DLB, which does not feature in either ICD-10 or DSM IV. However, shortly after detailed clinical descriptions of case series were reported, two sets of operationalized criteria were proposed (Byrne *et al.* 1991; McKeith *et al.* 1992). These were broadly similar, although the criteria of Byrne *et al.* specified parkinsonism as mandatory for diagnosis. Subsequently, both groups and others agreed on consensus criteria at an international workshop held at Newcastle in 1995. These are shown in Table 14.5 (McKeith *et al.* 1996), though it is important to note that neither the two original sets of criteria nor the current consensus criteria have as yet been prospectively validated by clinical pathological study.

Clinical features

DLB may initially present with dementia, parkinsonism, or both together—the order of onset of mental and motor symptoms being highly variable, particularly in elderly people. Sometimes patients with classic Parkinson's disease develop a dementia characteristic of DLB. As with AD, onset of DLB is insidious and the disorder progressive. Some cases progress rapidly to an end stage of profound dementia and parkinsonism after 1 to 5 years, although in other cases the course may more closely resemble that of AD. The prevalence and demographic features of DLB still have to be accurately defined, though some evidence suggests that men may be more susceptible than women and also have poorer prognosis (Kosaka 1990).

Fluctuation in cognitive function is common and regarded by some as the hallmark of DLB. In the early stages, patients may show global deficits in cognitive function which alternate with periods of normal or near-normal performance. No typical diurnal pattern to this fluctuation has been identified and the periodicity and amplitude of fluctuations are variable, occurring

Table 14.5 Proposed Consensus Criteria For the Clinical Diagnosis Of Probable And Possible Dementia With Lewy Bodies (DLB)

1. The central feature required for a diagnosis of DLB is progressive cognitive decline of sufficient magnitude to interfere with normal social or occupational function. Prominent or persistent memory impairment may not necessarily occur in the early stages but is usually evident with progress. Deficits on tests of attention and of frontal-subcortical skills and visuospatial ability may be especially prominent.

2. Two of the following core features are essential for a diagnosis of probable DLB, one is essential for possible DLB.
   (a) Fluctuating cognition with pronounced variations in attention and alertness.
   (b) Recurrent visual hallucinations which are typically well formed and detailed.
   (c) Spontaneous motor features of parkinsonism.

3. Features supportive of the diagnosis are
   (a) Repeated falls
   (b) Syncope
   (c) Transient loss of consciousness
   (d) Neuroleptic sensitivity
   (e) Systematized delusions
   (f) Hallucinations in other modalities.

4. A diagnosis of DLB is less likely in the presence of
   (a) Stroke disease, evident as focal neurological signs or on brain imaging.
   (b) Evidence on physical examination and investigation of any physical illness, or other brain disorder, sufficient to account for the clinical picture.

Reprinted from IG McKeith *et al.* Consensus guidelines for the clinical and pathological diagnosis of dementia with Lewy bodies (DLB). *Neurology* 1996; 47: 1113–24 by permission of Lippincott-Raven Publishers.

rapidly (lasting minutes or hours), slowly (weekly or monthly), or both. In many cases fluctuation is so severe as to resemble episodes of delirium. As such, before making the diagnosis of DLB, it is important to exclude several conditions including medication toxicity, intercurrent illness, and vascular events as possible causes for the clinical picture. Fluctuation is often a difficult symptom to elicit and quantify but it is helpful to ask carers for detailed descriptions of the patient's mental abilities and functioning at their best compared to their worst. Caregivers frequently report that patients with DLB are somnolent, show reduced awareness, and have episodes of going blank or switching off.

Visual hallucinations are reported in over 90 per cent of cases of DLB. They are typically recurrent, well formed, and detailed and appear to be the only psychotic symptom which reliably distinguishes DLB from AD or VaD (McShane *et al.* 1995). Themes are often of people and animals intruding into the patient's home though inanimate objects and abstract perceptions such as writing on walls and ceilings are not unusual. Some degree of insight into their unreality is often present. It is the persistence (over several months) of visual hallucinations in DLB which helps to distinguish them from episodic perceptual disturbances which may occur transiently in other dementias or during a delirium.

Spontaneous motor features of parkinsonism, typically mild, are frequently present. Rigidity and bradykinesia are the usual symptoms while hypophonic speech, masked faces, stooped posture, and a slow shuffling gait may also be seen. Resting tremor is less common. As parkinsonian signs may be found in advanced AD and other dementias, parkinsonism appearing for the first time late in the course of the dementia is consistent with a diagnosis of DLB, but not specific for it. An adverse and extreme reaction to neuroleptics is suggestive of DLB and has been found in up to 50 per cent cases in some series.

Personal and social function, as well as performance in daily living skills, may be markedly impaired, even in the early stages of the illness by a combination of cognitive and neurological disability. Other features which would support the diagnosis of DLB include a history of repeated falls, syncope, and transient loss of consciousness with no other definable cause as well as systematized delusions and hallucinations in other modalities (see Table 14.5).

Neurological signs consistent with parkinsonism, as described above, may be found but are not essential for the diagnosis. Focal neurological signs are absent. Their presence, with a history of fluctuating cognitive impairment, should raise the suspicion of a VaD. As with AD, a variety of non-localizing neurological signs may be present in DLB patients with advanced dementia.

Fluctuation in cognition should, where possible, be demonstrated by documenting variability in cognitive performance over time using standardized cognitive tests such as the MMSE. It may be possible during mental status examination to observe attentional impairments and infer the presence of hallucinations from a patient's behaviour. This is most likely if the patient is observed passively, as both will diminish during a conversational interview. Cognitive testing either performed in the office or with the assistance of a neuropsychologist should include tests of memory, attention, visuospatial ability, and executive function (see also Chapter 7). While DLB patients have global impairments or dementia (by definition), they exhibit a profile of impairment quite distinct from those seen in AD. There are prominent deficits on tests of executive function and problem solving such as the Wisconsin Card Sorting Test, the Trail-Making Test, and verbal fluency. There may also be disproportionate impairments on tests of visuospatial performance such as block design, clock drawing, or copying figures. Memory may be less impaired (McKeith *et al.* 1996). However, with the progression of dementia, this selectivity may be lost, making differential diagnosis based upon clinical examination difficult in the later stages when deficits in memory, language, and other cognitive skills overlap those seen with Alzheimer's disease.

Atkins, G. Douglas and Bergeron, David M., *Shakespeare and Deconstruction*, London: Peter Lang, 1988.

Aubrey, John, *Brief Lives*, c.1667, ed. Richard Barber, Suffolk: Boydell Press, 1975.

Auerbach, Nina, *Ellen Terry: Player in her Time*, New York and London: Norton, 1987.

Auslander, Philip, *From Acting to Performance*, London: Routledge, 1997.

Bakhtin, Mikhail, *Rabelais and his World*, London: Blackwell, 1966.

——*The Dialogic Imagination*, Austin, Tex.: University of Texas, 1981 and 'The Formal Method in Literary Scholarship', 1928 reprinted in Pam Morris (ed.), *The Bakhtin Reader: Selected Writings of Bakhtin, Medvedev and Voloshinov*, London: Edward Arnold, 1994.

Barker, R.P. and Kamps, Ivo, *Shakespeare and Gender*, London: Verso, 1996.

Barrymore, John, *Confessions of an Actor*, New York, 1926.

Barthes, Roland, 'From Work to Text' and 'Introduction to the Structural Analysis of Narratives', in *Image, Music, Text*, trans. and ed. Stephen Heath, London: Fontana, 1977, pp. 165–75.

——*Textual Analysis of Poe's Valdemar*, 1973 trans. Geoff Bennington, in David Lodge (ed.), *Modern Criticism and Theory*, Harlow: Longman, 1988, pp. 172–95.

Barton, Anne, *Essays, Mainly Shakespearean*, Cambridge: Cambridge University Press, 1985.

Barton, John, *Playing Shakespeare*, London: Methuen, 1984.

——*Playing Shakespeare*, RSC/LWT/Channel 4, 1984.

Bate, Jonathan (ed.), *Titus Andronicus*, Arden III, London: Routledge, 1995.

Bate, Jonathan, Levinson, Jill L. and Mehl, Dieter (eds), *Shakespeare and the Twentieth Century: Selected Proceedings of the International Shakespeare Association World Congress, Los Angeles, 1996*, New York and London: Associated University Presses, 1996.

Beckerman, Bernard, *Shakespeare at the Globe*, London: Macmillan, 1962.

Bennett, Susan, *Performing Nostalgia: Shifting Shakespeare and the Contemporary Past*, London: Routledge, 1996.

Benson, Constance, *Bensonian Memories*, London: Butterworth, 1926.

Berger, Harry, Jr, *Imaginary Audition: Shakespeare on Stage and Page*, Berkeley and Los Angeles, Calif.: 1989.

Berkoff, Steven, *I am Hamlet*, New York and London: Faber and Faber, 1989.

——*Coriolanus in Deutschland*, London: Amber Lane, 1992.

Bernhardt, Sarah, *The Art of the Theatre*, trans H.J. Sherring, London: G. Bles, 1924.

Berry, Cicely, *Voice and the Actor*, London: Harrap, 1973.

——*The Actor and His Text*, New York: Charles Scribner's Sons, 1988.

Berry, Ralph, *On Directing Shakespeare: Interviews with Contemporary Directors*, London: Hamilton, 1989.

Bevington, David, *Action is Eloquence: Shakespeare's Language of Gesture*, Cambridge, Mass.: Harvard, 1984.

Bingham, Madeleine, *Henry Irving and Victorian Theatre*, New York and London: Stein and Day, 1978.

Blau, Herbert, *Take Up the Bodies: Theatre at the Vanishing Point*, Urbana, Ill.: University of Illinois Press, 1982.

——*To All Appearances: Ideology and Performance*, London: Routledge, 1991.

Bloom, Harold, *The Anxiety of Influence*, Oxford: Oxford University Press, 1973.

——*The Western Canon*, London: Macmillan, 1996.

Boal, Augusto, 'Aristotle's Coercive System of Tragedy', in *Theater of the Oppressed*, trans. Charles A. and Maria-Odilia Leal McBride, New York: Theatre Communications Group, 1979.

——*The Rainbow of Desire*, trans. Adrian Jackson, London: Routledge, 1995.

Bogdanov, Michael and Pennington, Michael, *The English Shakespeare Company: The Wars of the Roses*, London: Nick Hern, 1990.

Boose, Lynda, E. and Burt, Richard, *Shakespeare, the Movie: Popularising the Plays on Film, TV and Video*, London: Routledge, 1997.

Booth, Edwin, 'A Few Words about Edmund Kean' in Brander Matthews and Laurence Hutton (eds), *Actors and Actresses of Great Britain and The United States: From the Days of David Garrick to the Present Time*, New York: Cassell and Co., 1886, 3 vols, vol. 3.

Borges, Jorge Luis, *Labyrinths*, trans. D.A. Yates and J.E. Irby, Harmondsworth: Penguin, 1974.

Bradley, A.C., *Shakespearean Tragedy*, with an introduction by John Russell Brown, London: Macmillan, 1905, 3rd edn, Harmondsworth: Penguin 1992.

Bradley, David, *From Text to Performance in the Elizabethan Theatre: Preparing the Play for the Stage*, Cambridge: Cambridge University Press, 1992.

Branagh, Kenneth, *Hamlet, by William Shakespeare: Screenplay, Introduction & Film Diary*, London: Chatto and Windus, 1996.

——(director/adaptor), *Hamlet*, cast includes: Kenneth Branagh, Derek Jacobi, Kate Winslet, Julie Christie. Rank/Castle Rock, 1996.

Brecht, Bertolt, *Brecht on Theatre: The Development of an Aesthetic*, ed. and trans. John Willett, New York: Hill and Wang, 1984.

Brennan, Anthony, *Onstage and Offstage Worlds in Shakespeare's Plays*, London: Routledge, 1989.

Bristol, Michael D., *Carnival and Theatre: Plebeian Culture and the Structure of Authority in Renaissance England*, London: Methuen, 1985.

——*Big-Time Shakespeare*, London: Routledge, 1996.

Brockbank, Philip (ed.), *Players of Shakespeare 1*, Cambridge: Cambridge University Press, 1985.

Brook, Peter, 'Private Experiment – In Public', interview by Simon Trussler, for *Plays and Players*, November 1964.

——*The Empty Space*, Harmondsworth: Penguin, 1968, reprinted 1972.

Brown, John Russell, *Shakespeare's Plays in Performance*, New York: Applause, 1993.

——'Chekhov on the British Stage: differences', in Patrick Miles, ed. and trans., *Chekhov on the British Stage*, Cambridge: Cambridge University Press, 1993, pp. 6–20.

——*New Sites for Shakespeare: Theatre, the Audience and Asia*, London: Routledge, 1999.

Bulman, James, *The Merchant of Venice*, Shakespeare in Performance, Manchester: Manchester University Press, 1991.

——(ed.), *Shakespeare, Theory and Performance*, London: Routledge, 1995.

Burke, Kenneth, *A Grammar of Motives*, Los Angeles, Calif.: University of California Press, 1969.

Burnett, Mark Thornton and Manning, John (eds), *New Essays on Hamlet*, London: A.M.S. Press, 1994.

Burns, Edward, *Character, Actor and Being on the Early Modern Stage*, London: Macmillan, 1990.

Butler, Judith, *Gender Trouble*, London: Routledge, 1990.

——*Bodies That Matter: On the Discursive Limits of 'Sex'*, London: Routledge, 1993.

Buzacott, Martin, *The Death of the Actor*, London: Routledge, 1991.

Bygrave, Stephen, *Coleridge and the Self*, London: Macmillan, 1986.

Calderwood, James L., '*Hamlet*: The Name of Action', *Modern Language Quarterly*, vol. 39, no. 4, December 1978, pp. 332–62.

Callaghan, Dympna, *Shakespeare without Women*, London: Routledge, 2000.

Callow, Simon, *Being an Actor*, London: Routledge, 1991.

——*Henry IV*, ed. Colin Nicholson, Actors on Shakespeare series, London: Faber, 2002.

Calvert, Louis, *An Actor's Hamlet*, ed. Metcalfe Wood, London: Mills & Boon, 1912.

Campbell, Thomas, *The Life of Mrs Siddons* (2 vols), London, 1834.

Carlson, Robert, 'Theatre and Dialogism', in Janelle Reinelt and Joseph Roach (eds), *Critical Theory and Performance*, Ann Arbor, Mich.: University of Michigan Press, 1992, pp. 313–24.

Cartwright, Kent, *Shakespearean Tragedy and its Double: The Rhythms of Audience Response*, Philadelphia, Penn.: University of Pennsylvania Press, 1991.

Case, Sue-Ellen, *Feminism and Theatre*, London: Macmillan, 1988.

——*Performing Feminisms: Feminist Critical Theory and Theatre*, Baltimore, Md.: Johns Hopkins University Press, 1990.

Cave, Richard, Schafer, Elizabeth and Woolland, Brian, *Ben Jonson and Theatre: Performance Practice and Theory*, London: Routledge, 1999.

Chattuck, Charles, *The Hamlet of Edwin Booth*, Urbana, Ill.: University of Illinois Press, 1969.

Church, Tony, ' "The Centre Cannot Hold": An Actor's View of Some of Shakespeare's Political Characters', *ISA Occasional Paper no. 3*, Oxford: Oxford University Press, 1985.

——' "Jack and Jill": A Consideration of *Love's Labour's Lost* and *A Midsummer Night's Dream* from the Point of View of an Actor and Director' in Murray Biggs, Philip Edwards, Inga-Stina Ewbank and Eugene M. Waith (eds), *The Arts of Performance in Elizabethan and Early Stuart Drama*, Edinburgh: Edinburgh University Press, 1991, pp. 135–47.

Cicero, *De Oratore*, trans. E.W. Sutton and intro. H. Rackham, in *Cicero*, Cambridge, Mass.: Harvard, 1967, 28 vols, vol 1.

Cixous, Hélène, 'Sorties', 1975 in David Lodge (ed.), *Modern Criticism and Theory*, Harlow: Longman, 1988, pp. 286–304.

Cloud, Random, ' "The Very Names of the Persons": Editing and the Invention of Dramatick Character', in David Scott Kastan and Peter Stallybrass (eds), *Staging the Renaissance*, London: Routledge, 1991, pp. 88–96.

Cohen, Derek, *Shakespearean Motives*, London: Macmillan, 1988.

Cole, Toby and Chinoy, Helen (eds), *Actors on Acting*, 3rd edn, New York: Crown, 1970.

Collins, Michael, *Shakespeare's Sweet Thunder: Essays on the Early Comedies*, London: Associated University Presses, 1997.

Cook, Judith, *Women in Shakespeare*, London: Harrap, 1980.

——*Shakespeare's Players*, London: Harrap, 1983.

Coursen, H.R., *Reading Shakespeare on Stage*, London: Associated University Presses, 1995.

——*Shakespeare in Production: Whose History?* Athens, Ohio: Ohio University Press, 1996.

Cox, Brian, *Lear Diaries*, London: Methuen, 1992.

Cox, John D. and Kastan, David Scott (eds), *A New History of Early English Drama*, New York: University of Columbia Press, 1997.

Cox, Murray (ed.), *Shakespeare Comes to Broadmoor*, London: Jessica Kingsley, 1992.

Craig, Edward Gordon, *The Theatre Advancing*, London: Bloom, 1947.

Crockett, Bryan, *The Play of Paradox: Stage and Sermon in Renaissance England*, Philadelphia, Penn.: University of Pennsylvania Press, 1995.

Davis, Derek Russell, *Scenes of Madness: A Psychiatrist at the Theatre*, London: Routledge, 1992.

Davis, Geoffrey V. and Fuchs, Anne (eds), *Theatre and Change in South Africa*, Amsterdam and New York: Harwood, 1996.

Dawson, Anthony B., *Indirections: Shakespeare and the Art of Illusion*, Toronto: University of Toronto Press, 1978.

——'The Arithmetic of Memory – Shakespeare's Theatre and the National Past', in *Shakespeare Survey 52*, 1999, pp. 55–67.

De Grazia, Margreta, Quilligan, Maureen and Stallybrass, Peter (eds), *Subject and Object in Renaissance Culture*, Cambridge: Cambridge University Press, 1996.

Derrida, Jacques, 'The Theatre of Cruelty and the Closure of Representation', trans. Alan Bass, in *Writing and Difference*, London: Routledge, 1979, pp. 231–250.

——'Racism's Last Word', trans. Peggy Kamuf, *Critical Inquiry 12*, 1985, pp. 290–300.

——'The First Session', 1972 reprinted in Attridge (ed.), *Acts of Literature*, London: Routledge, 1992, pp. 127–80.

——*Specters of Marx – The State of the Debt, The Work of Mourning and The New International*, trans. Peggy Kamuf, London: Routledge, 1994.

Desmet, Christy, *Reading Shakespeare's Characters: Rhetoric, Ethics and Identity*, Cambridge, Mass.: Harvard, 1992.

Dezseran, Louis John, *The Student Actor's Handbook*, London: Mayfield, 1975.

Diamond, Elin, *Unmaking Mimesis*, London: Routledge, 1997.

Diderot, Denis, *The Paradox of the Actor*, in *Selected Writings on Art and Literature*, ed. Geoffrey Bremner, Harmondsworth: Penguin, 1994.

Dobson, Michael, *The Making of the National Poet, Shakespeare, Adaptation, and Authorship, 1660–1769*, Oxford: Clarendon, 1992.

Dollimore, Jonathan, *Radical Tragedy*, Brighton: Harvester, 1984.

Doran, Gregory (director), *Titus Andronicus*, produced by Paul Kemp and Clive Rodel, SABC/Market Theatre/Channel 4, 1995.

Downes, John, *Roscius Anglicanus: or an Historical Review of the English Stage*, 1708, ed. Judith Milhous and Robert D. Hume, London: London Society for Theatre Research, 1987.

Drakakis, John, ' "*Jew*: Shylock is my name": Speech Prefixes in *The Merchant of Venice* as Symptoms of the Early Modern', in H. Grady (ed.), *Shakespeare and Modernity: Early Modern to Millennium*, London and New York: Routledge 2000, pp. 105–21.

Drakakis, John and Liebler, Naomi Conn (eds), *Tragedy*, Harlow: Longman, 1998.

Dutton, Richard, 'The Birth of the Author', in R.B. Parker and S.P. Zitner (eds), *Elizabethan Theatre*, Newark, Del.: University of Delaware Press, 1996, pp. 71–93.

Eco, Umberto, 'The Semiotics of Theatrical Performance', *Drama Review 21*, no. 1, 1977, pp. 110–11.

Edelman, Charles, 'Which is the Jew that Shakespeare Knew? Shylock on the Elizabethan Stage', in *Shakespeare Survey 52*, 1999, pp. 93–101.

Elam, Diane, *Feminism and Deconstruction: Ms. en Abyme*, London: Routledge, 1994.

Elam, Keir, *The Semiotics of Theatre and Drama*, London: Routledge, 1988.

Eliot, T.S, 'Tradition and the Individual Talent' in *Selected Prose*, ed. John Hayward, Harmondsworth: Penguin, 1953, pp. 21–31.

Else, Gerald, *Plato and Aristotle on Poetry*, ed. Peter Burian, Chapel Hill: North Carolina, 1986.

Evans, Maurice, *Maurice Evans' G.I. Production of Hamlet*, text edited by Charles Jasper Sisson, commentary by Maurice Evans, New York: Dell, 1958.

Eyre, Richard, *Utopia and Other Places*, London: Vintage, 1993.

——(writer/director), *Changing Stages: A View of British Theatre in the Twentieth Century*, BBC TV, 2000.

Falco, Raphael, *Conceived Presences, Literary Genealogy in Renaissance England*, Cambridge, Mass.: Harvard, 1994.

——*Charismatic Authority in Early Modern English Tragedy*, Baltimore, Md.: Johns Hopkins University Press, 2000.

Faucit, Helena, *Of Some of Shakespeare's Female Characters*, London, 1893.

Fielding, Emma, *Twelfth Night*, ed. Colin Nicholson, *Actors on Shakespeare* series, London: Faber, 2002.

Findlay, Alison, 'Hamlet: A Document in Madness', in Mark Thornton Burnett and John Manning (eds), *New Essays on Hamlet*, London: AMS Press, 1994, pp. 189–205.

Fineman, Joel, *Shakespeare's Perjur'd Eye*, Los Angeles, Berkeley, Calif.: University of California Press, 1986.

——*The Subjectivity Effect in Western Literary Tradition*, Cambridge, Mass.: MIT Press, 1997.

Fisch, Harold, *Hamlet and the Word: The Covenant Pattern in Shakespeare*, New York: Ungar, 1971.

Foakes, R.A, 'The Reception of *Hamlet*', in *Shakespeare Survey 45*, 1993, pp. 1–15.

Ford, Andrew, 'Katharsis: The Ancient Problem', in Andrew Parker and Eve Kosofsky Sedgwick, *Performativity and Performance*, London: Routledge, 1995, pp. 111–33.

Foucault, Michel, *Madness and Civilisation*, trans. R. Howard, London: Tavistock, 1965.

——*The Order of Things*, trans. A.M. Sheridan Smith, London: Tavistock, 1970.

——*The Archaeology of Knowledge*, trans. A.M. Sheridan Smith, London: Routledge, 1975.

Freedman, Barbara, *Staging the Gaze: Postmodernism, Psychoanalysis and Shakespearean Comedy*, Ithaca, NY: University of Cornell Press, 1991.

Freud, Sigmund, *The Interpretation of Dreams*, trans. J. Strachey, *Penguin Freud Library 4*, 4th edn, Harmondsworth: Penguin, 1991.

Frye, Roland Mushat, *The Renaissance Hamlet: Issues and Responses in 1600*, Princeton, N.J.: University of Princeton Press, 1984.

Fuchs, Anne, *Playing the Market*, Amsterdam and New York: Harwood, 1990.

Gainor, J. Ellen (ed.), *Imperialism and Theatre: Essays on World Theatre, Drama and Performance*, London: Routledge, 1995.

Gallop, Jane, *The Daughter's Seduction: Feminism and Psychoanalysis*, Ithaca, N.Y.: University of Cornell Press, 1982.

Garber, Marjorie, *Shakespeare's Ghost Writers: Literature as Uncanny Causality*, London: Methuen, 1987.

——*Vested Interests: Cross Dressing and Cultural Anxiety*, London: Routledge, 1992.

Garrick, David, *An Essay on Acting: In which will be considered the Mimical Behaviour of a Certain Fashionable Faulty Actor, to which will be added a Short Criticism of His acting Macbeth*, London: L. Bickerton, 1744.

Gay, Penny, *As She Likes It*, London: Routledge, 1994.

Gellrich, Michelle, *Tragedy and Theory – The Problem of Conflict since Aristotle*, Princeton, N.J.: University of Princeton Press, 1988.

Gevisser, Mark, 'What's Wrong with Relevance? *Titus Andronicus* at the Market Theatre', *Mail and Guardian* II, 15, 7.4.95, reprinted in *Shakespeare in Southern Africa*, vol. 8, 1995, pp. 83–4.

Giannachi, Gabriella and Luckhurst, Mary (eds), *On Directing*, New York and London: Faber, 1999.

Gielgud, John, 'The *Hamlet* Tradition: some notes on costume, scenery and stage business', in Rosamond Gilder (ed.), *John Gielgud's Hamlet, A Record of Performance*, London: Methuen, 1937.

——(director), *The Richard Burton Hamlet*, produced by William Sargent and Alfred Crown, Atlantic Programmes Lt. Broadcast 1964. Reissued and restored by Paul Brownstein, Onward Productions, 1996.

Gielgud, John with Miller, John and Powell, John, *An Actor and His Time*, London: Clarkson, 1980.

Gielgud, John with Miller, John, *Shakespeare: Hit or Miss*, London: Sidgwick and Jackson, 1991.

——*Acting Shakespeare*, London: Pan, 1997.

Girard, René, 'Mimesis and Violence', in James G. Williams (ed.), *The Girard Reader*, London: Crossroads, 1996, pp. 9–20.

Goldman, Michael, 'Characterising Coriolanus', in *Shakespeare Survey 34*, Cambridge: Cambridge University Press, 1981, pp. 73–85.

Goldsmith, Oliver, *Retaliation*, in Arthur Friedman (ed.), *The Collected Works of Oliver Goldsmith*, Oxford: Clarendon, 1966, 5 vols, vol. 4, pp. 352–62.

Goodman, Lizbeth, *Feminist Stages*, Amsterdam and New York: Harwood, 1996.

Goodman, Lizbeth and De Gay, Jane (eds), *The Routledge Reader in Gender and Performance*, London: Routledge, 1998.

Gosson, Stephen, *The School of Abuse*, London, 1579; Shakespeare Society Reprint, 1841.

Granville-Barker, Harley, *Preface to Hamlet*, London, 1937, reprinted by Nick Hern, 1993.

Greenblatt, Stephen, *Renaissance Self-Fashioning: From More to Shakespeare*, Chicago, Ill.: University of Chicago Press, 1980.

——(ed.), *Representing the English Renaissance*, Los Angeles, Calif.: University of California Press, 1988.

Greville, Fulke, *The Prose Works of Fulke Greville, Lord Brooke*, ed. John Gouws, Oxford: Clarendon, 1986.

Gross, John, *Shylock*, London: Chatto and Windus, 1992.

Grossman, Edwina Booth, *Edwin Booth: Recollections by his Daughter*, New York, 1894.

Grossman, Marshall, *The Story of All Things*, New York: Associated University Presses, 1998.

Guntner, J. Lawrence, '*Hamlet, Macbeth* and *King Lear* on Film', in Russell Jackson (ed.), *The Cambridge Companion to Shakespeare on Film*, Cambridge: Cambridge University Press, 2000, pp. 117–34.

Gurr, Andrew, *The Shakespearean Stage, 1574–1642*, Cambridge: Cambridge University Press, 1980.

Habib, Imtiaz, *Shakespeare and Race: Postcolonial Praxis in the Early Modern Period*, Lanham: University Press of America, 1999.

——*Shakespeare's Pluralistic Concepts of Character*, London: Associated University Presses, 1993.

Hagen, Uta with Frankel, Haskel, *Respect for Acting*, London: Macmillan, 1973.

Halio, Jay L. (ed.), *The Merchant of Venice*, Oxford: Oxford University Press, 1993.

Hall, Peter, *Peter Hall's Diaries: The Story of a Dramatic Battle*, London: Limelight, 1985.

Hanson, Elizabeth, *Discovering the Subject in Renaissance England*, Cambridge: Cambridge University Press, 1998.

Hapgood, Robert (ed.), *Hamlet, Shakespeare in Production*, Cambridge: Cambridge University Press, 1999.

Hawkes, Terence, 'Telmah' in Patricia Parker and Geoffrey Hartmann (eds), *Shakespeare and the Question of Theory*, Brighton: Harvester, 1986, pp. 310–33.

——(ed.), *Alternative Shakespeares 2*, London: Routledge, 1996.

Hazlitt, William, *A View of the English Stage*, 1818 in Duncan Wu (ed.), *The Selected Writings of William Hazlitt*, London: Pickering and Chatto, 1998, 9 vols, vol. 3.

Helbo, André et al., *Approaching Theatre*, Bloomington, Ind.: University of Indiana Press, 1991.

Heywood, Thomas, *An Apology for Actors* (1612), London: Shakespeare Society reprint, 1841.

Hill, John, *The Actor: A Treatise on the Art of Playing*, London: R. Griffiths, 1750.

Hillman, Richard, *Intertextuality and Romance in Renaissance Drama: The Staging of Nostalgia*, London: Macmillan, 1992.

——*Self-Speaking in Medieval and Early Modern English Drama – Subjectivity, Discourse and the Stage*, London: Macmillan, 1997.

Hodgdon, Barbara, *The End Crowns All: Closure and Contradiction in Shakespeare's History Plays*, Princeton, N.J.: University of Princeton Press, 1991.

——'Race-ing Othello: Re-engendering White-out', in Lynda Boose and Richard Burt, *Shakespeare, the Movie: Popularising the Plays on Film, TV and Video*, London: Routledge, 1997, pp. 23–45.

——*The Shakespeare Trade: Performances and Appropriations*, Philadelphia, Penn.: University of Pennsylvania Press, 1998.

——' "Making it New": Katie Mitchell Refashions Shakespearean History', in Marianne Novy (ed.), *Transforming Shakespeare*, New York and London: St Martin's Press, 1999, pp. 13–35.

Holcroft, Thomas, 'The Art of Acting', *The Theatrical Recorder*, vol. II, no. VII, 1805.

Holderness, Graham, *The Shakespeare Myth*, Manchester: University of Manchester Press, 1991.

Holland, Peter, 'The Resources of Characterisation in Othello', in *Shakespeare Survey 41*, Cambridge: Cambridge University Press, 1989, pp. 119–34.

——*English Shakespeares*, Cambridge: Cambridge University Press, 1997.

——'Film Editing', in Grace Ioppolo (ed.), *Shakespeare Performed*, London: Associated University Presses, 2000, pp. 273–99.

——'*The Merchant of Venice* and the Value of Money', in *Cahiers Elisabéthains 60* (October 2001), pp. 13–31.

Holledge, Julie, *Innocent Flowers: Women in the Edwardian Theatre*, London: Virago, 1981.

Honigmann, E.A.J. (ed.), *Othello*, Arden III, London: Thomas Nelson, 1997.

Howard, Jean and O'Connor, Marion (eds), *Shakespeare Reproduced: The Text in History and Ideology*, London: Routledge, 1987.

Hubert, Judd D., *Metatheatre: The Example of Shakespeare*, Lincoln, Nebr.: University of Nebraska Press, 1991.

Hughes, Alan, *Henry Irving, Shakespearean*, Cambridge: Cambridge University Press, 1981.

Huxley, Michael and Witts, Noel (eds), *The Twentieth Century Performance Reader*, London: Routledge, 1996.

Irving, Henry, Preface to *The Paradox of the Actor*, reprinted in Diderot/Archer, *The Paradox of Acting/Masks or Faces?*, New York: Hill & Wang, 1957.

——'An Actor's Notes on Shakespeare', in *The Nineteenth Century*, vol. 1, May 1877, pp. 524–30.

——*Impressions of America*, London, 1884.

Irving, Henry and Marshall, Frank, A. (eds), *The Works of William Shakespeare*, London: Blackie, 1895, 2 vols.

Irving, Lawrence, *Henry Irving: The Actor and His World*, London: New York and London: Faber, 1951.

Jackson, Russell (ed.), *The Cambridge Companion to Shakespeare on Film*, Cambridge: Cambridge University Press, 2000.

Jackson, Russell and Smallwood, Robert (eds), *Players of Shakespeare 2*, Cambridge: Cambridge University Press, 1988.

——(eds), *Players of Shakespeare 3*, Cambridge: Cambridge University Press, 1993.

Jameson, Mrs, *Shakespeare's Heroines*, London: Dent, 1832.

Jameson, Fredric, *Signatures of the Visible*, London: Routledge, 1990.

Jewell, John, *A Replie unto M. Harding's Answer*, London, 1611.

Jones, Ann Rosalind and Stallybrass, Peter, *Renaissance Clothing and the Materials of Memory*, Cambridge: Cambridge University Press, 2000.

Jones, Emrys, *Scenic Form in Shakespeare*, Oxford: Clarendon, 1971.

Joseph, Bertram, *Acting Shakespeare*, London: 1960, reprinted by Theatre Arts, 1989.

Joughin, John J. (ed.), *Shakespeare and National Culture*, Manchester: University of Manchester Press, 1997.

Jowett, John (ed.), *Richard III*, Oxford: Oxford University Press, 2000.

Kamps, Ivo (ed.), *Materialist Shakespeare: A History*, London: Verso, 1995.

Kemble, Frances, *On the Stage*, London, 1863.

——*Notes Upon Some of Shakespeare's Plays*, London, 1882.

Kemble, John Philip, *Macbeth and King Richard III: An Essay in Answer to Remarks on Some of the Characters of Shakespeare*, first published in 1786 by T&J Egerton, reprinted 1817.

Kennedy, Dennis, *Looking at Shakespeare: A Visual History of Twentieth-Century Performance*, Cambridge: Cambridge University Press, 1993.

Kiernan, Pauline, *Shakespeare's Theory of Drama*, Cambridge: Cambridge University Press, 1996.

King, T.J., 'Shakespeare to Olivier: A great Chain of Acting, 1598–1935', *Notes and Queries*, September 1986, pp. 397–8.

Knapp, Robert, *Shakespeare, the Theatre and the Book*, Princeton, N.J.: University of Princeton Press, 1989.

Knowles, Richard Paul, 'Shakespeare, Voice and Ideology: Interrogating the Natural Voice', in James Bulman, *Shakespeare, Theory and Performance*, London: Routledge, 1995, pp. 92–113.

Kobler, John, *Damned in Paradise: The Life of John Barrymore*, New York: Atheneum, 1977.

Krafft-Ebing, Richard Von, *Psychopathia Sexualis*, trans. Franklin S. Klaf, London: Bell, 1865.

Kristeva, Julia, 'Women's Time' in Toril Moi (ed.), *The Kristeva Reader*, London: Blackwell, 1986, pp. 197–214.

Kruger, Loren, 'That Fluctuating Moment of National Consciousness' – Protest, Publicity and Postcolonial Theatre in South Africa', in J. Ellen Gainor (ed.), *Imperialism and Theatre: Essays on World Theatre, Drama and Performance*, London: Routledge, 1995, pp. 148–163.

Lacan, Jacques, 'The Mirror Stage', in *Ecrits*, trans. Alan Sheridan, London: Tavistock, 1977, pp. 1–8.

Lacou-Labarthe, Philippe, *Typography*, trans. Christopher Fynsk, Stanford, Calif.: University of Stanford Press, 1998, originally published in French in 1979.

Landry, Donna and MacLean, Gerald, *Materialist Feminisms*, London: Blackwell, 1993.

Langtry, Lillie, *The Days I Knew*, London, 1925.

Laroque, François, *Shakespeare's Festive World: Elizabethan Seasonal Entertainment and the Professional Stage*, Cambridge: Cambridge University Press, 1991.

Lee, John, *Shakespeare's Hamlet and the Controversies of Self*, Oxford: Oxford University Press, 2000.

Leech, Geoffrey and Short, Michael, *Style in Fiction: A Linguistic Introduction to English Fictional Prose*, Harlow: Longman, 1981.

Leggatt, Alexander, *Jacobean Public Theatre*, London: Routledge, 1992.

Lenz, Carolyn, Greene, Gayle and Neeley, Carol (eds), *The Woman's Part: Feminist Criticism of Shakespeare*, Urbana, Ill.: University of Illinois Press, 1980.

Levinas, Emmanuel, 'Transcendence and Height' and 'Peace and Proximity', in Adriaan T. Pepezak, Simon Critchley and Robert Bernasconi (eds), *Emmanuel Levinas: Basic Philosophical Writings*, Bloomington, Ind.: University of Indiana Press, 1996, pp. 11–33, 161–71.

Lewes, G.H., *On Actors and the Art of Acting*, Leipzig: Bernhard Tauchnitz, 1875.

——'Foreign Actors on Our Stage', in *On Actors and the Art of Acting*, Leipzig: Bernhard Tauchnitz, 1875.

Lickendorf, Elizabeth, 'The Verse Music of Suzman's *Othello*', in *Shakespeare in South Africa*, vol. I, 1987, pp. 69–71.

Linklater, Kirstin, *Freeing Shakespeare's Voice*, New York and London: Theatre Communications Group, 1992.

Lodge, David (ed.), *Modern Criticism and Theory*, Harlow: Longman, 1988.

Loomba, Ania and Orkin, Martin, *Postcolonial Shakespeares*, London: Routledge, 1998.

Lowe, N. J., *The Classical Plot and the Invention of Western Narrative*, Cambridge: Cambridge University Press, 2000.

MacAloon, John J., *Rite, Drama, Festival, Spectacle: Rehearsals Toward a Theory of Cultural Performance*, London: Institute for Study of Human Issues, 1984.

McClintock, Anne and Nixon, Rob, 'No Names Apart: The Separation of Word and History', *Critical Inquiry 13*, 1986, pp. 140–54.

MacDonald, Joyce Green, *Race, Ethnicity and Power in the Renaissance*, Madison, Wis.: Fairleigh Dickenson University Press, 1996.

McGee, Patrick, *Cinema, Theory and Political Responsibility in Contemporary Culture*, Cambridge: Cambridge University Press, 1997.

McIntyre, Ian, *Garrick*, Harmondsworth: Penguin, 1999.

McMillin, Scott, *The Elizabethen Theatre and The Book of Thomas More*, Ithaca, N.Y.: University of Cornell Press, 1987.

McMullan, Gordon (ed.), *Henry VIII*, Arden, 3rd series, London: Thomas Nelson, 2000.

Macklin, Charles, 'The Art and Duty of an Actor', in James Thomas Kirkman, *Memoirs of the Life of Charles Macklin, Esq, principally compiled from his own papers and memorandums*, London: Lockington, Allen and Company, 1799, 2 vols, vol. 1, pp. 362–6.

Macready, William, *The Journal of William Macready*, ed. J.C. Trewin, Harlow: Longman, 1967.

Madden, John (director), *Shakespeare in Love*, screenplay by Marc Norman and Tom Stoppard; cast includes: Joseph Fiennes, Gwyneth Paltrow, Geoffrey Rush. Miramax Films/Universal Pictures, 1998.

Maher, Mary Z, *Modern Hamlets and their Soliloquies*, Ames, Ia.: Iowa State University Press, 1992.

Mahood, M.M., *Playing Bit-Parts in Shakespeare*, London: Routledge, 1992, reprinted 1998.

Mamet, David, *True and False*, New York, London: Faber, 1997.

Mangan, Michael, *A Preface to Shakespeare's Comedies*, Harlow: Longman, 1996.

Mann, David, *The Elizabethan Player: Contemporary Stage Representation*, London: Routledge, 1991.

Manvell, Roger, *Sarah Siddons, Portrait of an Actress*, London: Heinemann, 1970.

Marowitz, Charles, *Recycling Shakespeare*, New York: Applause, 1991.

——*Lear Log*, in D. Williams (ed.), *Peter Brook: A Theatrical Casebook*, London: Methuen, 1992, pp. 6–23.

Marx, Karl, *The Eighteenth Brumaire of Louis Bonaparte*, in David McLellan (ed.), *The Selected Writings of Karl Marx*, Oxford: Oxford University Press, 1977.

Maus, Katherine Eisaman, *Inwardness and Theatre in the English Renaissance*, Chicago, Ill.: University of Chicago Press, 1995.

Mazibuko, Doreen, 'Theatre – The Political Weapon in South Africa', in Geoffrey V. Davis and Anne Fuchs (eds), *Theatre and Change in South Africa*, Amsterdam and New York: Harwood, 1996, pp. 219–24.

Melberg, Arne, *Theories of Mimesis*, Cambridge: Cambridge University Press, 1995.

Miller, Jonathan, *Subsequent Performances*, New York and London: Faber, 1986.

Mills, John A., *Hamlet on Stage: The Great Tradition*, Westport, Conn.: Greenwood Press, 1985.

Mitter, Shomit, *Systems of Rehearsal*, London: Routledge, 1992.

Montaigne, Michel de, *The Complete Essays*, ed. and trans. M.A. Screech, Harmondsworth: Penguin, 1991.

Montrose, Louis, *The Purpose of Playing: Shakespeare and the Cultural Politics of the Elizabethan Theatre*, Chicago, Ill.: University of Chicago Press, 1995.

Moretti, Franco, *Signs Taken For Wonders, Essays in the Sociology of Literary Forms*, trans. Susan Fischer, David Forgacs and David Millar, London: Verso, 1983.

Mullaney, Steven, *The Place of the Stage: License, Play and Power in Renaissance England*, Chicago, Ill.: University of Chicago Press, 1988.

Mullin, Michael, *Design by Motley*, Newark, Del.: University of Delaware Press, 1996.

Munday, Anthony, *A Second and Third Blast of Retreat from Plays and Theatres*, London: Henry Denham, 1580.

Murphy, Andrew (ed.), *The Renaissance Text*, Manchester: University of Manchester Press, 2000.

Murray, Peter B., *Shakespeare's Imagined Persons: The Psychology of Role-Playing and Acting*, London: Macmillan, 1996.

Newman, Karen, *Fashioning Femininity and English Renaissance Drama*, Chicago, Ill.: University of Chicago Press, 1991.

Nietzsche, Friedrich, *The Genealogy of Morals*, trans. Walter Kaufmann, London: Vintage, 1969.

Norman, Marc and Stoppard, Tom, screenplay for *Shakespeare in Love*, New York and London: Faber, 1999.

Novy, Marianne (ed.), *Transforming Shakespeare*, New York, London: St Martin's Press, 1999.

Nuttall, A.D., *A New Mimesis*, London: Methuen, 1983.

Oddey, Alison, *Performing Women: Stand-ups, Strumpets and Itinerants*, London: Macmillan, 1999.

Olivier, Laurence (director), *Hamlet*, screenplay by Alan Dent; cast includes: Laurence Olivier, Eileen Herlie, Basil Sydney, Jean Simmons. Rank/Two Cities, 1948.

——*On Acting*, London: Wheelshare, 1986.

Olshaker, Mark (writer/director), *Discovering Hamlet*, narrated by Patrick Stewart, Unicorn/PBS Home Video, 1990.

Orgel, Stephen, 'Shakespeare Imagines a Theater', in *Poetics Today 5*, 1984, pp. 49–61.

——'The Play of Conscience', in Andrew Parker and Eve Kosofsky Sedgwick, *Performativity and Performance*, London: Routledge, 1995, pp. 134–52.

——(ed.), *The Winter's Tale*, Oxford: Oxford University Press, 1996.

Orkin, Martin, *Shakespeare Against Apartheid*, Jeppestown, S.A.: Donker, 1987.

——*Drama and the South African State*, Manchester: University of Manchester Press, 1991.

Paris, Bernard J., *Character as a Subversive Force in Shakespeare*, London: Associated University Presses, 1991.

Parker, Andrew and Sedgwick, Eve Kosofsky, *Performativity and Performance*, London: Routledge, 1995.

Parker, Patricia, *Shakespeare from the Margins: Language, Culture, Context*, Chicago, Ill.: University of Chicago Press, 1996.

Parker, Patricia and Hartmann, Geoffrey (eds), *Shakespeare and the Question of Theory*, Brighton: Harvester, 1986.

Parker, Patricia and Quint, David (eds) *Literary Theory/Renaisance Texts*, Baltimore, Md.: Johns Hopkins University Press, 1986.

Pavis, Patrice, *Theatre at the Crossroads of Culture*, London: Routledge, 1992.

Pechter, Edward, 'Remembering Hamlet: Or How it Feels to Go Like a Crab Backwards' *Shakespeare Survey 39*, 1987, pp. 135–49.

Pechter, Edward (ed.), *Textual and Theatrical Shakespeare: Questions of Evidence*, Ames, Ia.: Iowa State University Press, 1996.

Pennington, Michael, *Hamlet: A User's Guide*, London: Nick Hern, 1996.

Plato, *The Republic*, ed. and trans. Desmond Lee, Harmondsworth: Penguin, 1955.

Potter, Lois, 'Nobody's Perfect: Actors' Memories and Shakespeare's Plays of the 1590s', *Shakespeare Survey 42*, 1989, pp. 185–98.

Powell, Kerry, *Women and Victorian Theatre*, Cambridge: Cambridge University Press, 1997.

Quinones, Ricardo, *The Renaissance Discovery of Time*, Cambridge, Mass.: Harvard, 1972.

Ransome, Eleanor (ed.), *The Terrific Kemble*, London: Hamilton, 1978.

Redfield, William, *Letters from an Actor*, New York: Cassell and Co., 1966.

Redgrave, Corin, *Julius Caesar*, ed. Colin Nicholson, *Actors on Shakespeare* series, London: Faber, 2002.

Redgrave, Michael, *The Actor's Ways and Means*, with an introduction by Vanessa Redgrave, London: Nick Hern, 1995.

Redgrave, Vanessa, *Antony and Cleopatra*, ed. Colin Nicholson, *Actors on Shakespeare* series, London: Faber, 2002.

Reed, Robert, *Bedlam on the Jacobean Stage*, Cambridge, Mass.: Harvard, 1952.

Reynolds, Joshua, *Portraits by Sir Joshua Reynolds*, ed. Frederick W. Hilles, New York: McGraw-Hill, 1952.

Ricci, Digbi, 'Titus topples into the Relevant Pit', first printed in *Mail and Guardian* II, 14, 31.03.95, reprinted in *Shakespeare in Southern Africa*, vol. 8, 1995, pp. 81–3.

Rich, Adrienne, *On Lies, Secrets and Silence: Selected Prose, 1966–1978*, London: Virago, 1979.

Richards, Jeffrey (ed.), *Sir Henry Irving: Theatre, Culture and Society – Essays, Addresses and Lectures*, Keele: Keele University Press, 1994.

Richards, Sandra, 'Lady Macbeth in Performance', *The English Review*, vol. 1, issue 2, November 1990.

——*The Rise of the English Actress*, London: Macmillan, 1993.

Roach, Joseph, *The Player's Passion: Studies in the Science of Acting*, London and Toronto: Associated University Presses, 1985.

Robbe-Grillet, Alain, 'Nature, Humanism and Tragedy', in *Snapshots and Towards a New Novel*, Paris: Editions de Minuit and London: Calder & Boyars, 1965.

Robson, Flora, Introduction to *The Winter's Tale*, in *Introductions to Shakespeare: Being the Introductions to the Individual Plays in the Folio Society Edition, 1950–76*, London: Michael Joseph, 1978, pp. 225–33.

Rodenburg, Patsy, *The Right to Speak*, London: Methuen, 1992.

——*The Need for Words*, London: Methuen, 1993.

Rosenberg, Marvin, *The Masks of Hamlet*, New York and London: Associated University Presses, 1997.

Rouse, John, 'Brecht and the Contradictory Actor', in Philip B. Zarilli (ed.), *Acting, (Re)Considered*, London: Routledge, 1995, pp. 229–42.

Rutter, Carol, ed. Faith Evans, *Clamorous Voices: Shakespeare's Women Today*, London: The Women's Press, 1988.

Rutter, Carol Chillington, 'Kate, Bianca, Ruth and Sarah: Playing the Woman's Part in *The Taming Of the Shrew*', in Michael Collins, *Shakespeare's Sweet Thunder: Essays on the Early Comedies*, London: Associated University Presses, 1997, pp. 176–215.

——*Enter the Body – Women and Representation on Shakespeare's Stage*, London: Routledge, 2001.

Sachs, Albie, 'Preparing Ourselves for Freedom: Culture and the ANC Guidelines', in Ingrid de Kok and Karen Press (eds), *Spring is Rebellious: Arguments about Cultural Freedom by Albie Sachs and Respondents*, Johannesburg, S.A.: Buchu Books, 1990, p. 19.

Salingar, Leo, 'Shakespeare and the Ventriloquists', *Shakespeare Survey 34*, 1981, pp. 51–61.

Salkeld, Douglas, *Madness and Drama in the Age of Shakespeare*, Manchester: University of Manchester Press, 1993.

Salter, Denis, 'Acting Shakespeare in Postcolonial Space', in James Bulman (ed.), *Shakespeare: Theory and Performance*, London: Routledge, 1995, pp. 113–33.

Schafer, Elizabeth, *Ms-Directing Shakespeare*, London: The Women's Press, 1998.

Schechner, Richard, 'Introduction: The five avant gardes or ... [and] ... Or none?' in *The Future of Ritual, Writings on Culture and Performance*, London: Routledge, 1993, pp. 5–21.

Senelick, Laurence (ed.), *Gender in Performance: The Presentation of Difference in the Performing Arts*, Hanover: University Press of New England, 1992.

Shellard, Dominic, *British Theatre Since the War*, New Haven, Conn.: Yale University Press, 1999.

Sher, Antony, *The Year of the King*, London: Methuen, 1984.

——'On Playing Shylock', *Drama 4*, 1987, pp. 27–30.

Sher, Antony and Doran, Gregory, *Woza Shakespeare! Titus Andronicus in South Africa*, London: Methuen, 1996.

Showalter, Elaine, *The Female Malady: Women, Madness and English Culture, 1830–1980*, New York: Pantheon, 1985.

Shurgot, Michael, *Stages of Play: Shakespeare's Theatrical Energies in Elizabethan Performance*, London: Associated University Presses, 1998.

Sidney, Philip, *An Apology for Poetry*, ed. Geoffrey Shepherd, Manchester: Manchester University Press, 1973.

Siegel, Paul N., ' "Hamlet, Revenge!" The Uses and Abuses of Historical Criticism', *Shakespeare Survey 45*, 1993, pp. 15–26.

Sinden, Donald, 'Playing King Lear: Donald Sinden talks to J.W.R. Meadowcroft', *Shakespeare Survey 33*, Cambridge: Cambridge University Press, 1980, pp. 81–9.

Sinfield, Alan, *Faultlines: Cultural Materialism and the Politics of Dissident Reading*, Oxford: Clarendon, 1992.

Skura, Meredith Anne, *Shakespeare the Actor and the Purposes of Playing*, Chicago, Ill.: University of Chicago Press, 1993.

Slater, Ann Pasternak, *Shakespeare the Director*, Brighton: Harvester, 1982.

Smallwood, Robert (ed.), *Players of Shakespeare 4*, Cambridge: Cambridge University Press, 1998.

Smith, Emma, 'Ghost Writing: Hamlet and the Ur-Hamlet', in Andrew Murphy (ed.), *The Renaissance Text*, Manchester: University of Manchester Press, 2000, pp. 177–91.

Solomon, Alisa, *Re-Dressing the Canon: Essays on Theater and Gender*, London: Routledge, 1997.

Soule, Lesley Wade, *Actor as Anti-Character*, Westport, Conn.: Greenwood Press, 2000.

Soyinka, Wole, 'Shakespeare and the Living Dramatist', *Shakespeare Survey 36*, Cambridge: Cambridge University Press, 1983, pp. 1–11.

Sprinter, Michael (ed.), *Ghostly Demarcations*, London: Verso, 1999.

Stafford-Clark, Max, *Letters to George: The Account of a Rehearsal*, London: Nick Hern, 1989.

Stallybrass, Peter, 'The World Turned Upside Down: Inversion, Gender and the State', in Valerie Wayne (ed.), *The Matter of Difference*, Brighton: Harvester, 1991, pp. 187–222.

Stallybrass, Peter and White, Allon, *The Politics and Poetics of Transgression*, London: Methuen, 1986.

Stanislavsky, Konstantin, *An Actor Prepares*, trans. Elizabeth R. Hapgood, London: Theatre Arts, 1936.

——*Building a Character*, trans. Elizabeth R. Hapgood, London: Theatre Arts, 1950.

——*Creating a Role*, trans. Elizabeth R. Hapgood, London: Theatre Arts, 1963.

States, Bert O., *Hamlet and the Concept of Character*, Baltimore, Md.: Johns Hopkins University Press, 1992.

Sterne, Richard, *John Gielgud directs Richard Burton in Hamlet: A Journal of Rehearsals*, New York: Random House, 1966.

Stevenson, Juliet, 'Theatre in Thatcher's Britain: Organising the Opposition', NTQ Symposium, *New Theatre Quarterly*, May 1988, pp. 113–23.

Stokes, John, Booth, Michael R. and Bassnet, Susan, *Bernhardt, Terry, Duse: The Actress in Her Time*, Cambridge: Cambridge University Press, 1988.

Suchet, David, 'Talking about playing Shylock – A Personal Essay by David Suchet', in Gamini and Fenella Salgado (eds), *The Merchant of Venice*, Harlow: Longman, 1986, pp. xii–xviii.

Summers, Claude J. and Pebworth, Ted-Larry (eds), *Representing Women in Renaissance England*, University of Missouri Press, 1997.

Suzman, Janet, 'Hedda Gabler – The Play in Performance', in Errol Durbach (ed.), *Ibsen and the Theatre*, London: Macmillan, 1980, pp. 83–105.

——'*Othello*, A Belated Reply', in *Shakespeare in Southern Africa*, vol. II, 1988, pp. 89–96.

——(director), *Othello in Johannesburg*, produced by Eric Abraham and David Pupkewitz, Othello Productions/Channel 4, 1988.

——*Acting With Shakespeare: Three Comedies*, New York: Applause, 1996.

——'South Africa in *Othello*', in Jonathan Bate, Jill L. Levinson and Dieter Mehl (eds), *Shakespeare and the Twentieth Century: Selected Proceedings of the International Shakespeare Association World Congress, Los Angeles, 1996*, New York and London: Associated University Presses, 1996, pp. 23–40.

——*The Free State: A South African Response to Chekhov's The Cherry Orchard*, London: Methuen, 2000.

Taranow, Gerda, *The Bernhardt Hamlet – Culture and Context*, London: Peter Lang, 1996.

Taylor, Anya (ed.), *Coleridge's Writings*, vol. 2, 'On Humanity', p. 33, London: St Martin's Press, 3 vols, ongoing.

Tennenhouse, Leonard and Armstrong, N. (eds), *The Violence of Representation*, London: Routledge, 1989.

Terry, Ellen, *The Story of My Life*, London: Hopkinson, 1927.

——*Four Lectures on Shakespeare*, ed. Christopher St John, London: Hopkinson, 1932.

Terry, Ellen and Shaw, George Bernard, *A Correspondence*, ed. Christopher St John, London: Constable, 1931.

Thompson, Ann and Thompson, John O., *Shakespeare: Meaning and Metaphor*, Brighton: Harvester, 1987.

Thompson, Ann and Roberts, Sasha (eds), *Women Reading Shakespeare 1660–1900, An Anthology of Criticism*, Manchester: Manchester University Press, 1997.

Thompson, Ann and Taylor, Neil, ' "Father and Mother is One Flesh": Hamlet and the Problems of Paternity', in Lieve Spaas (ed.), *Paternity and Fatherhood: Myths and Realities*, New York and London: St Martin's Press, 1998, pp. 246–59.

Thomson, Peter, *Shakespeare's Theatre*, London: Routledge, 1983.

——'Rogues and Rhetoricians: Acting styles in Early English Drama', in John D. Cox and David Scott Kastan (eds), *A New History of Early English Drama*, New York: Columbia University Press, 1997, pp. 321–35.

Thorne, Alison, *Vision and Rhetoric in Shakespeare*, London: Macmillan, 2000.

Tilley, Vesta, *Recollections of Vesta Tilley*, London, 1934.

Todorov, Tzvetan, ' "Race", Writing, Culture', trans. Loulou Mack, in *Critical Inquiry* 12, Autumn 1986, pp. 170–82.

——*Genres in Discourse*, Cambridge: Cambridge University Press, 1990.

Toolan, Michael, *Narrative: A Critical Linguistic Introduction*, London: Routledge, 1988.

Truffaut, François (director), *La Nuit americaine*, screenplay by François Truffaut and Suzanne Schiffman; cast includes: Jacqueline Bisset, Jean-Pierre Aumont, Jean-Pierre Léaud. Films du Carosse, 1973.

Tushingham, David (ed.), *Live 2: Not What I am, The Experience of Performing*, London: Methuen, 1995.

Valéry, Paul, 'The Crisis of the Spirit', 1919 in James R. Lawler, trans. and ed., *Paul Valéry: An Anthology*, London: Routledge, 1977, pp. 94–107.

Vickers, Brian, *Shakespeare: The Critical Heritage*, London: Routledge, 1979, 6 vols.

——*In Defence of Rhetoric*, Oxford: Clarendon, 1998.

Videback, Bente, *The Stage Clown in Shakespeare's Theatre*, Westport, Conn.: Greenwood Press, 1996.

Walker, John (ed.), *Halliwell's Filmgoer's Companion*, 12th edn, London: HarperCollins, 1997.

Walter, Harriet, 'The Heroine, the Harpy and the Human Being', *New Theatre Quarterly*, spring 1993, pp. 110–17.

——'On Playing the Duchess of Malfi', in Martin White, *Renaissance Drama in Action*, London: Routledge, 1998, pp. 88–100.

——*Other People's Shoes*, London: Viking, 1999.

——*Macbeth*, ed. Colin Nicholson, *Actors on Shakespeare* series, London: Faber, 2002.

Walton, Kendall L., *Mimesis as Make-Believe*, Cambridge, Mass.: Harvard, 1990.

Wayne, Valerie (ed.), *The Matter of Difference*, Brighton: Harvester, 1991.

Weill, Herbert, 'On Expectation and Surprise', *Shakespeare Survey 34*, Cambridge: Cambridge University Press, 1981, pp. 39–51.

Weimann, Robert, *Shakespeare and the Popular Tradition in Theatre*, Baltimore, Md.: Johns Hopkins University Press, 1978.

——'Mimesis in Hamlet', in Patricia Parker and Geoffrey Hartman (eds), *Shakespeare and the Question of Theory*, London: Methuen, 1985, pp. 275–91.

——*Authority and Representation in Early Modern Discourse*, Baltimore, Md.: Johns Hopkins University Press, 1996.

——*Author's Pen and Actor's Voice: Playing and Writing in Shakespeare's Theare*, Cambridge: Cambridge University Press, 2000.

Wells, Stanley and Taylor, Gary (eds), *The Complete Works of William Shakespeare*, Oxford: Oxford University Press, 1988.

Wells, Stanley and Taylor, Gary, with Jowett, John and Montgomery, William, *William Shakespeare: A Textual Companion*, Oxford: Oxford University Press, 1988.

Wesker, Arnold, *The Merchant*, London: Methuen, 1983.

West, Shearer, *The Image of the Actor: Verbal and Visual Representation in the Age of Garrick and Kemble*, London: St Martin's Press, 1991.

White, Martin, *Renaissance Drama in Action*, London: Routledge 1998.

Whiteside, Anna, 'Self-Referring Artefacts', in Michael Issacharoff and Robin Jones (eds), *Performing Texts*, Philadelphia, Penn.: University of Pennsylvania Press, 1988, pp. 27–37.

Wilde, Oscar, *The Picture of Dorian Gray*, 1891, in *The Complete Plays, Poems, Novels and Stories of Oscar Wilde*, London: Magpie, 1993.

Wiles, David, *Shakespeare's Clown: Actor and Text in the Elizabethan Playhouse*, Cambridge: Cambridge University Press, 1987.

Wilkes, Charles, *A General View of the Stage*, London, 1759.

Willems, Michele, ' "They do but jest", or do they? Reflections on the ambiguities of the space within the space', in F. Laroque (ed.), *The Show Within, Dramatic and Other Insets: English Renaissance Drama, 1550–1642*, Montpellier: University of Montpellier, 1992, 2 vols, vol. 1, pp. 51–63.

Williams, David (ed.), *Peter Brook: A Theatrical Casebook*, London: Methuen, 1992.

Williams, Gordon, *Shakespeare, Sex and the Print Revolution*, London: Athlone, 1996.

Williams, Raymond, *Modern Tragedy*, London: Chatto and Windus, 1966.

——*Culture*, London: Fontana, 1981.

Woddis, Carole (ed.), *Sheer Bloody Magic: Conversations with Actresses*, London: Virago, 1991.

Woods, Leigh (ed.), *On Playing Shakespeare: Advice and Commentary from Actors and Actresses of the Past*, Westport, Conn.: Greenwood Press, 1991.

Worthen, W. B, *The Idea of the Actor: Drama and the Ethics of Performance*, Princeton, N.J.: University of Princeton Press, 1984.

——*Shakespeare and the Authority of Performance*, Cambridge: Cambridge University Press, 1997.

Zarilli, Philip B. (ed.), *Acting (Re)Considered*, London: Routledge, 1995.

Zucker, Carole, *In the Company of Actors*, London: A&C Black, 1999.

Zunder, William and Trill, S. (eds), *Writing and the English Renaissance*, Harlow: Longman, 1996.

Website: *Hamlet on the Ramparts*: < http://shea.mit.edu/ramparts2000 >

Index